Praise for Angus Peacock

SISU: A Series of Epic Adventures hurls the reader into a world where the only rule is simple: refuse to break. Drawing on the hard edges of broken institutions, military life, police corruption, and brutal nature survival, these stories drag the reader through a dangerous, "Dark London", across the French Alps and Europe to Mongolia, before finally collapsing into a burgeoning, volatile China. The journey tests not only courage but the costs of clinging to one's own moral compass; this is endurance stripped bare—writing that is raw, relentless, and impossible to walk away from.

— KINCAID, COO BIOTECH & AI ENABLED OPS

SISU A Series of Epic Adventures is a journey through dangerous physical and emotional terrain. Gritty and fascinating, the protagonist moves boldly away from the life he was born to. Who is this man from dark London and how will his life's trajectory change as he takes those early survival skills into the larger world?

A bold nature and a need for cash gets our hero into dangerous situations around the globe, along with true adventure, and some romance. The question remains, is he changed?

— JANET STARCEVICH, OUTDOORSWOMAN & RANCHER

SISU is rooted in lived discipline rather than theory. Angus' stories show why SISU and sang froid still matter, especially when modern life offers distraction instead of direction.

— ZACH RIVERA SPECIAL FORCES ENGINEER (RET.)

Sisu: a heartfelt exploration of the quiet determination that can carry us far beyond where we begin.

— A.P-ADAMS, TALENT ACQUISITION MANAGER

From the first chapter to the last, it's a fearless testament to grit - Sisu - hope with teeth. A powerful reminder that resilience—Sisu—isn't loud, it's relentless.

— PAUL CHAMBERS, LABOR ORGANIZER

Peacock's vast lived experience shines through in this page turner.

— RICHARD LAMONDIN, CO-FOUNDER & CEO OF ECOFI

A humble and honest work that will change your view on life. SISU by Angus Peacock is a must read!

— JP, SECURITY MANAGER

Angus is a world class adventurer speaking French, Chinese and, of course English.. Angus saved me from a Chinese jail by intimidating the corrupt police in Shanghai with his presence and command of the language.

— PETER HARRIS, PROFESSOR (RET'D)

SISU is the wild journey of Angus Peacock, a man learning to be good in a hard, corrupt world. Inspiring!

SISU is the wild journey of Angus Peacock, a man learning to be good in a corrupt world. Inspiring!

SISU is the wild and inspiring journey of Angus Peacock, a man learning to be good in a corrupt world. Buckle up!

— MICHAEL L, TRANSLATOR

ANGUS PEACOCK

SISU

A Series of Epic Adventures

SISU

A Series of Epic Adventures

First Edition

Published by Tactical 16 Publishing

Colorado Springs, Colorado

www.Tactical16.com

ISBN: 978-1-966413-17-2 (paperback)

ISBN: 978-1-966413-41-7 (ebook)

Thank You's and Recognition

Writing is difficult. Words are hard. And closing out a book is complex.

Like the author, this story has already traveled the globe. From the Pacific West Coast, across the Rockies, into Britain, through Italy, over to Japan and back to the U.S.A., the story of SISU is almost as resilient as its writer and contributors.

Bottom Line Up Front: any success derived from SISU is thanks to the collaboration and cooperation of a multitude of people; conversely, any flaws, failings and fractures herein must be self-owned for I have had every opportunity to polish my own words.

Obvious gratitude and respect must be given to Chris, Cindy, and Kristal at Tactical 16 Publishing. They are industry stalwarts without whom I could not bring this story to life. My questions, feedback, push-back and eccentricities have all been managed with patience and professionalism.

The "beta test" readers, of whom there were many, come from within and outside the worlds of uniformed service providers. My direction arrived with their guidance.

Particularly though, I must tip my hat to the following people:

To Mike, who significantly influenced my growth as a person and as a writer.

To Janet, who, in the way of grandmothers everywhere "forced" me to confront my own feelings and challenged my attitude to writing about "love interests." (No good book is without one apparently.)

To Amber, who rebuilt bridges that were previously considered irreparable.

To the "Two Paul's": British Paul for helping me authenticate Dark

London, rather than the "Mary Poppins" version, offering insights from north of the river. American Paul for helping me authenticate that the world outside our bubbles can be both unbelievable and real.

To all the people who lived with my dysfunction and offered healing from the combined curses of shame and imposter syndrome. Particularly Marissa who has endured stoically and in her own glamorous fashion.

To Kincaid, without whose help, I am not sure I would have finished this book. Your empathy for the combustible state of Anglo – American grammar nuances and your engagement with the story was unparalleled and beyond expectation.

To the Alumni of Westminster, for you will never fully realize how much, as the torch bearers of friendship, you illuminated the darkness.

To Ivor. Erudite, avuncular and the most sustainable of male mentors, you kept the standards bar high for many decades. Decreed by Fate, you showed up at critical moments before I disappeared too far back down the rabbit run of dysfunction.

Contents

Foreword

"A Testament to Human Resilience and the Power of Mental Toughness"

Reading this book felt less like consuming an adventure story and more like walking alongside someone who has deliberately chosen the hard road, again and again, to understand himself. Angus Peacock doesn't just describe extreme environments or difficult journeys; he invites you into the mindset required to survive them. At its core, this book is about sisu: the quiet, stubborn resolve to keep going when quitting would be easier, more rational, and completely understandable.

This is not a polished hero's narrative. It's raw, uncomfortable at times, and deeply honest. The Writer writes openly about trauma, betrayal, violence, and failure, and he doesn't rush past those moments to get to the victories. That willingness to stay in the discomfort is what gives the book its credibility. As a reader, I trust him, because he never pretends the journey was clean or linear.

WHAT IT FEELS LIKE TO READ THIS BOOK

From the beginning, I found myself emotionally invested. The Writer's reflections on his past are handled with a level of vulnerability that immediately pulled me in. When he describes moments of fear, isolation, or doubt, whether in Arctic cold or desert heat, I don't just understand them intellectually; I feel them. There were sections where I noticed myself physically reacting: tightening up during moments of danger, slowing down during periods of exhaustion, and feeling genuine relief when he made it through.

What stood out most was the emotional range. There are moments of grit and determination that are genuinely inspiring, but they are balanced by failure, self-questioning, and exhaustion. That balance keeps the book grounded. It never turns into a motivational slogan or a fantasy of invincibility. Instead, it reflects real human experience—messy, uneven, and often unresolved.

More than once, I caught myself reflecting on my own life: times I gave up early, avoided discomfort, or convinced myself I had reached my limit when I hadn't. That quiet self-examination is where the book's impact really lands.

LESSONS THAT EXTEND BEYOND ADVENTURE

What makes SISU particularly valuable is how applicable it is to everyday life. The Writer makes it clear that mental toughness isn't reserved for explorers or endurance athletes. The same principles apply when facing career uncertainty, strained relationships, financial stress, or personal loss.

The frameworks he shares, like the OODA Loop (Observe, Orient, Decide, Act)— are practical without feeling forced. They offer a way to stay grounded and make decisions under pressure, whether that pressure comes from an expedition or a sudden life disruption. His reflections on integrity, selective trust, and learning from betrayal felt especially relevant in professional and personal contexts alike.

One of the most useful takeaways is his view on failure. The Writer treats setbacks as information, not verdicts. That shift, from seeing failure as something to fear to something to analyze, feels both realistic and empowering. It encourages curiosity instead of shame, and persistence instead of paralysis.

WHY COACHES AND ATHLETES SHOULD READ THIS

As someone who thinks deeply about coaching and overly passionate about development of young athletes, I found this book particularly compelling in a sporting context. The Writer's journey mirrors what many athletes experience: growth through discomfort, progress through repetition, and confidence earned, not given.

His "Plan, Do, Conclude, Review" approach aligns naturally with effective coaching practice. It reinforces the idea that development happens when preparation meets adaptability. Conditions change, bodies change, minds fluctuate—and good coaching, like good expedition planning, must account for that.

Most importantly, SISU highlights the mental barriers that often limit performance long before physical limits are reached. Injury recovery, performance anxiety, competitive pressure—these are spaces where sisu matters. The book is a reminder that coaching is not just about drills, exercises and conditioning, but about helping athletes build the inner resilience that sustains long-term growth. It subtly challenges coaches to "think out of the box".

FINAL THOUGHTS

SISU asks an uncomfortable but important question: how do we respond when things stop being manageable? The Writer doesn't offer or suggest that there are easy answers or shortcuts. Instead, he demonstrates, through lived experience, that resilience is something built deliberately, often in silence, and usually in moments we would rather avoid.

This book will resonate with anyone facing adversity, guiding others through challenge, or simply questioning what they are capable of when comfort is removed. It's not about becoming fearless or invincible. It's about learning to continue; thoughtfully, ethically, and with purpose, when perseverance alone is no longer enough.

–Johan Botha

Preface

Dear Reader,

I never intended to write this book.

I wanted to write about China and the upheaval of global trade in the crushing clash of ideologies that temporarily united the Eastern and Western hemispheres. The Middle Kingdom offers so much experience and opportunity for the curious; it has become a lodestone for writers and chroniclers across the world.

But that story begged so many questions from friends and colleagues that I was forced to reframe my aspirations and, unlike George Lucas, write the prequel before the sequel. So, another journey began in a world far, far away.

In writing this story, it demanded that I open a "Pandora's Box" of complex problems and interwoven issues whose consequences rippled across decades. It forced me into a dark place, a form of personal hell, out of which I had to walk (not for the first time).

Attributed to Winston Churchill is the quote, "If you are walking through hell, keep walking." Sound advice. And, in so doing, I rediscovered my own SISU and a spiritual attachment to Finland, the love of nature, of light, and of the odd drink or two.

SISU – A Series of Epic Adventures is, in some senses, a test piece. A brand-new adventure and my first publication, which explores the old trope of light vs dark in a modern setting.

The perpetuation of fear and anger is a natural human condition. When words are articulated out loud, they have ten times the impact of those left unsaid. When those words are negative, rather than positive, they have three to seven times more impact. I learned this from an interview with an NFL mindset coach. Positivity, therefore, is a labor of love, under constant threat of erosion by the twin traits of negativity: fear and anger.

Recently, on a milestone birthday, looking at the stars from the top of a mountain, I had a moment of clarity. Checking in with my own physical and mental state, I realized that not only was I still alive, but I was also still living a life. This came as something of a surprise.

Out in the physical darkness, it was apparent that the constant conflict between yin and yang is not something to be feared. Rather, it is a challenge to be embraced. The beauty of the night sky is the reminder that there is light around the corner.

In that light are the strengths of the human condition.
Within the human condition are authentic kinships.
Within authentic kinships are the fortitude of friendships and the causality of commonality.

The "Dark Side" serves a purpose. It reminds us that there is a "Light Side," and that we can leverage the behaviors of the weak peddlers of anger to become better people. Positivity may appear to be a mathematical improbability. Still, it stands to reason that the more we wrestle with the equation, the stronger we become.

In my experience, the human condition exists equally in all countries and cultures, no matter what the ideology.

After many years of professional and personal travel, I adopted the phrase "beware the indignation of the righteous." Draped in the flag of duty, righteous folks are often harbingers of darkness. They are a healthy reminder that some people can never allow others to grow, nor will they ever "bury the hatchet," unless it is in the body of their opposition. However, as far back as 1775, Samuel Johnson held a mirror up to false flag waving with the words "Patriotism is the last refuge of the scoundrel."

Commonality is a strength of the Light Side. Conversely, it is the fuel that authoritarians fear, be they politicians, principals, or policemen. I learned once, from a wise man, that fear and anger are no basis for sound business decisions. He taught me that the sustainability of your journey is rooted in the defiance of those emotions, and therefore those people.

Today, thanks to my adventures, not only have I sustained, but I also speak a personal patois that taints the lingo and taunts the grammar aficionados, much like "the Urban Dictionary". You will discover this as you turn the page and join my journey. Part of this adventure is to discover new words, new thinking, or even new opinions, just like I did.

So, at this juncture, I thank you in advance for engaging with my story.

And I encourage you to "tarry a while" to learn more about SISU.

For life is not a dress rehearsal.

And this is no ordinary book.

This is a story of resilience and realization. It is also an exploration of optimism and the human condition.

What is Sisu?

Sisu is the ability to act in the face of adversity and continue moving forward. It is a Finnish trait about never giving up, whatever the odds. An almost mystical strength, Sisu goes beyond the boundaries of determination and grit.

It is the "second wind" of mental toughness, after an individual has reached the limits of their observed mental or physical capacities. – Emilia Lahti

Where resilience ends, Sisu begins.

If you're walking through hell, keep walking – Winston Churchill

If you recognize any similarities between these adventures and the people, places and circumstances described within, characteristics, traits or situations, it is purely coincidental.

To all the people across the world on a journey.

Introduction

Fate determines the trajectory of our lives. In my case, an unfortunate act of excessive violence, a murder to be precise, triggered a series of horrific experiences that changed me forever. The murder was brutal and opened the door to a world of further brutality which offered two choices: move on or break down.

Move on, define my own destiny, and create a better existence.

The alternative? Be broken down by the force of a determined group of people for whom justice was a luxury others enjoyed.

I did not commit the murder, nor was I party to that. To this day it is not known who delivered the fatal blows. That said, the scars from the fallout of that experience are etched deep into my soul. I was collateral damage in an explosion that destroyed my universe; an explosion of force that concurrently destroyed all the institutions – law, education, and society - in which I was raised to believe.

In the event of emergency or pressing need, institutions failed me. The beliefs with which I was raised were found wanting when the frailty of civil society was exposed. Falling through the meshed fabric of rules and regulations that bind us together, friends and relationships dissolved into nothingness and hopelessness.

Life is a struggle, particularly if you grow up in a world of dysfunction. British society prefers not to speak to dysfunctions, even those in plain sight. "Keep Calm and Carry On" is a form of English stoicism akin to "stiff upper lip" and similar mantras that, at best, point out the national trait of being cool in the face of adversity. At worst, it points to a national trait of repressive emotion. I learned back then that people recoil in horror when the ugly underbelly of civilization is exposed. None more so than "the chattering classes."

Those "chattering classes" are the folks who enjoy the comforts of a first world nation. The steady revenues, regular employment, and good schooling that are taken for granted if you are lucky enough not to be impacted by dysfunction or, as is the case of many, able to turn a blind eye to dysfunction. The chattering classes are a subset of society preaching outwardly about upward social mobility if you just try harder. *"Pull yourself up by your bootstraps"* is the mantra easily peddled by people who never have had to do that.

For upward mobility to occur, there must be downward mobility and, as I discovered, many folks would do anything rather than reach down and make room for you. At the extreme, they will lie, cheat, and steal just to preserve the sanctity of their comforts. Upward mobility is the myth, and the minute you contest the perceived veneer of wealth people will maintain a limpet like chokehold on their station.

To make significant change in your own life, you must be prepared for the hardest of contests. To meet those changes, you are going to have to take the gloves off and get bloodied in the fight for growth. To sustain those changes, you must prepare for a lifetime of challenge. Change is uncomfortable. Gains are incremental. Mobility is often unattainable.

For this reason, many folks give up, preferring to accept the status quo. Some, however, halt their own descent through the meshed fabric of society and walk a path less travelled. These are the adventurers, entrepreneurs, and social misfits who know that life is not a dress rehearsal. These are deliberate people who choose not to be squashed or accepting but spark change and forge a new destiny.

I chose to be one of those people. A dreamer by birth and a fighter by necessity.

Believing in my heart that validation would arrive through non-conformity, (an action that in my mature years could best be described as folly), I stepped out of my lane and embarked on a series of epic adventures that furthered my education and achieved some degree of enlightenment.

These same adventures took me all over the world. Like the protagonist in the books I loved to read as a young boy - part pirate, part commando, part spy – I crossed seas and mountains, oceans and deserts, fuelled by curiosity and fearful of ignorance.

En route, I discovered many things. Not least of all is that business is never really what it seems, and that the law is a funny animal. While business can be hard or soft, the law is a chameleon concept which is accorded the luxury of interpretation. It changes colour for country, context, and circumstance. The law protects society from itself yet is discerning about who it serves. The laws of society change by ideology and culture, and if you are far enough away from a judicial environment, the law of society disappears completely, replaced by the laws of nature, and failing that, the man with the biggest fists.

The rule of law, like many things in modern life, is essential; equally, like many man-made things, it is also fickle and malleable.

I was ill equipped for my journey. Survival required that I suck every ounce of new knowledge from each experience. Learn fast, analyse with alacrity and apply immediately. Reflecting deeply, often disregarding conventional wisdom, I would push boundaries as far as I dared, sometimes at the risk of my own life. My intent was always one of discovery; my guiding regulations were to be law abiding, (even in the face of criminal intent) and be pain relieving (by not being the architect of someone else's pain). The OODA loop - Observe, Orient, Decide, Act (something I learned later in life)- became part of my intrinsic life philosophy which carried over into a coaching philosophy that includes "Plan, Do, Conclude, Review."

My family, like many British families, is a hybrid of cultures.

Migration is in our genes. We are Anglo-Scots on my father's side; my paternal grandmother was descended from Highlanders, poor folk who were economic migrants to London. Via the Limehouse docks, for centuries the entry point of commoditised folk, they followed the path of French Huguenots, European Jews, African Slaves, Colonial Indians who got their first taste of London through this part of the East End.

Gran and her sisters married into English families, survived two World Wars including rationing, the Blitz of London by the Germans, and many other hardships. They all smoked many cigarettes, drank whisky or brandy, fought like cats, and lived tough lives into their seventies and eighties. The Anglo side of our family were farmers, likely descended from Dutch immigrants who drained the fen lands east of Cambridge. Tough folk with a history going back to horse drawn technology through the transition to steam engines and into the management of diesel machinery.

My father is the most vehement of Englishmen. Feasting on the stories of Empire. He donned the uniform of "Law Enforcement" from where he could forcibly preserve his Anglo-Empirical view of the world. My grandfather, also a policeman, died in a "Dark London" that was smashed by German bombs. He died on the "domestic frontline," where a civilization bent under Nazi bombing raids, sometimes broke, and resorted to dysfunctions never publicly, or even openly, discussed. My elder brother, following the footsteps of our father and grandfather, joined the ranks of law enforcement professionals, cementing a family heritage across three generations.

My mother was different. An economic migrant from Finland, she worked as a Red Cross nurse and, for a short time, an au pair in London. Introduced to my father through mutual friends, she remained in England and settled in London. Finnish people are rare, we seldom notice them as a country or a society, yet their impact on history has been significant thanks to their own level of tacit stoicism. The veins of this national trait run even deeper than any other stoic form of which you may have heard.

Finnish stoicism, Sisu, is the product of a nation occupied and reoccupied over history by Sweden and Russia. Finland eventually gained independence in 1917. Shortly thereafter, the Finns faced down the might of the Soviet Russian military machine. Stalin's attempts to annex their country were fought to a standstill by men and women protecting the independence of their young nation. Finland, abandoned by the allies, fought alongside Germany on the Eastern front in the cruellest of cold temperatures. Many Finnish families were broken by the conflict, annexed by the Russians in lost territory, or simply disappeared. In the village where my mother lives, a statue of an unknown soldier is dressed in a German stormtrooper uniform.

He overlooks the graves of the fallen. The names of the fallen in this tiny village are Finnish, Swedish, and German. In other villages, some are English. These were freedom fighters who fought against Russian empire building. Authentic unsung heroes who received no coverage in the stories of Hollywood.

Like many of her country folk, my mother is stoic and resilient.

My father divorced my mother in a vitriolic and scarring battle of wills, winning custody of his children. Like many men, he then excused himself from the responsibility of upbringing, which he bestowed upon my grandmother, the Highlander. He was not present emotionally or mentally.

Like many Finns, my mother endured stoically and was determined to be present, even from a distance. She always made time for phone calls, cards, and small gifts even when she could not be close to her children. She took interest in our education, hobbies, and music to stay connected and relevant to my brother and me. As a young boy, I did not always offer sufficient recognition of, nor grace for, the determination and the disciplines of my mother and my grandmother; that said, thanks to them, I grew up with respect for all people, and an appreciation for the resilience of women in a man's world.

With no male mentors in my formative years, the influences of my mother and grandmother were defining. Both my grandfathers had been killed at a young age, and my father was a law unto himself. To become a real man, I learned about courage, stoicism and resilience by observing my Scottish grandmother and my Finnish mother. Their traits illustrated ways to behave that were missing in my male influencers. What mum and gran lacked in traditional male knowledge was supplemented by the extensive reading of comic strips like "The Beano", "Tintin", and the war focused "Commando." Such reading material laid the remaining foundations of my early learning. Hungrily, I devoured these comics and others like them, creating a dreamscape with which real life could never compete.

The ability of both mum and gran to demonstrate generosity and kindness against the odds, even when they had nothing, remain with me today. Spiritually, thanks in part to these matriarchal influences, I matured more with a sense of being Finnish or even Finno-Scots than English. This is not cultural misappropriation. This is the reality of British-ness for many folks. Britain, after all, is a hybrid nation of jumbled families and an agglomeration of cultures. Personally though, the values of solidarity, kindness and love, as well as an appreciation of nature, are all linked to matriarchal influence. Whereas Englishness, thanks to patriarchal influence, became attached to fear, anger, and hubris. The nationality of righteous indignation. My internal conflict was real and ultimately became the fuel in a journey of discovery. The discovery of identity, purpose and knowledge.

This story then, is a modern novel. It is a story of growth, adventure, and struggle that I share with you in the hope that it brings enjoyment, engagement, and some form of education.

This is also a story of integrity and humour in the face of adversity.

It is a story of resilience.

It is a story of Sisu.

Trans Alpine

YEAR OF THE RABBIT

Rabbit people are elegant and courteous with keen senses. They are surprisingly savvy in business and finance. They adore abundance and cannot tolerate boredom constantly hopping from one excitement to another. Gentle in nature, they can be jumpy and cautious, yet analytical and diplomatic. Rabbit people need to learn how to manage their emotions to survive.

THE FRENCH ALPS

AM I GOING TO DIE? Possibly, if I don't get my act together.

The snow bites my skin, as the blizzard whips my trembling body. If I make a wrong decision now, the possibility of death becomes a probability. I have cheated death a few times. Not by choice but by circumstances, some of which were self-made, others of which were imposed. I am not sure if I can cheat it this time.

What are my choices now?

Standing there, semi-naked, in white out conditions, I could climb up to the peak of the mountain where there may be a refuge with food and drink. This is France after all, and a well-stocked refuge is not uncommon on their mountain tops. Alternatively, I could head down to the road, invisible beneath me, which might be the safer option. Wearing summer hiking gear, a vest, shorts, socks and boots, I carry a few provisions in my rucksack. Half a baguette, a small hunk of cheese, and a bottle of water for food. A few extra clothes for warmth and some basic camping gear for shelter. It doesn't sound like much but collectively all these items weigh about twenty kilograms. Not an insignificant weight to carry on a mountain hike which is now entering day five. Or is it day four? It is so cold now I cannot remember when I started or where I am headed. Here I am, stuck in a blizzard, contemplating my own end and, even with nobody around, feeling stupid.

I am embarrassed at a predicament which could lead to my untimely death.

This is not the first time I have faced death; or at least the threat of death. I know death as a continuum of existential threats ranging from raging storms in the South Atlantic and raging men in London's pubs. I am still surprised that the world finds me intact and fully fit. Internally though, I struggle with a turmoil perpetuated by a search for peace of mind.

In the heart of the French Alps, at the mercy of nature's fickle friendship, I once again face my potential demise, though less violent than some of the previous encounters. That's one blessing.

As a natural optimist, I like to count my blessings.

"Onwards and upwards" says the devil on my shoulder, tempting my ego. The devil wants me to forge ahead, peak the mountain, and be a hero. That would be a story to tell in the bars and brewhouses.

The temptation is real.

The angel, on my other shoulder, is a counsel of caution and wisdom. She recommends descending. Go find shelter and improve your chances of survival. "Funny", I think in the moment, "how devils are male, and angels are female". That might be my own implicit bias and possibly a product of upbringing. Clearly though, there are still some sparks firing in my synapses and decisiveness is not beyond my current capability.

With renewed optimism, I know two things with certainty: there is no point changing clothes until I find shelter and can dry my body, and this is no time to question my own life choices. If you're not moving, you're dying. I am already shaking, almost uncontrollably. As my body temperature is plummeting, it's obvious that I have to get going.

Thinking is hard; hypothermia is harder.

DARK LONDON

Smash!

The plate glass picture window explodes into a million little pieces. A fire extinguisher is the missile which caused this offense. It has done a thorough job. Inside to out or outside to in, the trajectory of the fire extinguisher is unclear. The glass splatter will tell that story later, but once the yelling melee of scrambling people clears the decks I see carnage. Either way, it is going to be expensive. The artwork on the window was hand painted and cost a few hundred pounds. The glass is easily another few hundred. That's most of a grand gone right there. The remaining costs include shattered furniture, glasses and, destroyed inventory. Then there's the emotional cost of lost business until the dust settles. The final account will easily be a few grand plus extras.

More glass shatters as people try to clear out. In the panic, clenched fists rain blows and flashing blades draw blood. Welcome to "Dark London."

The world of my early twenties - in the territories between Crystal Palace and Croydon - is a conflict zone. This is Dark London, where the destruction of trusted societal institutions has created a war between the yin and yang of my own philosophies. The struggle between Light and Dark is reduced to a binary state: the exploitation of stupid people (as upward mobility feels unattainable) vs the wrestle with instilled values (often spoken by men yet walked by women). This is further distilled; temptations vs rewards. Or simply put, profit over enlightenment.

I exist on Maslow's bottom rung, earning enough money to pay some bills but not enough to feel safe.

Friday nights in the southeast of London are volatile, complex, and uncertain. This is the arena where a hard world pauses, refuels, and refreshes. The punters are mostly local, but others come down from the West End or the southwestern boroughs looking for action and an escape from the sanitized post codes of less colourful sanctuaries. Whilst outward appearances have changed, the fundamentals of the human condition remain the same. And just like in Roman gladiatorial times the desire of the chattering classes to see the big fight have not gone away. And so we say to those modern gladiators:

> "Those who are about to die, we salute you!"

Some nights it is quiet and there is opportunity to speak with customers or enjoy the trade. Yet, in those quieter moments, there is also the threat of pending anarchy. Silence here is a rare commodity, and peace does not last for long. If this was ancient Rome, then southeast Londoners are gladiators in the arena, fighting for survival; they are also decompressing in their dysfunction with pints of lager, shots of spirits, and slivers of substances that we know but do not see. This substantive cocktail is the catalyst in a countdown that will, at some point, trigger a round of flailing fists, flashing blades, or worse. The darkness of London stretches back through the novels of Conan-Doyle, Dickens, and Shakespeare. For centuries the fuel in the fight has been "entertainment after dark." This is not a new concept and when it all kicks off, the collateral damage is significant.

The citizens from more affluent post codes are the spectators in this Colosseum. They bring the cash and make it rain. Looking for inked arms, mean muscle, and bloody engagement, they drink from the top shelf looking down upon the huddled masses. Being here is edgy enough, but the prospect of bloodshed adds a frisson of excitement to an electric environment. I must assume they are here for the entertainment. The booze they drink is available up West, as are the hostelries, which are also cleaner and generally safer, which makes them more boring perhaps. In rare cases, one of the local warriors gets to walk into the night with a princess on his arm. Whatever the motivations and desires, whatever the expected outcomes, Friday nights in the southeast boroughs provide rich material for stories that fuel the fires of Monday morning chats over coffees.

And if Friday night is dull, there's always Saturday night for a rerun. And failing that, good gossip feeds the mythology of an escapade undertaken. After all, never let the truth get in the way of a good story.

Drinking and fighting are good for business. Up to the point when a bomb goes off.

"Are you not entertained?"

But let's come back a couple of steps.

I work here for my father, his buddies, and a bit of coin. The price of family loyalty means I get to manage their bar and defend myself against local gangsters who, it is rumoured, want to take over the venue for their own criminal purposes. I've been in plenty of bars around the city and beyond. I have also worked a few. It is not my choice of profession, but it is an easy way into London life. In the absence of career opportunities there's always pints to be pulled and drinks to be drunk.

This is one of the border bars.

British bars are cultural hotspots and often more than mere drinking dens. Like mile markers on roads, they are signs indicating destinations and directions. Some are more polished than others. Most are weather beaten, bearing the scars of history. Others are border markers indicating whose territory you are now entering. The pubs and bars of London have a history going back hundreds of years and you best be careful where you set foot, particularly if you are on the edge of someone's territory. My bar, situated on the eastern edge of a western district, on the border of Palace turf – Crystal Palace that is - is feisty with live entertainment tonight. Palace must be playing at home.

This is the second visit in as many weeks by the local robber barons. They want this property as part of their turf and their distribution network. Today's violence appears mindless but is pre-meditated. These are warnings of their power rather than mutually assured destruction. They want to retail their product in the bar, but papa and pals said no. They, the business owners, casually mention the situation to me in passing. A warning, without HR representation, that I might want to be aware of pending trouble. At this moment in time, I am stuck at the back of the back bar where there are no exits. I wait calmly. As the bodies thin out and the business settles down, I will be able to get out front. The cool night air flows through the broken window.

The hyenas who scavenge for the robber barons are servicing the crowd. Manhandling bodies, pushing people around, and intimidating those who resist. Resistance is futile. One of the hyenas is close to me. T-shirt, jeans, wiry lean and mean, he has his hand in his jacket. I can smell him from here, sweat and cheap scent. He is eyeing me up, ready to attack, made brave with his pack close by. Adrenaline pumps through my body. Time slows down, and I wiggle my toes ready to strike. Hit and run is the only way out of here. Otherwise, I am trapped in the back and could be carrion for the whole pack. His hand starts to pull out from his jacket. I can probably land one blow before he retaliates but I eschew violence. Even in the face of criminal intent I wish to avoid lawbreaking behaviours. It is stupid, I know, but it is a code by which I have chosen to live. Not a code of pacifism, just a code whereby violence is the absolute last solution to any perceived problem. It is hard to maintain this code, which has become a real discipline and, as the boundaries of behaviour are stretched, so is the respect of my own code.

These guys are mean. Dirty cheap muscle hired to help a faceless evil, they are amped on coke and maybe pills. They will wreck the joint in exchange for a few lines and some free beers. They are not worth fighting. When you wrestle with dogs you can guarantee that you will be bitten and probably end up in the shit.

Taking the high road is not easy, also I don't want my mom to know I've been fighting.

I am genuinely scared. Breathing slowly and deeply I work hard to remain calm, waiting for an exit opportunity. Do not panic, otherwise, this will not end well.

The hungry hyena opens his jacket. I see a dark shape. Is it a blade? It looks like a gun. I can't be sure in the half-light. I just know that either option will be painful. This little piggie is tooled up. This situation is messed up.

Then the plink, plink fizz of gas fills the air.

Ever the optimist I like to count my blessings, thank goodness for that bomb. Fast on the tail of the fire extinguisher, a CS gas canister skids across the floor bumping up against the guilty red cylinder that smashed the window. I hate being gassed, it hurts. This is not the first time. The gaseous agent spews out across the floor and will soon fill the space. The spew is further agitating the excitable audience who, eyes wide open with adrenaline pumping, are sucking down large gulps of air tainted with tear gas. The impact is maximized. The crowd starts to scream and kick its way through the window and doors.

I feel the gas bite my flesh as it crawls up my body and leaves its residue on exposed skin. This malevolent ghost traces thousands of indelible scars like the poisonous stings of so many wasps. Bodies crushed in small spaces are trying to escape the pain and the hyena grimaces, and leers at me. I assume he's on coke, rather than tabs or anything stronger, as the gas seems to be hurting him, too. Coke gives him confidence to carry but hopefully not pull the trigger or run his blade into my body.

The tear gas hurts, yet it offers a reprieve from imminent violence. I embrace the opportunity it presents to exit this moment of theatre.

The clean handkerchief in my pocket is old-fashioned and applied over my face. It is a simple measure that stops the residue entering my nose and mouth. My eyes are stinging, but I know not to rub them.

Time to move.

Incapacitated by gas, the lean meanie, bent over with eyes streaming, is less menacing now. Whilst the effect of terror is writ large among the paying customers, in my case the gangsters have scored an own goal. Although it is unclear if I am an intended target or just part of the collateral, the tactic gives me time and space to get out. Unwilling to wait around and find out more of their intentions, I move away from lean meanie towards fresh air.

One bomb has been enough to shatter this evening's crowd and disperse the people. The spectators got their money's worth, though, and Monday morning coffee time gossip will be spicy with stories now.

I know not to rub my eyes but can feel burning residue on the back of my hands, seeping through the pores in my skin working through the powerful adrenaline that is keeping me alert.

Pushing people aside, I step around choking and bleeding bodies, past the weeping faces and out through the broken window. I cross the road into a safer darkness. Stepping on to new territory and in the lee of darkened shop fronts I can finally breath cleaner air. Wearing dark clothes, standing still in dark shadows, my safety is relative, and I watch the street theatre continue to unfold.

Shattered glass twinkles. People disperse along with the gas as the bullet heads smash a few punters and a few other windows before they disappear. By the time that police, fire, and ambulance services arrive, the crowd is mostly gone, and they are left with street detritus and a handful of broken frightened people to manage. Hugging the shadows, I am sure that the robber baron gang is gone. Stepping out onto the pavement I turn away from the trouble and walk up the hill looking for my car. Parked in a nearby safe zone, I still scan the terrain for threats. Safety is not guaranteed on "live entertainment" nights, but I think the bullet heads are whooping it up in the next pub now. They are fifty metres down the street in the opposite direction. There, they can celebrate the anarchy, with a fistful of dollars and a pledge of allegiance to the man with the biggest fists, whoever he may be. The distance of this pub is far enough for plausible deniability should curious police officers come around asking questions.

Safety is relative. Fifty metres is a long way on a London street. Standing still, I take a final look over and around the car, unlock the door, fire up the engine and pull away. I have suffered no major damage, but this is wearing thin. These safety routines are necessary. The car is a trap after dark, and I regularly change locations. Breaking up patterns of behaviour is a habit now, an essential skill to remain free from harm. Sadly necessary, I learned the skill from reading spy books by John le Carre. Espionage stories about bad actors in other peoples' territories. It never occurred to me that I would have to use these techniques in my own back yard.

I am trying to earn a living and find my way in life. This is too spicy and was never really part of the plan. London is a great city, with an amazing history and culture; a great place for earning and learning. "Dark London" is its evil twin, the underside of that history and culture with a great capacity for struggle and violence.

I eschew violence naturally, except as a last resort; family loyalty has plunged me into this heart of darkness, which I resent as I am stuck here now. Stuck in a London which may be going into, or coming out of, another recession, I am not sure which as recessions seem to be almost as common as IRA bombing threats.

I count the days until I can leave and find a better place.

THE OLD GANGSTER LEANS IN. He's bigger than me, not taller, broader. A massive chest and fists like hams are the signs of bare-knuckle fights. Part of a former life where he had to fight to survive. His tattoos are etched in a faded prison blue. A fork tailed songbird, rests on the "v" of forefinger and thumb. He's done time inside. The swallow is symbol of being locked up, or "doing a bit of bird." Etched with blue ink and a blade, I have seen these tattoos before. Not just around here. I also saw them when I was younger. Administered in school with a sharp pointed compass, they were badges of honour for a subset of the student population. They are not my cup of tea; my skin is tattoo free.

OG has tattoos on his fists and forearms. Maybe on other parts of his body. He's built like a beast, unsurprising for a bare-knuckle fighter and one-time apprentice butcher. Training back then was unsophisticated, mainly involving machetes and cow carcasses. High school was irrelevant for there was money to be made in butchery (either in the ring or in the shop). School is for academic learning, which is the wrong kind out here, where learning for the purposes of survival starts at an early age. The toughest survive using street wisdom. Academia is a luxury concept.

His backstory is impressive and daunting. People like the OG, as seen on T.V., are not meant to be real. They are meant to be characters in movies and shows where the good guy always wins. Sat here in front of me, he is very real. Larger than life and twice as wide, the

OG fills my whole field of vision and can easily capture my attention.

Even more impressively, the OG can do business math in his head. He teaches me numbers at high speed - fast calculations that help you survive and keep you alive. The streets are his market and, in that world, anything can be bought or sold.

The OG captivates my young mind. Unlike the folks of social standing who have influenced my life prior to murder, the OG is authentic. The genuine article. His massive frame fills the social void in my world.

He is a product of the post war baby boom; the OG has seen many things and fears nobody. Except maybe the Russians. But that's another story. This is our story:

> "You'll be alright Angus. From our side of the house that is. You're trusted to tell the truth. Stay square and you'll come through. Ever since my old man came back from Crete our type has been on the wrong side of the house. Killing Germans for King and Country didn't make our lives better. The people who unleashed the dogs of war, made good use of this community. At the end they just wanted us to go back in the cage. We tried to live normal lives; some got a ribbon from the King but there was no real reward for 'blitz spirit' in the aftermath of war. Everything was broken. The city was wrecked."

Southeast London is full of characters. Gangsters and survivors like the OG. History books celebrate the end of the war, yet nobody speaks to the destruction of society and the struggle to rebuild the boroughs and buildings. The OG's father served in occupied Greece. Living in bushes, eating berries by day, he would emerge at night to spear the Nazi occupiers and push them off cliffs. The precursor to special forces warfare, theirs was a glorified industry that rarely speaks to consequence. You don't read about that in the comic books or the history books.

> "We put the knives and guns away. Went about our business. The business of survival. They trained us to live like animals, to fight and to kill

for the love of country. For freedom and independence. And, not for the first time, when the people came home, the officers got the bank jobs, the government positions, and the industry accolades. For the rest of us, they tried to put us back in the box. They wanted us to be a civil society but brought the fight home, to squash us down. The thing is, once the cat is out of the bag, you can't put it back in again."

I believed him then, and some of his teachings have proven to stand the test of time.

Belief is my weakness. So is trust. These two attributes make me vulnerable and, even in the face of contrary evidence, I want to believe what people tell me. All people. I take everyone as I find them as I find the alternative to be horrible. A world of distrust, cynicism, fear, and hatred is a colourless world without hope. In spite of prejudice it is important to believe that people fated by birth, are intrinsically good. This is a principled foundation of my own behaviour which can be painful to maintain.

Also, I have no choice now. There is nowhere else to go for help, and he is authentic. Speaking truth to reality, the OG is the most genuine male mentor I have known for many years. This is a new experience, and I am cautious about the lessons learned. But where else do I go? Once upon a time I could go to the police. That is no longer an option. The waters are muddy, since the murder; some are even poisoned, and it will take time to find clear water for I am not sure how to navigate this world. After all, how do you tell a policeman that you need protection from other policemen?

What about a doctor?

I am not ill; scarred, yes. But I sought help from a doctor, only to be pushed away with a rebuke. My problems are imaginary, unbelievable for one so young. Yet they are very real to me, and I know enough to understand I am not equipped to manage life on my own. The return for being vulnerable though is a rebuke. Judged for being young by a member of the chattering classes with a shortage of life experience. What does this doctor know? I came here for help, and the offered solution is a prescription for anti-depressants to help my imagination and to suppress the pain. No better than a drug dealer, the doctor offers an escape from reality and no advice on how to rebuild your life in the aftermath of destruction. There's no medication for that. Unbeknownst to him, the doctor seals my fate and that of all institutions.

Leaving the doctor's office I realize that my last light of hope in societal institutions has just blinked out. As I walk alone up the road, the pain of loneliness sears a hole in my heart. I am totally alone now. Nothing and nobody matter anymore, just survival. It is from this day I become an observer in my own life. I exist outside the shell that is my body and rarely engage on an emotional level with anybody. Connections lead to trust, trust may lead to love, love and trust combined are the enemies of truth. As I cut loose from all acquaintance, I realize that I can stay sharp mentally and physically. It is a chilling realization, but it works. The preservation and protection of self is in the cold world of disassociation.

What about a lawyer?

I have no money, nor have I committed a crime. For as long as I have known, the law is administered by men in uniform. Lawyers are something you see on T.V. generally working for the well-heeled. If I needed a lawyer, I wouldn't have the money to pay for one. There is a system out there somewhere, the Crown Prosecution Service maybe or a similar organization, that is supposed to help the vulnerable. I don't know how to find it, nor who to ask for help or guidance. Fundamentally though lawyers fall into the same resource pool as doctors now. It is highly likely that their response to my vulnerability will be similar, exacerbating the shame of my current predicament, and so I will carry this burden alone.

What about family?

They are mostly gone or scattered to the four winds. My grandparents are dead. My mother, a foreign émigré, lives several hundred miles away. I cannot share with her my current predicament. This is my fate. She knows something is going on, but she has suffered enough pain as a policeman's spouse. Forced out into the cold, thanks to decisions by divorce court judges, she has been separated from her children in a fight that my father cared only to win, by any means. My brother is a serving policeman, and it would be wrong to solicit his assistance. I believe, rightly or wrongly, that we are tainted by sins of the father, and it would not be right or proper to mix my brother into this affair. My stepmother and youngest siblings are stuck in the middle of the very same predicament, doing their best to survive the onslaught. They have no bandwidth or capability for support.

What about friends?

I thought I had many but, in this new world, they seem to have gone cold, too. The human condition in action. Friendships are fickle and fragile, particularly when you are in real trouble. I do not really know who to ask for help nor for what help I might be asking. Feeling alone, my friends seem very distant now. This is my perception and perception is reality. Why would they have any concern for me when their perception is that I am an accessory to something they do not want to be around. Only one man reaches out. A Navy guy who has seen hardship provides support, guidance, and a friendly chat in my hours of need. He's seen struggle, bears no ill will and suspends judgement. There's a couple of others like him, but I cannot pull on them forever. It's just good to be around them in the bar or after a rugby match where I get a temporary reprieve from this nightmare world.

Alone in the dark mostly, carrying a triple burden (protection of my own innocence, the conviction of truth and the protection of family), I strive for validation at work, on the sports field, and in society, yet little changes over time. The social construct requires that you stay in your lane, which means there is no way out, and upward mobility is not for me. In this topsy turvy world, where all my institutions - education, law, and the church - are broken, merely flimsy products of the chattering classes. Full of righteous contradictions, these are places where the chattering classes stay safe in their sanctuaries, and I am left unsupported, navigating a new world where there is no meaning, and trust has vanished.

Where old relationships are flawed and new ones impossible to maintain, I learned there is always hope. My dog Oscar brings that hope in the form of canine loyalty and playfulness. Outside of the OG he is my other mentor and the remainder of my support network. Oscar represents a gentler aspect of life with a form of empathy that I feel but do not understand. The OG represents the harsher realities of the world and shares truths hitherto untold about social constructs and the attributes of power. He shows me respect, mainly because I fight my own battles. In addition, we are both aware that my testimony puts him in a place and time that undermines police evidence. My statements made to investigating officers present obstacles to the swift conviction that they are seeking and which, therefore, bring a world of pain down on my head.

This is my actual crime. There is no place for honesty and integrity in their world. Intimidation is their method. Everyone is guilty until proven innocent and I am an obstacle to progress. Young and naïve, I believe in truth and integrity. Weirdly and, in contradiction to my upbringing, the OG is the representation of those values. The policemen are not. I am not a suspect in their investigation, that has been made clear. Nevertheless, I am an obstacle to progress, and they intend to crush all obstacles. That has also been made clear.

The OG and my father have been arrested and released. They have been held in prison cells, interviewed aggressively and doggedly pursued. When they are restrained or out of sight, police officers seek me out determined to bend my will and rewrite aspects of history.

Thanks to my version of events, I have been stalked, threatened, cajoled, and tracked across town, all to force a change of opinion, to rearrange the facts and to give the police what they want. A few sentence changes here and there, a couple of time adjustments and location alterations will suffice. *"Come along now Angus, you know it makes sense. We've written it for you anyway. All we need is a little signature here and it all goes away."*

The language at the beginning was soft and cajoling. Friendly and encouraging. Nevertheless, it was intimidation in the form of grooming. What I know is that I don't know what I don't know. If I do what I am told by the police, an autocratic rule I have lived my life by, then the OG and my father may be off to jail for the murder of their business partner. This does not seem right when I am being coerced to pen statements that would contravene my life principle to respect the rule of law. Instinctively, I know that perjury is bad and if I lie in a statement for the police, then they control my narrative. So, I can obey the police – like I have been brought up to believe. Or I can disobey the police and respect the rule of law, which I feel is the strongest priority.

A Hobson's choice. Play their game and have no life except under their control. Or do the right thing and have them destroy my life through intimidation and worse. I choose to do the right thing, not fully realizing the extent to which these people will go.

The pressure is real and heavy and singular.

I trust my gut and stick to the rule of law. I will not lie in court, nor in testimony, which puts me at odds with the policemen who regularly visit our house. It is the right thing to do. I imagine standing in front of a judge, swearing truth on the bible, knowing that I cannot lie for anyone. Trapped between might and right, the conflict is real. So is the pain.

What a mess.

Life as I know it is over. There is no coming back from this. When the OG has been released, he tells me what's occurring. Often in loco parentis, he remembers me when my father is absent.

Yet, there is a quid pro quo. The OG teaches me how to survive "Dark London." He teaches me what he knows about surviving the odds, after all he learned to survive at a young age. It is a brutal business school with a vertical learning curve on cost, value, and consequences.

Quid pro quo is new to me.

In business and in politics, it is an exchange for goods and services.

Business is all about quid pro quo.

And London is all about business.

The OG delivers and in return, I tell the truth and pay the price The world is frightening and sometimes painful; sometimes his umbrella opens for protection but mostly I must weather the storm alone. In the jungle that is "Dark London", he knows who's who in the zoo and is respected by them. This zoo is busy; business is costly, and exits are hard to find.. People have been burned. Others are out of pocket. A few others are also in the pocket of the extended web of vendors, suppliers, and facilitators that keep the zoo running. In this zoo, there have been actions and there will be consequences.

Thanks to OG though, his side of the house will leave me alone.

Shame that doesn't go for the men of law.
My father's side of the house.

THE FRENCH ALPS

In my twenty-eighth year now, I have found an exit from that world of pain. The influences of dark London are pervasive though and I remain an observer in my own life. I feel like I exist outside of myself. Like a child looking at the world through a clear window everything is new and needs to be learned again. Adrenaline rushes provide emotional highs and lead to risk taking. Neural scarring, and deeply ingrained memories are by-products of violence which perpetuate trust issues. The lived experience of multiple traumas haunt me still. I am alone in my healing which seems to be the safest place. I have tried many things to escape "Dark London" and discovered that being unbending in my values is where survival lies. Courage, resilience, and integrity are my iron triangle. They are the hard-earned medals from a time spent in a hell where every day was a fight to survive.

Hope came in the form of service, the Navy had started a new recruitment campaign; before long I was in uniform, a different one to that of my forebears, yet it feels good. For many, service life is tough. For me, the structure and process bring hope of a new future. I learn new skills, enjoy regular meals, get regular exercise, and not least of all, gain new experiences. This leap of faith is real. It teaches me to trust process, trust engineering, and trust total strangers that have no prior influence in my life.

Before long I am deployed across the Atlantic, down into the Persian Gulf, and out across the Baltic Sea. Epic weather sees our ships shuddering in gale force winds, crushed under the weight of grey, concrete like waves, or rolling in blue azure like currents. Navigating through icebergs we explore the coves and shores of Grytviken, a whaling station ghost town populated by elephant seals and penguins.

Sailing through Suez, we disembark in Egypt, Djibouti, and the countries of the Middle East, exploring the deserts and the seas of

Northeast Africa and the Arabian Peninsula. Floating through the fogs of the Skagerrak and the Kattegat, we slip silently into the brackish waters separating Soviet Union satellites from their Nordic neighbours and the boundaries of Cold War nations. In these environments the relearning of trust continues. It is easier than before. People here are professional, and friendships are forged in foreign affairs and shared circumstance. Service life creates some peace of mind in the preparations for war and, as someone who shuns violence, the irony is not lost on me. It also pays a living wage.

And it is thanks to the Royal Navy I acquire skills, knowledge, and experiences which can support me through the rest of my days. Yet, out here in the military world, the scars of conflict are visible in the substrate of society. Every country is war torn to some degree, and the sadness is real. Worse still, in our attempts to offer aid, we encounter victims of trafficking, including children. Heartbreaking conditions and disturbing images that make unforgettable memories re-open deeper scars and add another layer to my own sense of dismay at the human condition. Worst of these is the grisly memorial of a concentration camp with gas chamber intact serving as a museum that plumbs the depths to which humans can sink. Heaped up shoes and showcased memorabilia of summarily executed victims are all that remain of a human hatred that scorched the earth. Maybe if I had not suffered from the dysfunction of the human condition I would have brushed off these experiences. Undeniably though, the benefits of service made me worldly and simultaneously cast a light upon the hidden truths of humanity.

But the Navy also exposed the rawness of nature, and nature is the gift that keeps on giving.

Crashing seas in the South Atlantic and baking suns in the Middle East are without compare. The power and forces of nature are on full display when transiting oceans and seas. There is no experience more frightening than the pounding of the sea when it shakes the rivets of your ship, where icebergs and growlers are your last view of the world as gigantic salty waves pummel the bridge. Temporarily submerged you learn a new prayer, cursing the engineers who built this thing, only to praise their expertise as you resurface once more, ready for the next flurry of blows from the oceanic pugilist. And conversely, there is no magic like a sunrise on the water, sitting above the bow, admiring the agility of dolphins as they dive through your bow wave, and surf your wake, feeding and playing in their family pods.

On land too, nature nourishes the soul. Foggy Dartmoor, the rain drenched Brecon Beacons and the briny coves of Devon and Cornwall offering their hiking trails, hillside climbs, and peaks with stone cairns that ultimately descend through jagged rock faces onto sandy beaches by azure waters. Look beyond the discomfort of the squall or the heat of the sun and you will find a forever friend.

Back in civvy, life is softer. Here, I am studying modern languages, Chinese and French prose to be precise. Language is a gateway to culture and in the days spent studying, reading French and writing Chinese, I discover areas of expression I warm to rapidly. There is something both therapeutic and educational in the study of French prose and Chinese calligraphy which is particularly satisfying. At the end of my first year of study, a trek through the French Alps seems like a good adventure. I do miss the adventures of the military.

Fit, lean, and even with a heavy pack, I know that I can walk into Italy in a few days. Walking is easy and natural, the weather is great, and France is civilized. Travel in Europe is mostly fun. The physical challenge will be a good experience and the Alps, in my case, are uncharted territory. The exploration of the mountains offers the desired adrenaline rush, and the permanency of alpine exercise means a new adventure and an exploration of food, which is also an gateway to culture. With this vision in mind I head into the mountains. After all, it's just a bit of summertime back-packing, what could possibly go wrong?

Behaviour has consequences. I thought I was prepared for this expedition. Being a victim is not in my DNA, nor is complaining, but a blizzard in August is bullshit. It's just unfair. That said, indecision is the enemy of action and it's time to move now. No shelter. Just snow. No point standing still.

The icy, angry snow that bites my skin and tears my flesh reinforces the need for attention to detail, which gets harder as the onset of hypothermia reinforces my lonely state. Out here I own all my decisions and all of the outcomes.

Just yesterday, the summer heat was burning my back. The weather forecast this morning was uninformative. Clearly, I read too much French and have not learned to listen enough. A bit of rain greyed the skies outside my window which reminded me of Dartmoor, ringing no real alarm bells. Just some rain, that is all. A bit of breakfast, some hot coffee, and I'll tip over the Col d'Isere in no time.

That was plan A. Before the snow.

Time for plan B. After the snow.

I don't really have a plan B. I am still pissed off at the capriciousness of fate. But, this is no time to die, so, shaking uncontrollably, I decide that today I am on the side of the angel and will opt for wisdom over ego; ignoring the devil of temptation, starting my descent towards an invisible road that lies somewhere beneath my current position; biting my lip to generate pain, a bit of heat and some focus. I tread carefully through the snow looking for the downward path. If I find the road, I can find the town or maybe head up to the refuge faster. Then I can get whatever help I need.

We did wet and dry survival training before. Entry level expedition leadership and team training tested in controlled environments. Uncomfortable at times, it was also exhilarating, learning how much stress you can endure physically, emotionally and mentally. Some of that has been tested, on land and in the water. Today though is the real deal. There is no margin of error.

In cold like this, under pressure, and experiencing extreme stresses, decisions need to be simple. Reduced to option A or option B; complexity leads to analysis, followed by paralysis and nothingness. The cold here would freeze the balls of a brass monkey. Dressed in shorts, singlet and lightweight hiking boots, it is impossible to process variables anyway. Life is reduced to "pick one option. Up or down."

A voice in my head says, "Keep moving muppet." A physical training instructor I think, or maybe one of the survival guys. Marine or Navy, I am not sure which, but the voice is familiar, and the advice is sound.

Down it is.

Nearly snow blind, treading carefully, I fumble for the downslope trajectory and in a desperate attempt to find warmth and shelter move gradually towards the road I cannot see and the illusion of a safety that may or may not be there.

This is painful but I've known worse. Physical pain cannot trump mental or emotional pain. I ignore the cold biting my skin and sink into the core of my soul where secret stores of gratitude are hidden. Movement heals and I continue to step stumble through the blinding snow. This will make a great story, if I survive.

Will people believe me?

Who knows?

The adventure is real. I would rather regret what I have done than what I haven't done.

DARK LONDON

In the pre-dawn, I stand outside the house and look up at the darkened front door. I can see it is open, and I bite my lip to focus. The police cars outside are quiet, no flashes or splashes. They are dark, foreign and conspicuous by their uniformity. That means the men inside are plain clothes. The neighbours' houses are quiet, too. Today's visit is by low profile men of law who work in the shadows.

What are they up to now?

I do not visit here often these days. I know they turn up regularly as part of their intimidation strategy. Hoping to make someone crack, they put pressure on the family to cough up invisible information that their cynical minds believe is stashed away in the family home or tucked away in our collective consciences. They are neither subtle nor sophisticated. Just persistent.

Everyone is fair game to these leather-jacketed gorillas, including kids and women. I made my own survival arrangements; nevertheless, they still find me across London, often outside of their jurisdiction. Shake downs are inevitable and my first experience of these at the courtesy of a subset of the Metropolitan police is frightening. In tight corners in public spaces, they are clever and conspicuous with a sprinkling of low-level menace. I have experienced multiple shake downs across the world. Mostly by uniformed authority leveraging power. They leave an indelible impact and open your eyes to a bigger game with new rules. Here in London, members of the Met appear out of nowhere, get close, and form a shield close to a wall. Inside a bar or outside a shop, to outward appearances the encounter looks like a small group of friends having a conversation. The internal dynamic is different. Friendly words are wrapped around veiled threats to deliver spring loaded tension. Bound by some rules, the gorillas of the Met aim for provocation to justify a response. They hope to trigger you with insults, threats, and cajoling. If you lash out, they can strike hard and bring you into closer confines. It is dehumanizing and confusing. Sometimes they are so close I can smell their scent, the stale tea on their breath or the cheap scent on their bodies. Animal instinct – fight or flight – are natural instincts, hard to resist.

They know my predicament better than I do and leverage my family history against me .

I grew up with violence. From the youngest age a target of vitriol thanks to my father's role as a police officer. Now, I am a target of threats by the self-same force that he served, men with sticks and the ability to inflict more pain.

What they do not know is that I've lived this all of my life. Instinctively I know to stay calm and de-escalate. No posturing. "Be like a swan" is my mantra. Calm on the outside, furious on the inside. Eventually the shake downs are so common they diminish in impact. They reach a peak and gradually die away. Resigned to this pattern of behaviour, I give them nothing. Unsure which is worse, the blizzard of emotional pain or physical pain, the only course of action is to walk through hell and hope that I will come out the other side.

Today is cold and damp, standard London weather. Just another miserable day. It is mid-autumn, deep into rugby season, and the weekly physical poundings keep me battle hardened and toned. I play with an intensity fueled by the defiance of the odds, discovering my own form of Sisu. Unsure what this looks like from without, I continue to bleed blood, break bones, and rise out of the mud every weekend to face the filth that infected our lives. Rugby is my only surviving institution, it is the remnants of family, a gladiatorial arena for civil combat where truth and friendship are hard forged. No matter how much the rugby hurts, it is no match for the mental and emotional snowstorm of Met gorillas and gangster hyenas.

"Angus, come home please. The police are here; your brother and sister are frightened. We need help." The siren call of family loyalty is the voice of my stepmother on the other end of the phone. Loyalty is my other weakness. When I am on your team, I am on your team, through thick and thin. Last man standing in the trenches, I will be there for you. Loyalty is as much a purpose as it is an attribute. In the here and now though, it is at the heart of this conflict. I feel betrayed by life. I carry a triple burden: protection for a family I know not how to protect, helplessness in not knowing what to do or where to turn, and shame in the face of society and in this sense of conscious incompetence. I can fend for myself, up to a point, but just a few years out of full-time education, this should not be the load that I carry. That said, even with my limited education and upbringing, I cannot leave the defenseless in the hands of the unscrupulous. It is in these moments of fear that I forge a defiance which over time I realize is the Sisu of my Finnish forbears.

The men inside are bad actors. They are policemen and representatives of a darker fraternity who solve crimes through coercion and bullying. The OG has taught me many lessons about these gangsters (or gorillas?) in the guise of investigators. They solve crimes by tearing families apart. I'm conflicted. My father was a man of the law once. Was he one of them, too? My belief in the rule of law remains strong but the actions of these men have cracked my faith. They warned him, then arrested him and the OG for the murder of their business partner. They then released them in this game of cheap liberty played with flawed paperwork and fake warrants.

My father has been many things over the years: angry, bullying, and reckless are the first three that come to mind. He was also intimidating, cunning, and to many people in our universe, colourful and engaging. He is not; however, a frenzied murderer.

His business partner - stabbed multiple times in the back - bled out somewhere in the borough. He was discovered buried in a pit near the Masonic Lodge; his body had been eaten by lime and chewed by animals. The evidence to his ending was as flawed as his character; stabbed so many times he would have leaked like a sieve, yet not a single drop of blood was ever discovered. Connected to organized crime, prostitution, drugs, Freemasonry, and bent coppers, he is, was rather, a colourful character.

Business was quid pro quo, and other than bars and restaurants, he had fingers in many pies. Partnering with the OG and my father, they all played entrepreneur with their own version of a cocktail bar in the shadows of Crystal Palace. The same bar I was encouraged to work in for reasons of family loyalty, no matter what my own dreams and aspirations were.

The dead man traded with robber barons. Those men played entrepreneur too, though in much larger realms with much more influence and a lot more money. Often, they would appear in the bar, with protection, expensive smelling scent, women, and loads of lolly. Robber barons are frightening kings of the jungle. Lions who masquerade as real businessmen; they reek of power, and do not shy away from the application of force.

Owing money to legitimate breweries, our man in the pit also owed money for several kilos of uncut cocaine. He enjoyed salacious evenings with mistresses and courtesans, some of whom were attached to the robber barons. It was also rumoured that one was pregnant with his child. Networking voraciously between the criminal and civil communities, other rumours greased the grapevine. Most significantly, he may have been a grass. A snake in the grass is the worst kind of animal; whispering underworld intel to the police about the gangs or to the gangs about other gangs. Nothing good ever happens to a grass and without sustainable protection their preservation is far from guaranteed.

Grasses face one big challenge: in the absence of hard evidence, rumour and conjecture often serve to fill the void. Additionally, in the presence of hard evidence, rumour and conjecture often serve to supplement the truth.

No matter the truth though, perception is reality. Within this frame of reference, the life of a grass is invariably short and not very sweet.

The people of south London rub shoulders in the same markets, attend the same schools, and frequent the same speakeasies. Whether or not you wear a uniform makes little difference to those with whom you rub shoulders. It's a game of survival and one of leverage. The man in the pit has little power, but large aspirations. He has little leverage but a large lifestyle. There are many lions in this jungle, and the list is long of those who could have rendered death upon the man in the pit.

A local Inspector of Police whose mistress is being unfaithful, owners of breweries who are owed money, and a string of illicit affairs make death a possibility. When you add in the infringements upon a politician in Westminster, mad Freddie doing a ten stretch for armed robbery, and a patriarch of the Glasgow underworld whose family honour has been tarnished, possibility becomes probability.

The bloody execution is not really a surprise, except to his mother who puts on a good show with tears at the rendering of her family and her little boy.

Fair enough. We are all someone's angel after all.

It could be argued that my father and the OG had means but I'm not sure they had motive. But the ability of humans to argue a rationale is unparalleled and the whole legal industry thrives on rationale. The gorillas who storm through the doors and appear randomly "just for a quick chat" believe they have means and motivation. So, the gorillas of the Met haunt our family looking for easy prey, weak targets, and staged evidence.

They warned him, too. My father that is. After all, they were brother Freemasons and wore the same uniform. For this alone he deserved fair warning. The Freemasons, a society with a global network that raises funds and does good works for charity is also tarnished with cronyism, the protection of fraternity, and blurring the boundaries of conventions when it comes to covering up corruptions.

The warning was clear and obvious. "Step away. Justice will be served by convicting the OG and his brother for the murder of the man in the pit." For the gorillas it does not matter who actually committed the crime, nor whether that same person, or persons, will swing for the crime. But for the sake of our family now is the time to walk away and never look back.

To this day it is not clear why my father chose to die on this hill.

Yet, he made that choice and, in the process, brought down the wrath of the gorillas onto the heads of his own family. Here in the jungle, it was rarely clear what divided might from right.

MY FATHER IS MISSING today which is not unusual. He is often away looking after his own skin, leaving his family to fend for themselves. He and the OG have much in common. Fated by birth, they grew up in the same world, products of a generation where destiny was predetermined and, if you were lucky, you were offered an exit. My old man was lucky. He got a forever job with a uniform, pay, and power. Instead of being grateful, he became, and remains, a wrecking ball of relationships. His first wife, his second wife, his mother, his children: nobody was spared from his rages and cultivated hatred. Fellow Freemasons were the exception to the rule. No matter their creed, colour, or faith, Freemasons, were blindly accepted as the truest of true people. According to his lore, the peak of civilization were Freemason police officers who could create an echo chamber of opinions and beliefs that were unparalleled and undisputed.

A lone gladiator with the burden of protection. I am fighting battles that are not mine. At 23 years old I do not know how to protect my family from the wrath of gorillas or gangsters. The weight of responsibility is enormous. Living in the aftermath of bloody murder, navigating the shadows, balancing the purpose of protection with the hope of an exit, I am not trained nor equipped to handle this world.

I hold on tight to truth and integrity, which is all I have left.

Winston Churchill said: "If you are walking through hell, keep walking." And so, I do.

With this heavy burden, I manage to still walk upright with curiosity, learning how the world really fits together. Dopamine hits are common and essential to avoid being dragged into the pit, but the IV drip of adrenaline is also addictive and detrimental. Feelings of enjoyment are fleeting and swamped by depression, anxiety, and an almost unbearable pain. Even these sensations don't persist, instead they leave me numb and frozen to feelings.

The pain of an injustice inflicted by gorillas is linked to my evidence and testimony which is the spanner in their works. Their case for incarceration fails because of a single date and time when the OG and I are in a café drinking coffee. That single point of history unravels their case and creates rare moments of solitude and solidarity where the OG speaks, and I learn about London's worlds and underworlds. Fate has stuck us together in a weird twist that fuels the retribution of the policemen, like we just pissed in their doughnuts.

The gorillas apply a heat of pain designed to crush me spiritually, emotionally, and mentally. The kind of pain that lands no punches. The heat burns my skin, scoring white hot scars in the blackest of times.

In a desensitized world, murder apparently still has an impact. It is serious enough to create a ripple of reactions and recriminations. I guess this is good, that society gives face to the value of human life is something.

In this world, Oscar is my constant companion. He is a large, lean dog who brings joy just by being. Every day is a happy day for Oscar. Exercise, discipline, and love is all he needs. We can be found running together for miles across country, pumping dopamine in the pursuit of happiness. Four to five times a week; seven, ten, twelve miles through rolling English countryside, where nature provides a haven from the vagaries of people and offers an alternative life of peace, we run. When we stop, we sit or lie in the grass. Oscar rests against my body, wags his tail, licks the sweat on my face or hands then sleeps. Then we run again. We are silent buddies mostly. Oscar listens when I speak and, in dog fashion, shows empathy, loyalty, and friendship, particularly when I cry. This is a macho world so I cry alone, where nobody can see me. The best of friends, Oscar is always there, always happy, and always comforting. Often at the end of our energy we sit on the top of a hill looking out over the countryside enjoying the sounds of the natural world. Nature becomes my church and I savour every minute with my companion, knowing when this ends, we must return to a hell scape. In the embrace of solitude rabbits skip through the grass and dun coloured deer move silently through the trees. It is out here in the wilds that I can remain undisturbed and devise a strategy to solve my own problems. Tactically I am trying to avoid violence and coercion, and most sad of all, plan my own escape from everything I have loved and have known.

And then there is rugby, the ultimate sport, which gives me a role in a team.

Scrum, ruck, maul, attack, defend: the soldier making game is combative, competitive, and can be violent. Head butts, punching, and stamping are some of the extras you get in the English version for hooligans, played by gentlemen. Skills are important but take second place on the podium to physicality. This is a sport where you live at the "edge of the law," and in my case is imitating life. Somewhere on the muddy fields where we play the game, the camaraderie and solidarity fill many voids. Rugby fuels resilience and provides balance. In a tough, unforgiving world, it offers an emotional outlet and a safe space to vent. Rugby becomes my family and I cannot get enough. The men around me have no real idea of the internal combustion I deal with daily, nor are they aware how much I would give of myself to them, just for a few drops of kindness and camaraderie.

Violence finds its purpose in this new Dark London. In the drinking dens of the southeast boroughs, I have seen many smashed bodies and much broken glass. I have enjoyed the taste of tear gas. Here blood is drawn, scars are long, and the local bullet-heads and robber barons offer business owners the choice of cough up or carve up.

No spoon full of sugar here Mary Poppins, this is not a comedic cockney movie.

In the melee which follows the murder of the man in the pit, the gorillas take the path of least resistance. It is easier for them to threaten a vulnerable mother and her children than battle against authentic gangsters, in whose world justice is a luxury reserved for others. In this grey world, is seen only in the peripheral vision of the chattering classes, unless of course it can be played on their television screen.

Today I am tired. Too many shakedowns leave you twitchy. Too many adrenaline spikes create an exhausting rollercoaster of emotions.

Mentally and emotionally, I am not up for the fight today. In England's green country, in the world outside of London, I get a temporary reprieve, as the gorillas of the Met do not enjoy open space; exposed outside of their jungle. They wait patiently until the end of each run when the gravity of their universe drags me back in to Dark London.

Tactically I am confused at how to respond. A single hyena I could beat in a fair fight, but they have the advantage of numbers, and steel. While the gorillas leverage their power and do not wish for a fair fight. I hate bullies; cowards who hide behind a crowd or a veneer of power. Bullies are oxygen thieves who deserve no respect. They are the drains down which much garbage flows and as I look up at the dark house I know it is full of bullies.

I take a deep breath.

Physically sound, I cross the threshold, into the cold heat of menace.

Holding my breath at the door I pause before entry and am ready for confrontation. I turn off all emotions. With a practiced calm I offer up a steely edge to the gorillas in our home. They see a young man come in the door, muscled and agile, and stand up straight, sniffing the air.

Two children, my brother and sister, are crying. They are frightened which is no surprise. Young and defenseless, they have no other protections from the very real menace that fills their innocent world.

I challenge the gorillas. "What are you doing?"

"Looking for evidence," they snort.

There is no evidence here. What is it they even think is here: the blade that stabbed a man one hundred times, the blood he left in whichever location he died, a bundle of clothes, a series of incriminating letters perhaps?

Dumb fucks.

Their motives are transparent. This is not their first visit but a contrived search for the purposes of intimidation.

"Why are the kids crying?" I spit this challenge. "Do you think they are hiding evidence in their beds?"

Hannah is seven years old and holds my legs. I send her back upstairs with her brother Ross. He is thirteen years old, more aware, in shock. "Go back to bed," I suggest, quietly. "Stay in Ross' room, it's safe there." A temporary refuge. Whispers have reached the schools of the little ones; the resulting cruelty hurts their hearts and their bodies. The gorillas have a long reach and weaponize gossip throughout the schools. The chattering classes gorge on tittle-tattle and before long two small children are guilty by association.

What a mess!

Innocent children, hurt by failed institutions.

I turn on the two big gorillas staring out from the recesses of their leather jackets. Their energy is different, not totally on board with the ruckus maybe. I look closer to see if they are clean under the filth, but maybe it is just something I wish to see. This is no time for false friends though, so I say nothing.

"You are joining the army?" asks one, flipping through my own papers. "None of your business" is what I should say but I bite my lip and control the rage. It is true though. Joining the military and serving my country provides both an exit strategy and the hope of purpose. Calm is good. Icy cold is better. For now, I will face down the gorillas who prey on children. The damage borne of this business means trust contracts are broken; nobody gets a free pass, and everyone must earn goodwill. "Possibly," is my response. This feels like an olive branch. Maybe a search for commonality.

Other gorillas are tearing through our house, thumping around, and I don't know how many are here. Too many. I can only imagine the wreckage they are leaving.

Oscar is at my side. Smelling the air, he is sensing the trouble, and I feel comfort in his bulk under familiar fur. He runs around, seeking the children, showing them love. Ross and Hannah are his family too. He also disrupts the gorillas going about their business. Dogs don't see uniform; they smell energy, and Oscar knows who is producing the bad smells. He diffuses their odours with canine optimism and a wagging tail.

The gorillas show up when least expected, and here in the house they continue to verbalize their threats. The threats have become more prolific and precise now. They articulate concern for the safety of my mother and the wellbeing of my brother and his children. The more desperate they become to close out their case the more deliberate they are in their descriptions of the accidents and incidents which "may" happen if I don't play by the rules of their game.

They sink to any depth in their efforts to force me to lie. Even our pets are targets, dead and mutilated, they are left on the lawn, just in time for school. In the confusion I often wonder is it the police or is this intimidation coming from another source? One side wants us to talk, the other wants us to shut up. We assume it's the bad guys but who they are anymore? The gorillas or the gangsters?

I wonder at their own families and their behaviours at home. Do they have wives and children? Do they simply switch it all off after work?

The kids are hurt, the pets are dead, the family is smashed apart and the world is empty of hope. Here Sisu begins. The second wind of mental toughness, where perseverance and grit ends. These fuckers have overstepped the mark and from hereon I will defy them in my own way and break them through sheer determination.

I won't lie for anyone.

Least of all the kind of people who leverage power to hurt the vulnerable.

Dysfunction reins. The chattering classes are weak and devoid of functional help. Dark London is now a flickering firefight between right and fright, throwing up demons I must face alone. I want to protect my loved ones but do not know how.

The world is visceral. And there is nothing more painful than when the system eats one of its own. For then, all vestiges of respectability are gone, and all traces of the action must be totally erased so there can be no comeback. Destruction is total. There is no strength drawn from this type of pain, only lessons learned.

In the eyes of these gorillas, I am an easy target. They are not wrong. If I change my official statements they can close their case, regardless of truth and justice. *"Good job lads. Job well done! Let's head to the pub."* In this world, they would have me over a barrel and prosecute their targets of choice with no need for the veracity of authentic justice. My truth undermines their case. But my truth, unlike theirs, is real, and a hill upon which I choose to fight. The struggle is counter to everything I have been bought up to believe.

Beyond the OG, I am not sure who is on the other side of the house. If I fold for the gorillas what retribution could come? Who gets wrapped up elsewhere? The frequency of shakedowns, the threats, and the mutilated animals indicate that someone else is watching. Friends of Mad Freddie? Watchers from Glasgow? Brewery men? The jungle is dark and dense. It is difficult to see who might be impacted, who is interested, and even who is involved. So, the gorillas, lions, and the hyenas play a stalking game of threats and violence, while the chattering classes remain ever distant. In this world, friends become foes and foes become friends. The experienced people are from the world of the OG, or older men of law, or random people I barely knew existed. All of them are old bears who have foraged in the jungle and survived. These connections are unexpected and reach out like the OG to guide my way even though fate has decided I must eat crow. The old bears are wise; they sniff the air whenever they leave the cave. They teach, I learn, and to this day I can detect the odour of mendacity and the tang of trouble.

I now know to sniff the air everyday: when I leave home, when I exit my car, when I am out on the streets.

I want to be an old bear one day, with wisdom and education, like these guys.

WALKING DEEPER INTO THE HOUSE, I enter the kitchen. The gorillas have bought their furore into the family home today. Wrong move. A stout man, the fattest of the gorillas, wears a Burberry raincoat and menaces my stepmother. He is greasy, with bad skin - greyish like Gollum on a bad diet. She is pinned into a corner where she offers them tea and toast. It is such an English response.

Don't feed them, I think. *They're a betrayal of everything we believe in and give the rest a bad name*.

Burberry turns on me, his snout poking out of the recesses of his jacket.

"You need to leave our house," I say. "There's nothing here for you and you know it."

He glares, affronted. "I'm Detective Sergeant..." I don't hear his name and couldn't give a toss. *The children are hurting and you, DS Burberry, are a living abuse of trust. The garbage can of authority.*

He's waving a piece of paper. A search warrant. Fake? Possibly. Real? Possibly. Both have happened before; the paper is the only constant. I calm my inner rage and a desire to knock him down. I will myself to stare into his greasy face.

"Give us what we want, or we get you, and your family," he sneers. "Give us what we want or go down."

There is nothing to give. They know it. We know it. What they want is control of our lives and emotions in order to close their case. The tiniest crack will give them room to leverage their power. My head hurts. I want to vomit. Some of that is fear. Some of that is disdain.

"You need to leave. You are looking for evidence that you know is not here." My outer calm covers inner rage. Adult men must not menace women and children. That is a simple rule. It is too much to tolerate and in a moment, I envision simply knocking him down. After all, he's not a real policeman, not even a real man, just a fat gorilla in a rain jacket.

"You've made your threats, time to go. There's nothing here for you and you know it." I say with a calm determination and the authority of innocence. No violence is necessary. I choose to take the high road, trying hard to rise above the fray and bend them to my will. The gorillas are uncomfortable on the high road; it is not a place they travel. They want fear. They will get nothing.

Burberry peers up at me. His gorilla snout wrinkles, annoyed.

"Didn't you hear me? You have no rights. We will break you. Break you all. We will get your father and his friends."

They have all the cards, all the rights, and all the knowledge - which is terrifying. They think they have all of the power, but there is still nothing for them to find.

Have you ever tried to break a husk? Crack a walnut out of its shell? If so, you know the pressure that is required and hope that the fruit is worth the squeeze. The husk is the hardest part of a nut to crack and in my case, the husk is all that remains. They can squeeze as much as they like but this nut isn't cracking, which is a cause for concern for the gorillas, particularly as the dog is now bored of their odour.

Oscar growls. His muscles tremble under fur, his instincts are keen from chasing rabbits, deer, and birds. *Cry havoc and let slip the dogs of war!* quotes Shakespeare in a distant memory from those recent high school years. Oscar is gearing up to be that dog.

I chuckle.

"What you laughin' at?" Burberry is edgy.

"English literature fatty!" is what I should have said. A small shrug is what I give.

"Control your dog!" barks Burberry.

"I can't." I respond. "You're in his house see, threatening his family. He is doing what dogs do. It would be best for you to leave."

"I have a warrant." Burberry barks again. I don't read it or even reach for it. Fake or real, it may be either, but all movements are unnecessary as they are potential triggers for Burberry to overreact and create some collateral damage.

"The dog can't read," I respond.

Burberry is stuck. His next move could trigger pain...his own. Bullies fear pain. I don't want a record, but I'll hurt this guy before he harms my family anymore. Oscar, my proxy for violence, is rumbling, ready to spring as we stand off in the kitchen. I touch his fur, feeling raised hackles, and shush gently. The Burberry gorilla looks tasty, but a short-term gain would cause long term pain, plus the seizure and death of my constant companion. Oscar knows my touch and maintains his posture. There's been enough violence around here. I am not sure I would come back from the death of my beloved pet. He maintains his poise, but I can feel him retreating from the edge in incremental shifts the gorilla cannot see.

"Leave our house. There's nothing here for you. You know that too," I persist. One mother, one son stand face to face with these harbingers of dubious purpose. The tension is palpable. Burberry sweats some, stuck in the vice of his own making. His body language changes subtly as there is no justifiable cause for further action. He is probably skating on very thin ice, particularly if this warrant is illicit. Turning towards the front door he whistles up the other gorillas in their leatherjackets; they have trashed the house, delivered their threats, and created fear. Unaccountable men with no concern for the detritus left behind them, they are just here to shake up the jungle.

"We're going to hurt you," he spits out.

Words mean something and this is his sign off.

Burberry crosses the threshold, stands on the front porch turning long enough to stare.

Oscar rumbles and offers a flash of canines to encourage Burberry, who scuttles away after the gorillas who have already disappeared. I can breathe again and check the neighbours' windows. A few lights twinkle but no curtains are twitching. It is still early in the dark dawn.

I reach down and fuss with Oscar; it is time for a reward.

He loves human food. Tea and toast are his gift.

With the gorillas gone, I begin to wonder how much more I can take, how many more threats I have to handle, how many more traps I can avoid. This hell just goes on forever. Has it been months or years? Maybe it is just weeks. Time is abstract now, merely compressed into periods of light and dark. The minutiae of minutes and hours no longer make sense escape is essential.

The darkness seems to be growing, maybe even winning, but it will pass. All things must pass. Resilience is the game. Sisu will win.

And here in the pre-dawn darkness I decide to get out.

THE FRENCH ALPS

The escape from Dark London has begun.

Lying in lush mountain grass, three thousand metres up in the sky, the eagles fly looking for food. It's beautiful here in the heart of the natural world. It's quiet too, except for the sound of birds and the chatter of animals. It reminds me of happier times running the English countryside with Oscar. I reach out instinctively to feel his fur and am momentarily saddened by his absence. He has been the sacrifice made in the breach of that old world. The grip of Dark London is weaker these days and University life means I study in Marylebone and work in Chelsea and Westminster. While these boroughs are a short train ride from the denizens of the Southeast, culturally they are a million miles from the gladiators and their bloody arenas. With boutique shops on every street, designer labels on all the clothes, and the gleam of polish on all the cars, it is abundantly clear why upward mobility is a myth, as downward mobility would mean letting go of all of these trappings. Everything is more expensive and practical stores like supermarkets, hardware outlets, fast food outlets, and newsagents are missing. Replaced by flowers, clothes, cars, real estate, and cafés, all the frontages blend with the local architecture. Any hint of blue-collar lifestyles has been carefully erased so the eye remains unoffended by the world outside of this bubble. This level of wealth is way beyond my reach but, as a student with subsidized costs I can enjoy living here, temporarily at least (assuming I continue to work night and day, and all spare hours outside of my studies). I get to sup at the tables of the chattering classes, to shop in their shops, to drink in their bars, and to observe their way of life. This is the best of London. A rich tableau of international cultures, modern commerce, and historical influences all freely accessible to roam through and learn from. I like it but disguise myself with external skepticism. I do not want anyone to see my happiness which I feel is a weakness in my armour of self-preservation. Whenever possible I escape to the healing hills of England and broaden my horizons, visiting the towns and villages of the countryside. I notice how the international students seem to be laden with cash. A Chinese family pays a full year of rent, with wads of notes as thick as sandwich. Just in my locale, there are Italians, Vietnamese, Greeks, Indians, Americans, and Germans. Well dressed, articulate, and knowledgeable they all seem to be rolling in money, self-assured and totally at one with a London lifestyle which is out of reach to so many of the citizens here.

This world is new to me and while I instinctively dislike the chattering classes: I begrudgingly like it here, and I don't like that admission.

Brits, in general, have no care for, nor desire to hear about, the trials faced by the citizens of other countries. I am consistently surprised at the lack of curiosity about South American regimes, Middle Eastern conflicts, and closer to home, the impacts of Cold War dictators. Unexpectedly, Navy life provided faith and a sense of belief in myself to achieve more than I previously thought possible. Yet it also provided a worldly education which would leave as many scars as it would pay dividends.

Standing in the heartland of Brazil, a short but dangerous walk to uptown, via Salvador's harbour shanty downtown, the trauma of real human tragedy once more raises its ugly head. We are here to provide humanitarian aid to a Swedish run refuge. We clear the cemetery of debris, overgrowth, and garbage, uncovering Portuguese text on moss marbled headstones. We add fresh coats of paint to the internal walls and restore the aged carpentry of this wooden building that serves both as school and church. Children here get a free education in English, mathematics, and science. More importantly they get food and protection from the streets.

Beyond the safety of the refuge, crack cocaine is sold cheaply, for as little as a few cents per rock. Addiction is rife. We are warned not to wear jewelry or have anything remotely valuable on show as hold ups are prevalent. Adults are maimed and killed in street crimes which spike with the demand for this super addictive chemical. Worse still, small children are trafficked by their own substance addicted parents. Some of them are in this refuge. The ones without parents may be the luckier ones, as they avoid being trafficked by their own family. Others are forced to work the streets and pay the price of their education. To feed their mother's addiction, two small girls get education and prostitution on rotation. Time off for good behaviour means refuge, school, and food. Working weeks are on the streets where salacious men feed their predilections for a few cents, mother gets crack to supplement her diet, and the sister gets to go to school.

This is terrible. Heart rending and scarring. I think back to my own little brother and sister, menaced in their own home by uniformed gorillas. When adults hurt each other, that is one thing. The exploitation of minors, vulnerable and frightened, by adults and even their own parents, is the ultimate betrayal. The ultimate inhumanity.

I am not sure how my colleagues feel. The local chattering classes claim no knowledge, but they are wealthy and comfortable, living in secure compounds protected from the sight of orphaned children hawking cheap jewelry made from hammered tin. The kids are desperate for food and care.

Shutting out my real emotions, I maintain a steely exterior, trying to be a good military man - even though I know this erodes my desire to continue service.

The erosion continues in Eastern Europe. Gas chambers used by Nazi Germans are memorials to human horror marking time in Poland's wooded countryside. The clothes and shoes of the exterminated yell out their message across time as the cries of adults and children are almost audible from behind the display glass.

And the erosion deepens through Egypt, Djibouti, and into the Middle East. The scars of inhumanity are everywhere. Bullet marks on buildings, conversations with haunted locals, discarded belongings in uncleared rubble are just a short list of real sights.

People being shit to each other is not the problem. I am worldly enough to know how shitty people can be. It's the ripple effects of human "shitty-ness" which I cannot escape. Broken families, destroyed homes, and wrecked businesses are the remains of dysfunctional societies. The force multiplied effects of rationalized destruction by ideology or corrupted governance is evident everywhere.

Back on the ground, high up in the mountains, I am camped downslope from a small road running out of the body of the Hexagon – the geometric nickname for France - into Italy. France offers the combined enchantments of fresh air, clean skies, as well as good food and beautiful countryside. For me, it is a place of happiness. The contrasts with Dark London are significant and some of my earliest happy memories are from short trips to France. The shanty towns, trafficking, and criminality are far, far away. Fueled by a strong desire to escape the mundane, any opportunity to pull on a pack and explore the wilderness is a top priority. Exploration feeds curiosity which breeds education, which creates freedom, which perpetuates every time I discover something new. It feels good to be away from the horrors of the Dark as I consider my own membership application to the chattering classes.

Up here in the sky, there is lots to learn. Marmots scuttle, squeak, and disappear fast into their holes avoiding "death by eagle." An ignominious death, I suspect, and a common fear amongst the wildlife inhabitants of the mountain peaks. The eagles themselves patrol the skies. Feathered drones soaring ever higher, they scan the terre below, swooping down on the slightest movement of the unsuspecting rabbits, marmots, and even baby goats. Isolated or exposed in a cruel twist of fate, the animals are defenseless against the might and majesty of the authoritarian bird.

In the distance, barely visible, mountain goats are the hermits of the crags who graze at a distance sufficient for avoiding the twin dangers to ruminant life: humans and eagles. They remind me of the old bear, for they sniff the air and survive the dangers whose presence floats upon the wind. Fully grown, they are too heavy to be seized, but their babies are easy prey to reaching talons. Separated from the herd, young kids are vulnerable and can be snatched in an instant by the feathered predator, flown high up into the sky, then dropped onto the rocks below.

The brutal beauty of nature seems much more honest than the hypocrisy of human society.

Humans, smell bad and can be detected from far away. The odour warns of disruption and danger to the gregarious social lives of the mountain goats, and when I happen to see any, it is ever only at a distance. Here the colours, scents, and sights are overwhelming, and I drink it all in. Time means nothing, at the peaks of the Alps, where the world stands still, and Mother Nature decides all things, including who lives and who dies.

France is a magical land with new foods, freedoms, and cultures that are so distinct from Britain's sceptred isle. More than magical...it is magnetic, too. France, the temptress, who has caused so much pain for so many English folk, is, for me, a sanctity of anonymity. Some of my fellow countrymen are myopically noisy. They harbour narrow world views, hanker for better times, and fear the foreign influences of

Europe. So strange for a country whose own culture was influenced so heavily by the breadth of its own Empire.

At home, I choose not to speak out about my love of France as I cannot be bothered listening to the rhetoric. Yes, there have been wars across Europe, but in these years of peace there is so much to enjoy here. Not only can I learn the language of this belle dame, but I can taste her food, drink her wine, and enjoy her garden. France offers an affordable freedom of choice which I cannot get in London. Even more, she offers a release from the burdens of the society that imposed those restrictions. France is exotic, enticing, fragrant, and hypnotic, and here in the Alps, I am on top of the world. Unsupported except for superficial knowledge, this is the ultimate immersion. It is here on foot, hiking from village to village, from mountain town to mountain town, for days on end that the absence of England is the most noticeable; speaking, listening, observing, all things in a foreign language lets you see the world through a different lens. It is like bathing in an inexpensive luxury.

It started out so easily. Walking out from home, I jumped on a train to central London. From there I jumped onto the Eurostar train from London to Paris, and within a couple of hours leaving home we are rolling through the verdant Kent countryside. Dropping into the steely grey Channel, the train climbs from the water and out onto the verdant Normandy countryside, which may as well be England for all the differences between here and the county of Kent. These two countries, once conjoined, are now separated by a watery division which has become a constant tributary of taunts and tantrums. If you look back far enough in history, you can see we are all related. Former cousins, we all eat potatoes, fish, sausages, and cheese, in one form or another, and it is likely we have more in common than we care to admit. Nevertheless, true to human nature, the Channel has become a pissing pool of one-upmanship, which over the centuries, led to war, back to peace, war once more, and for now, for a little while at least, some more peace. Whilst nature abhors a vacuum, the human condition seems to abhor peace and will keep rivalry alive at any cost, preparing opportunities for the next war. Immigrants are the big issue today. A fuel added to the fire of nationalism.

The fields of Normandy roll by smoothly and before long, we arrive in Paris, which, like London, is a mirrored pool of architecture and art, film and entertainment, food and festivities. The City of Lights, entered via the Gare du Nord, is a gateway to a whole new world of destinations, the names of which flutter like the eyelashes of the Gallic temptress, whispering of new experiences in Montparnasse, Austerlitz, Versailles, and Poissy. Maybe five hours ago, I was at home in a London borough. Now I stand in the middle of Paris, and everything has changed. This is a place of dreams, a romantic adventure, and standing quietly, soaking up the atmosphere of the clattering station, I take a new bearing. Southeast seems good and, for no reason, I jump on to the train for Lyon. According to my map, it is close to the Alps, and I am sure that from there, I can walk somewhere, somehow.

Finding a seat, I relax with the rolling rhythm of the train and drop into a snooze.

Beautiful, generous, and abundant is the France in my dreamy bubble which bursts with a sudden resounding pop as the train stands still.

In Geneva.

In Switzerland.

Say what now?

Everybody off!

In London, I purchased a ticket for Paris with no extension or return. In Paris, I jumped on a train to Lyon, without leaving the station. Yet here I am, with no visa in my passport, nor ticket in my pocket, standing on the platform in Geneva. Looking hopelessly at my map, I can see that if you turn left at Lyon, head north a bit and take a nap, you soon reach the land of gold and chocolate.

This is my third country in one day. Should I be here?

Philosophically and legally, that's up for discussion. Physically, it's indisputable.

Several hours ago, this all seemed straightforward but now, like all good plans, the situation is completely messed up, a total fudge with a host of unforeseen complexities. My level of conscious incompetence is increasing, which is irritating. I'd rather be unconsciously ignorant than openly aware of my own stupidity. I know nothing of Switzerland.

It's a place for rich people who ski, show off their wealth, and evade the tax man.

We have nothing in common.

I walk down to Lac Leman which, like many beautiful things, offers inspiration without resolution. The streets are very clean but empty of people. Uncrowded and well ordered, the city feels soulless. I notice the frequency of public transport and that all the bus drivers are black men. Knowing I should not be here compounds the feeling that I do not want to stay. With just a handful of currency, no food, and no friends, I am left with very few choices. I was expecting to hike and camp on a budget, live like Sasquatch in the mountains and countryside of France, and fundamentally, hoped to do very little thinking. Now, I must navigate metropolitan Geneva and turning south in the late afternoon sun, I start walking. This part is easy. South takes me towards the border which I will have to cross and is out there somewhere. That part is more complex. An unknown border at an unknown distance with unknown legal implications as to my current situation.

If I'm lucky, the border will be in open country.

If I'm unlucky, well, then the border will provide an opportunity for creative problem solving. Surreptitiously crossing international borders is not high on my skills list. Optimistically though, I consider that I have plenty of time to work out a solution. Biting my lip for focus, I take a bearing and start moving.

Hiking is normal and an activity that I enjoy. Hitchhiking is alien as it generates feelings of vulnerability. Walking is human, natural, and allows me to feel in charge of my journey. That said, the realities of crossing an alien border after dark with no papers are daunting. Indecisive, and not sure of myself, I stick out my thumb and try to look endearing, the kind of person you want to take care of, which is difficult. At more than six feet tall, weighing over one hundred kilos, and carrying a pack, endearing is one of the last adjectives I would use to describe my own condition. And, as I have plenty of time to examine my life choices, I get to think on this for a while when....

Bingo!

Three young women in a small Peugeot slow, check me out, collectively smile, and stop.

The future looks bright as darkness falls. The Peugeot door is opened, I clamber in, and we continue southbound into the night. A night that brings beer, pizza, and casual chat at a local bistro. Their English is limited, so is mine. My French is worse. I impress them with limited verbal and expansive non-verbal cues, combined with the general air of a stranded puppy. Intimidatingly, they are intelligent, hot, blond and brunette, and with money. They speak the sing song melody blend of French and German Swiss, it is a beautiful sound; they also have the upper hand on looks, wealth, and I.Q. I have just one trump card and win on entertainment value. I engage them with my story which sounds incredulous, even to myself. Yet, here I am, lost in the heart of Switzerland, helpless to the ways of the world and clearly pulling off the endearing look as dinner deepens into darkness; we fumble our way through conversation until it is time to retire and dawn finds us at breakfast, bonding over black coffee in their collective apartment nearby.

They like me. I can stay for the week if I wish, which is a generous offer to a strange man who is randomly hitchhiking through your country. I cannot see that happening in England. The coffee is good and the apartment luxurious. The offer is tempting. The kindness of wealthy people is rare, so I keep the seat warm and accept more hospitality.

They will show me Geneva, feed me chocolate, give me gold, and make me a prince. I am sure that is what they said. It is my preferred interpretation of events. Such kindness is too generous and makes me feel uncomfortable. Deep down, I know that generous hospitality should never be taken for granted, not least of all because it creates warm fuzzy feelings that Englishmen are not supposed to entertain. This seems unfair. I do not feel very English. Anglo-Scottish with a Finnish twist makes me a mutt with a gentle combination of bumbling stoicism. Also, with a dry sense of humour that can be lubricated by beer, whiskey, or wine, I present a conflicted cocktail of Anglo-Presbyterian-Lutheran morality. Less than twenty-four hours from the start of a manly adventure, I have fallen into this honey trap, and, like an ever-hungry Winnie the Pooh, the honey looks good from here. Ethically though, would that make me a resident alien? Or an illegal alien? Surely, too, I have a moral obligation, at least to myself, that I complete my journey across the Alps. Good grief!

I cave in to pseudo religious morality and a set of values which have been hard earned. Feeling foolish, I mumble "I can't stay, I have to get to France."

"Why?"

"I am walking to Italy" is the best I can do. Totally irrational when said out loud.

Silence reigns.

They giggle. Rightly so.

This stupid Englishman got lost on a train to France and ended up in Switzerland. How on earth does he expect to walk into Italy?

I get it.

And then there is the opportunity of free bed, board, and possible bordello, for a week versus the foot blistering yomp through the Alps. Well, if you put it like that, my life choices are clearly strange. Except to me. As this is a part of my escape form Dark London.

I snort; they giggle more. Smiling like Goofy, I blush. More giggling.

"The call of the journey is stronger than the destination," is what I want to say. A garbled philosophy perhaps, but truth be told, I feel like an imposter amongst kindness, wealth, and a seemingly carefree lifestyle. These are uncharted waters in which I do not know how to swim. Comfortable in the lap of Mother Nature, forests or mountains, seas or sounds, I am most uncomfortable around people, particularly the generous kind. Mother Nature, I am learning, has a buddy. Fate.

And Fate will tempt you.

Fate always plays a canny hand to see how connected you are to your cause, trying to pull you off course, creating an internal struggle, and littering your life choices with temptations.

My life goals are arbitrary and, therefore, easily dispensed with. Still in my twenties, I have survived a dozen deaths and seem to be permanently stuck on the bottom rung of Maslow's hierarchy of needs. Always on the drop of discomfort, at the edge of feeling alive, comfort is the gateway to fat, dumb, and happy - or so I believe. Fate has opened this door to an oasis of generosity which I graciously accept for a few more hours. Those lessons from London and the belief in quid pro quo are deeply etched into my psyche. I have no ability to repay this hospitality and the combined effects of a pseudo religious morality and belief in quid pro quo means I must soon be on my way. So, we drink coffee, chat, laugh, and plot the "Great Escape." Before long the Peugeot is unleashed from its mooring and soon, we are zipping towards the Swiss border, which, thanks to my amazing language skills, I still have no idea how we plan to cross.

Many images run on a loop through my imagination like so many scenes from Hollywood movies: crashing through the border control at high-speed, cuffed and stuffed over the front of the car, or abandoned bodily in a cell are some just some of my imagined scenarios. At any time now I could say stop and give in to the delights of "bed, board, and bordello". Be fat, dumb, and happy for a week or so. But the beautiful women are happy in their adventure and who am I to spoil the romp. Chatting away in the car, these three Bonnies to my solitary Clyde are as carefree as ever. We are co-conspirators in the escape from Geneva and having pulled the trigger on my own exit, I shrug internally and optimistically hope for a positive outcome.

It is in this moment that I decide Swiss prison is unlikely to be too bad. The trio of Bonnies are in charge now, and truth be told, they do not seem stressed. My immediate future is in their hands. As the border heaves into view, I am unaware of the irony that my fate is in the hands of complete strangers. I know nothing about Switzerland, the administration, laws, or culture. Like a sailor trapped in the allure of siren songs, I careen towards the rocks with no care for the dangers around me. After all, what is the worst that can happen? Interrogations by beautiful people? Rations of chocolate and coffee, with guilt laden visits from hot women? That's preferable to what I suffered at the hands of my own people, so with my imagination colouring my judgement, the border crossing appears to be a risk worth taking.

I just needed to stay the course. There is another upside which I will not admit out loud. If, for whatever reason, I am trapped in Switzerland, at least I have a solid reason for not crossing the Alps. Completing my manly adventure is not totally ego fueled. I have some trepidation about stepping into an unknown wilderness and testing myself to the edge of my own knowledge and experience. An authentic fail-forward opportunity. Alternatively, being a fugitive in Swiss prison could be an equally compelling story with which to regale any audience and, if all things end in the next few minutes, there would be the prospect of far fewer blisters, and I would have still made it through three countries in as many days.

A win-win either way is the rationale for my young mind. Running the gauntlet across the border brings a frisson of excitement and outward calm, not in control of my own destiny, the racing beat of my heart is inversely proportional to the speed at which we drive straight towards a blue uniform looking out from the guard post.

Stepping out.

Facing the car.

He raises his hand.

The melody chatter of the Bonnie trio rises. The sirens are like a chorus of songbirds, and I am totally spellbound by the melodic Swiss language. For goodness' sake, their freedom of care is inspiring and right now seems absurdly unnecessary. Still, if mythological Greek sailors are anything to go by, I am merely human after all and therefore on the right side of history. I hold my breath, bite my lip for focus and wait for alarms, gunshots, sirens, and a showdown. The Bonnies are all smiles and laughter and with no idea what is happening now brace for impact as the car does not appear to be slowing down. Making no attempt to stop:

We sail into France.

No bumps, no bullets.

As blue uniform waves a cheery greeting to the small car full of hot women.

The women return the wave and laugh out loud at my tortured expression. Sighing for the hard of intellect, which would be me, they explain slowly and clearly that Switzerland to France is what we do, "you silly English man." Love's great adventure turns out to be just another Saturday shopping spree for them. Apparently, the citizens of Geneva regularly whizz across the border. With Swiss Francs to burn and cheaper prices over there, they can buy their way through the next town in a frenzy of retail thrills and be home in time for fondue. Who knew?

This was not quite the dangerous adventure I thought we were heading into, but the environment was charged and as the adrenaline rush subsides, I chalk it up to experience. Still unsure on the legalities of my time in Switzerland, here in France, I am on solid legal ground. Tacitly forgiving my hosts and chauffeur for being wealthy, intelligent, and beautiful, I administer an internal benediction to their loveliness and enjoy the remainder of our short time together. Parking up in Annecy, we make a fond farewell with a gentle bisou from each lady I turn my back forever to bed, board, and bordello, and turn south to face the peaks. As we go our separate ways, I reflect on their unwarranted and unsolicited generosity. Kindness such as this is a heartwarming reflection on the best of humanity, something I would not have anticipated in London. Stepping out into the bright sunshine, I start the climb up towards the distant mountains trying not to wonder if I should have stayed in the honey trap.

Several days later, I am still walking. Hiking upwards towards the sky the endeavour is real. The heat is intense; my clothes stink and muscles burn. Sweat runs in rivers down my spine and sternum as my thighs, shoulders, and back muscles burn from the combined weight of the backpack and steepness of inclines. The days are simple. Seven to eight hours, eleven, twelve, thirteen miles a day I climb, then drop, then climb again. Some days the ascent is a few hundred metres, others a thousand or more. More than that though, the descents mean multiple ascents each day and the altitude means my lungs are burning – an experience I have never enjoyed at walking speed. Yet, my stubbornness prevails. I try to avoid people and stay off road, hiking through forested terrain. When I am back on road, to avoid unnecessary complications, I can see the stares of vehicle bound tourists wondering at the climber under his load. Nevertheless, my purpose is personal and always climbing towards the peak of Val d'Isere: my only point of focus is the crossover into Italy.

Switzerland and the honey trap have become a surreal experience. It was only a few days ago but could have never happened. The sensation of a goodness that breeds kindness, and a kindness that is unwarranted, is more of a dream than a reality. Yet, the more I travel, the more I encounter good people. The kindness of strangers is often the most meaningful and the depth of that meaning is directly proportional to the extremes of your situation. At the edge of your condition, even the smallest gesture brings out the warmest sensations. I have plenty of time to reflect on this in the hours of solitude. Openness and a lack of guile breeds trust and for every step forward that I take, I bury another demon on the road. Not totally buried, but for now I have closed the door on some horrors witnessed and tapping into my inner Finn, I keep myself busy with learning and adventure.

Italy is a few days hiking. More of an endurance march as I yomp at speed, pushing and punishing myself in what has now become a one-person competition. Without the distractions of T.V. and music and other artificial tropes that keep us hooked on society, I make the most of France: mountains, trees, and grass; cheese, bread, tomatoes, oranges; scents, sensations and solitude; honey, wine, and walking. These are all the treasures in the world and all the wealth I need. The food here is the culture and I notice the quality I can buy for the price. It tastes so good, is affordable, and there seems to be no real distinction between organic and industrial. Here in France, I taste food and flavours; back in England, we just seem to eat food and have bowed to the sugar laden industrial might of America.

Scanty in singlet, shorts, and hiking boots it is too hot to wear any other clothes. When the mountain slopes are too steep or the paths hard to find, I stop and sit in the shade. I drink water, eat a piece of cheese or half a tomato whilst I get my bearings. Up is the only real direction. Path or no path, I tread carefully knowing that eventually I will break out of the forest and stand at the edge of a ridge or road. From there I can redirect myself towards a small mountain town or find a refuge in which to shelter for the night. Sometimes I am forced to bivvy under the trees, brew tea from my backpack, and eat the remaining bread and cheese from my rations. Hot tea solves many problems and provides solace in the toughest times.

The remaining weight in my pack includes books, maps, and a cumbersome tent which I never use. I prefer to sleep wrapped in a blanket under the stars. There are some spare clothes, too: long pants and a shirt just in case I need to dress for dinner. I carried the extra camping gear as a perceived necessity but now it is just ten kilos of unnecessary dead weight. The rewards on a good night are always in the form of food. When I find a manned shelter, in a town or on a peak, that refuge serves their own specialty dish. Boeuf bourguignon with polenta and red wine, in a tented kitchen attached to an inn. Thin crust pizza with cream cheese, arugula, and red wine at a small chalet with room and hot shower. Bread and cheese served al fresco under the stars. And more wine. There is always plenty of wine, whatever you desire. Blood red, granite pink, golden white there is so much choice, and available in half litre carafes, it beats ibuprofen as a cure for the aches and pains of the day. Good food and good wine are the reward for struggle. A little piece of heaven served every day.

Sleeping under the stars is intimidating at first but remains a special activity even to this day. Boxed up in houses and apartments we soften our bodies and minds becoming fearful of the great outdoors. When you survive your first night in the bush, unaided and unsupported, you step into a different realm that has been the preserve of shepherds and soldiers across centuries of history. Daytime ascents and descents at altitude are unknowingly the best exercise. Five hundred, one thousand, fifteen hundred metres, steadily climbing, descending and climbing again forces you to cast all woes, superstitions, and troubles away. The altitude burns, breathing can be laboured, but in the pauses between Albertville, Bourg St. Maurice, Tignes, and Val d'Isere, your goals become simple and singular. Life becomes very pure and with each step forward towards the Col d'Iseran, I know that every incremental gain brings Italy one metre closer. As arbitrary goals go, this is a good one.

I miss Oscar. My biggest sadness in the mountain wilderness is a lack of companionship. There is nobody with whom I can share this experience. Oscar was my constant companion but up here, I am totally alone. There is nobody with whom to share the beauty, the food, the memories, and the experiences. The sadness of loneliness is real. At the time of planning, everyone thought I was mad and those I know mad enough to join me were occupied elsewhere. Oscar would be happy here chasing rabbits, marmots, and anything he could slobber over. I know he would love the cheese and bread and from our experience on other hikes, he would also enjoy a cup of tea. He would not drink the wine, just water for him. In my heart though I know he is in good hands, looking after family and bringing happiness to others. A dog with purpose is a good dog. The children are older, but everyone is scarred by Dark London; Oscar helps to bind and heal us all with unflagging loyalty and unfailing happiness. He is older, too, and needs love, care, and a lifestyle more sedentary than climbing mountains and running hills.

Maintaining human relationships has become difficult. I cannot stay close to anyone for long and even though the nightmares of Dark London are far behind me, I still have nightmares and struggle to get close to people. Strangers and strange lands are a safer prospect than anything close to home and the combined dysfunctions of betrayal and violence have left deep neural scars in my psyche. Adrenaline and adventure are therapy and medicine. The harder the adventure the more I can cut away from the sensations of loneliness and hopelessness. Adventure gives me purpose and for now, it is here in the French Alps. Yomp by day, eat well, read until sunset, and fall into a rhythmic life of physical hardships and simple luxuries. Even with my tiny budget, France provides manna from heaven and an escape from loss.

Every morning, I wake before dawn and put a brew on: tea and remnants of bread, cheese, maybe some honey, or a piece of orange serve as my meal. It was rinse and repeat, every day. It is less than a week since I crossed the Swiss border but, in the great outdoors, it feels like I have been here much longer. Brown skin and sun-bleached hair make me feel foreign. My physique is lean, muscles are long, and I feel powered by a super strength that makes me feel I could go on forever. The glances of women in the mountain towns are welcome, a bonus and a temptation. But now I am deep into this commitment and like a Hannibal without elephants, I am determined to complete the crossing into Italy. The burning heat of the Alpine summer brooks no distractions and I plug my ears against the Siren songs that would see me dashed on the mountain rocks.

Late one afternoon, at nearly two thousand metres, I decide to pack up. Exhausted, entering a campsite, I purchase a berth. Under the long limbs of a large tree, I set up a simple bivvy using the outer tent and some bungee cords. A thin mat covers the ground protecting me from damp and I sit in my sleeping bag with back against the broad trunk. People peer at me from their caravan windows. I feel vulnerable and a little exposed, preferring the wilderness to the camp site. There is hot water here though which means I can wash, body and clothes, for the first time in a while.

The friendly attendee warned, "attention a l'orage." A storm is coming. You are not kidding. Falling asleep just before sunset, the skies are clear of clouds, and the stars blink down serenely. The world is at peace until the roar of thunder splits the skies just before midnight. A storm rages around us, smashing the skies and tearing the clouds. Mother Nature is pissed; seriously angry, as a party of gods are wrecking her house in a furious titanic battle. Casting down forks and sheets of lightning, mad at the heat of the day, they are lashing out in flashy anger. Holy cow! Mesmerised, I watch from the flimsy protection of my temporary shelter. The mountains, cloaked in rain, are humbled by the aggressive storm. The last time I witnessed such a tempest was during a squall at sea in the South Atlantic. Humans love to mess with the planet but weather fronts like this remind us how small we really are. Even the mountain giants stand still, waiting for the rage to pass. They are wise. Under my shelter the tea is hot, and the mat keeps me dry. The weather is everything and the only thing. Sitting is all I can do, watching and hoping the drama will subside. Nature heals, fate tempts us, then nature reminds us of our temporary lease on life with a smack down like this display of power.

For the next few hours, everything else ceases to exist and in the pre-dawn light, the gods burn out, nature cleans house, and the sun slowly rises. I drink more tea amongst the debris of the campsite. Tree limbs are scattered everywhere. Anything that was not tied down is gone and other campers traipse around looking for belongings and recovering their dignity along with lost items. My simple bivvy shelter is the same now as it was before the storm. It takes me no time to pack having enjoyed a shower the previous evening, I feel ready to climb the silent mountain sentry standing closest to my position. As the debris laden campsite fades away, I soon find a path into the lush mountain grass. The storm has abated, and a silence cloaks the world once more. But this silence is new: a strange silence with a different energy.

Not the warm silence of ambient mountain meadows.

Nor the expectant silence of a pre-storm mountainside.

But a low-level menacing silence with a warning.

Stopping, I squat down to examine my senses and discover the difference between now and what went before. There's an absence. An absence of birds and beasts.

Total stillness.

Like death.

I scan the horizon and check my surroundings. Nothing. No wind, no people, no life.

The world is still. Has it stopped turning? Time has slowed, no longer running round the face of my watch, rather it drips like molasses from a spoon. I feel the stillness on my skin and screw my face up trying to get a handle on the sensation. Where have all the birds gone? Where have all the animals gone? This is weird. The grasses move, as do the branches, but they seem to make no sound. I wonder if the storm made me deaf but recall the ambient noises a short while ago at the start of this climb. Whatever is about to happen, it is something new and alien.

Then, like a slowly extinguishing flame, the light that gives us life fades away and the world on top of the mountain goes dark as the moon glides across the face of the sun. Sticky minutes drip through the hourglass of time as sunlight grip the edges of the moon.

And then the sun is gone.

The animals are gone, too.

The world is in the embrace of darkness as the moon eclipses the sun. One of the most viewed solar eclipses in Europe is happening above me and I can see how superstitious folks in centuries past would consider this a bad omen. In a time before science, this would have been seen as a message from the gods and a precursor for troubles. What happens next? I do not know. Even today a solar eclipse creates drama and excitement. But, up here in the mountains, there's nobody to tell me the rules. The first visible eclipse from Britain for seventy years has switched out all the lights here in France. So, in the spirit of

"Keep Calm and Carry On," I drop down and brew some tea. The gladiator refrain springs to mind: "For those about to die, we salute you!" If this is the last thing I am destined to see, I might as well enjoy the view. Tea brings solace as I sit back against a rock and let the world work out its own agenda.

The moon and the sun maintain their fiery embrace for many minutes. I want to look. Like staring at the Medusa or glancing at scantily clad ladies (so I've been told), the danger is palpable, and I might turn to stone. Or worse.

Looking into the middle distance, trying to resist glancing at the embrace of celestial bodies, I sip tea wondering awkwardly. I really want to stare at this enigma and see the full impact of the moon cloaking the sun. Everything around me is dark and the temptation is real, but I know that as the earth rotates on its axis the momentary copulation of heavenly beings will end almost as quickly as it began. I have absolutely no desire to be staring straight into the sun as it emerges to restore daylight to the world.

I notice that the birds and the bees have disappeared too. I feel like the solitary voyeur to this brief encounter. Gracefully the moon starts her exit and maintaining a watch on the middle distance, indirectly viewing from the corner of my eyes, I see the sun restored to its full glory. Does it glow brighter than before the moon's seduction or is that my imagination? Overwhelmed by the phenomenon, I wonder if I shall see anything like this ever again. Owing to my unique location, the experience of this solar eclipse will never be topped, which I am soon to discover, in more ways than one.

As I sip the remaining dregs of tea, time is reinstalled to the fast-track beat of minutes and seconds. And as the last tasty tannins trickle across my tongue, the animals return to business as usual in the mountain tops, two thousand metres above the sea.

BLIZZARD

The snow fills the sky. It fills my eyes, ears, and nose. It stings like a swarm of angry bees, bites my skin and whips my face. The magnificent beauty of yesterday's solar spectacle has been eclipsed by the magnificent ferocity of today's snowy storm. Descending towards an invisible road, I move too slowly to keep warm. Before long the ice is biting my bones: deep, crunchy bites down to the marrow. I know that I must move faster to heat up, but I cannot see the ground beneath my feet and risk of tripping is high. Stuck between Val d'Isere and the Col d'Iseran around three thousand four hundred metres above sea level, the remaining distance to the peak should be easy. One lap of the track in real terms even at altitude this is achievable, if I could see properly.

My head hurts too. Arriving in town the evening before, the bar of my hostelry is manned by the son of a famous opera singer. An English guy, I do not know the name. Opera is not my strongest subject, but I am willing to listen. The barman is generous with the Stella Artois, which hits hard at altitude. Like the French rugby team who are training here in preparation for the World Cup. The barman lives here semi-permanently. He carries the burden of fame. He can never match the achievements of his famous father, who has brought so much wealth to the family. My knowledge of opera singers stops at buxom German ladies and portly Italian men. Beyond that I am totally out of my depth. The barman, as generous with his emotions as he is with the Stella pours, is the embodiment of first world problems. Summers in the Alps and Winters in wherever with a stipend from a trust are burdens I would happily carry. I sit at his bar in the thin mountain air, listening to his woes trying to remember details. English opera singers are a rare phenomenon, so I vow to enlighten myself at the earliest opportunity. Then the rugby team arrives. In peak physical condition, they start their own party and the beer continues flowing. Carried away in the excitement of it all, I do not notice the combined impacts of altitude and alcohol.

Until now.

My head and stomach hurt. Some bread and coffee at breakfast provide fuel. I want to get over the peak before lunchtime, so I hustle out of the hostel early. A litre of water and some more bread sit in my backpack and I decide no further provisions are necessary. The light rain outside is preferable to a baking sun and I move out fast. Climbing towards the peak, I believe there is a refuge up there then the drop will begin my descent into Italy. Moving with determination I know that the hangover will soon recede. In my standard uniform of singlet, shorts and boots, despite the chill in the damp air, my body starts to warm up. Until, roughly halfway to the peak, rain becomes sleet, and sleet turns into snow. The snow plays havoc with my senses. Sight, sound, and sense of direction are all diminished.

"Where's the bloody road?"

Failure is not an option and is pushed from my mind as I consider my direction. The prospect of returning home without reaching the end brings enough shame to propel me forward and ignites my competitive spirit. Also, if the worst happens, who will tell my mum? Or anyone else for that matter.

Before I left England, mum had already asked, "What makes you think you can do this stupid hike?" Concerned, she knows well the challenges of the natural environment. Growing up in Finland, winter months and short days see temperatures twenty Celsius degrees below zero .

"I don't know" is the honest answer. I am not sure I can do this hike, but I need a challenge. Without any real purpose beyond my studies, the prospect of just surviving, grinding out a life, is unappealing. Fundamentally I am determined to do something different, something more than eke out an existence in, what I call, the "culture of no." Mainstream society is riddled with rules and littered with regulations. For as long as I can remember the world is tightly bound by "no." "Don't do this, mustn't do that, shouldn't do the other" are the refrains of voices in civvy society. A fire of curiosity burns in my belly and has triggered an attitude of "get to it, give it a go and why not?" I hate being constrained, by rule makers who seem to be the hypocritical arbiters of power. So here I am, stuck on the side of a mountain, in a blizzard, questioning my life choices. I have nothing to lose out here and everything to gain but, if it all comes to an end here at least I lived my life.

Or died trying.

Wrapped in a blanket of snow, I can hear my mum's concerns. "What if I die?" I promised her I would not. Bloody hell. If ever there was a spur to getting a task done, it was the thought of letting your mum down. Surrounded by white fields, white caps and whiteout, options are fast disappearing. I can already here the chorus song of the classes that chatter. *"That poor woman, did you hear what her son did? Stupid boy, fancy doing that to your mother."* And so on, and so forth. Right now, most people's opinions can go hang but as my brain shuts out thoughts, there are two rules of society as yet unbroken: 1 – don't disappoint mum and, 2 – never piss off grandma (anyone's mum or grandma for that matter).

With these two rules blinking on my inner dashboard, I better sort my shit out. If I walk out of this predicament nobody will be any the wiser and I can keep the secret to myself. Everybody has their own memories of basic training, and some of my strongest recollections were forged in the gym and on the moors. Already fit upon entry to the Navy, I was nevertheless surprised how much more we could physically achieve under the guidance of Royal Marine physical training and survival instructors. Rope climbs, box jumps, long trail marches, and managing the elements were just a handful of new experiences which punctuated the hundreds of push ups, the miles of running, and hours spent training. This is where my real inspiration comes from. I know from them, that we humans can always do more than we believe we are capable of.

Here in the Alps, I get to finish my ultimate test.

The instructor's voice booms out from history, loud and clear through the medium of memory: *"Keep moving muppet!"* A strong message. Clear and concise, he has shown up a few times on this journey but was never more needed than right now.

Where did that come from?

Not just the prospect of disappointing mother and grandmother, but also the disdain of the corps of PT Instructors who, across the years, whipped all of us young men into shape.

At the point of maximum fatigue, and utmost shiver, when it would be easy to just stop and flop, the voice reaches out and with a chuckle, recharges my flagging spirit. It is there resonating with firm concern, always behind me, urging me forward, allowing no weakness and giving no quarter. There is more care too, as this is not just an exercise in discipline, it is also an exercise in survival. Stumbling and fumbling, crashing into drifts, I keep moving. Down is good, up is bad, so down is where we go. The die is cast. The solar eclipse has played a cruel trick. Overnight, the summer heat has evaporated into a winter cold. And as the heat fades from my core, and the flames go out, I dig deeper into the gift of Sisu. A genetic gift from my Finnish forbears. This is almost like a spiritual force drawn down from the lakes, forests, and rocks which are home to wolves, bears, and reindeer. They are the survivors of white winters and green summers in Finland. This is the spirit that reignites the flames that burn in my soul.

Which levels the playing field.

Moments of spiritual clarity in periods of extreme adversity are a very human construct. Literature is littered with moments of awakening through the most extreme of circumstances. This is mine. The strength of rock and river, snow and ice, forests and fields will carry me through today.

I will win, and Fate can eff off.

With a capital F and a resounding OFF!

Reserves depleted, I dig deeper into a wellspring of energy that I learned of in Dark London, drop down into a small crag, stumble some more metres and keep moving until, there beneath my feet, is the hard comfort of a concrete road. The single solitary road which winds through the mountains now lies beneath my feet and means I can speed up, warm up, and hopefully get picked up. This little piece of terra firma also means cars and cars mean safety.

Behind a large rock I strip naked. Pinching my skin -the hurt creates some heat – I then dry my body with a towel from my pack. Rubbing my limbs hard to generate more heat I do not want to be naked too long. Firstly, I tuck my hands in my armpits and jump up and down. Feeling appropriately ridiculous, I reach into my pack, pull out some lightweight trousers and a shirt. Dressing as fast as my trembling body allows, I find dry socks too. Tucking my hands into my armpits again, I jump up and down some more. With no care for appearance, I feel like a possessed pogo. A second pair of socks covers my hands like mittens and, low on energy, in the lee of the mountain I creep up the road. Not noticing the change of direction in the falling snow, I am walking towards possible refuge instead of down to a guaranteed town. Some cars crawl by slowly. Learning from Switzerland, I stick out my thumb. Hitching and hoping, I just keep moving.

Right about now, I think about the honey trap. I could be languishing in a chocolatey heaven being pampered by beautiful people. As I consider my life choices once more, a few more cars drive by. Soulless people with no love for their fellow human sit warm inside.

Teeth chattering like a cartoon cat, I discover enough energy to make the cold air bluer. Curses fill the skies around me.

"Aaaargggh!" I scream and shout at the sky.

Shouting loud it feels like a new warmth fills my lungs.

Mad at Fate and the games of destiny, I roar again. My skin hurts so much the pain is like a white heat. In this moment I turn up and walk towards the top of the mountain. Down is guaranteed safety, the town, a bar and some Stella Artois. Up promises nothing more than the guess of safety. The hope of a refuge that may or may not be there.

Onwards and upwards I climb. Not feeling the pain, just numb with cold. Knowing not to stop, as the internal instructor keeps up his mantra "Keep moving muppet!" And as the heat ebbs from my body, a small car, similar in size and shape to the charabanc of three Swiss ladies, pulls over to the side of the road and a door opens. The three Bonnies are here to rescue me, unbelievable luck. A few tears of gratitude leak out onto my cheeks and freeze on my face. The trio of blonde and brunette have finished their shopping trip and decided to stay in France for a few days. Knowing the foolishness of my escapade, they have come looking for me, will return me to the honey trap, feed me up, and give me a soft bed to sleep in. Just a few metres ahead, heaven awaits, and I push my freezing limbs the final few steps uphill to the car. Falling into the back seat in full hallucination, I embrace the heat and with the last of my ebbing energy whisper a cheery hello. Hurting with cold and aching from the freeze, I nearly puke in the new heat. Silence surrounds me and I open my eyes slowly. Concerned eyes look down. Soft brown eyes. Two women.

Not Swiss.

Spanish.

They speak a melodic song which reminds me of the three Bonnies. The tones are gentle with concern. Like an upturned turtle, flat on the back seat, I climb out of the webbing of my rucksack. Shoving the pack to one side, I sit up awkwardly, nod and put my hands together in the universal symbol of prayer.

Mumbling gracias, gracias, gracias, I quickly exhaust the few words of Spanish I know.

The socks on my hands keep my fingers warm. The kind eyes in front of me linger on my person. The heat in the car is high, and I curb the urge to vomit as the impact shocks my system. Feeling embarrassed in the spotlight of kindness, stupid even, I notice a pattern of behaviour emerging. Rescue by beautiful women appears to be the theme and long may that last. The real question however is: How much dumb shit do I have to do for that pattern to sustain? At what point does this become terminal? These philosophical thoughts flutter around as my eyes get heavy, and I start to slumber. The soft brown eyes linger, a soft voice speaks, and the car begins moving. As adrenaline subsides, a painful ache prevents slumber from turning into sleep. Spanish words softly spoken reach my ears and even with no comprehension of their meaning, there is a kindness within which releases fuzzy emotions. Socially awkward, in an typically English way, I keep my eyes closed. The company of foreigners is preferable to my own country folk. Cultures bring learning and language and food which is a stark contrast to that from home, where the residual hurt of scars from another time has created a distrust of my own kin. I no longer know where I belong or who I should be. Distrust now drives curiosity and my global journey where seeking validation seems to take me further and further away from my upbringing.

Slumbering, I mutter "gracias" again and fold into myself. Saying a silent prayer of thanks to Spain and the Spanish, I tuck sock mitten hands into my armpits and let the ache of slumber compete with the hot puking sensation. A short while later we stop at the Col d'Iseran. Rallying, I climb out of the car to take photos of the storm at the peak. The wind and cold bite my skin again. Needles tear at the pores of my skin. This does not feel like a wise choice but, worried that nobody will believe my story, I want evidence of this crazy blizzard. At the edge of focus, just out of range I can see the refuge that would have been my intended destination. It is closed. No cars, no people. Reaching the peak would have been a pyrrhic victory and possibly a fateful decision. Reaching there I would have been truly in the merde with no shelter. Soft brown eyes above gentle smiles look my way. My Spanish rescuers are friendly, and their concerns are diminished by my upright demeanour. Arguably they have saved my life, but I am still cold to the core. Like an ice block has replaced the space behind my sternum. Climbing back into the car we chat a little. With my death no longer imminent, we can all be friends. Unable to speak Spanish though, I feel foolish. Mostly mumbling "gracias" between simple English phrases I soon get tired in the warmth and safety of the car which rapidly brings sleep. Nodding, smiling, and mumbling awkwardly, sleep takes over, while the car wends its way carefully along the snowy road and on to the next town.

The small mountain town of Bonneval-sur-Arc is where we part ways. We say fond farewells. The Spanish women smile some more. Their warm fingers hold my hands and transmit a new heat through the tips which are still chilled. They utter words which, although incomprehensible, feel kind. I choose to believe in their kindness as it makes me feel better about the human condition.

Physically clumsy and emotionally awkward I turn away, for there is a new sensation within.

Until now I was cold resilient, often found in shorts and tee shirt in the depths of winter, it was a rare day when I wore a hoodie or sweater. Now, the enduring impact of this storm is an ice block in my core. A cold that nestles like a virus and never goes away. A cold that will come back to life in wind, water, or winter and remind me forever of this day at the top of a mountain.

The Spaniards may have saved my life, and I really do not know how to process the feelings. The blizzard was cold, judgmental, and without empathy. Much like the England I know and therefore, weirdly, a kind of comfort zone to struggle through, it is also an experience I cannot forget.

"Viva Espana!" I should cry but words which would articulate my feelings are hard to find. Surrounded for days by "foreignness." I have discovered great foods, greater kindnesses, and a different outlook on life. I am loyal to my country but wonder if I love it anymore. Foreign lands bring discovery, adventure, and new experiences. They offer an alternative to fear and loathing and may even be a place to realize dreams.

Bonneval-sur-Arc is a market town of stone buildings. A handful of shops, a laundromat, some houses, and an internet café; life here is simple. As the cold eats at my bones, my actions are simple too. Eat and heat.

I break out some coins.

Buy a tin of condensed milk from the store.

Enter the laundromat.

Stripping down for the second time in a couple of hours, I push all of my clothes into the tumble dryer.

Money goes in the slot, pushing the big start button, I press my face against the glass door feeling heat from the working dryer. Nearly two hours have passed since I escaped the blizzard, but the cold still permeates to my core. Whilst I have stopped shaking, the ends of my fingers and toes are still numb, affecting dexterity. My entire body feels like it is wrapped in a clammy cold sheet, as if I will never be warm again. I climb atop the rumbling machine. The heat from the motor pushes up combatting the cold in my core. I start ladling condensed milk into my mouth, moving slowly as I struggle to hold the spoon. The dryer heat creeps across my skin moving slowly towards my outer edges. The thick sugary milk steadily restores energy and provides a relief from the dull ache created by a biting freeze that still nests in the marrow of my bones. Absorbed in this world, a thin towel covers my dignity, and I fail to notice the silence around me.

Not the silence of nighttime in the mountains, nor the silence of a solar eclipse extinguishing all the natural noise, a silence of a human form. For it is laundry day in Bonneval and looking up my eyes meet those of my audience. Old ladies, and younger old ladies, stare at my naked torso. Condensed milk drips from the spoon missing my open mouth as another moment of awkwardness surrounds me causing a flush in my face. Hustling for heat and an escape from the cold I had paid no heed to the room. Stripping down rapidly, the ladies of the town have enjoyed a show. Not vaudeville nor burlesque, but free nevertheless, and mildly entertaining, I hope. My dignity is protected by a thin camping towel which barely reaches around my waist. More ladies show up and from their glances I know the local grapevine is at work. The absence of laundry baskets for some is also indicative. After a short while, there are more women than machines and the heat of the room is almost at a level of the dryer under my butt.

This is embarrassing, every item of clothing is still wet and cold in the drying cycle.

The town matriarchs are clearly curious as the blizzard on the peak has not reached down this side of the mountain. In the absence of context, my actions are clearly those of a deranged man. Sitting statue like, except for the steady motion of spoon to mouth, the view through their eyes is hopefully more comedy than caution. Exposed to their examination, life feels somewhat ruthless as the gentler concerns of the Spanish women fade with the cold. Hiding my growing embarrassment, I pretend I am in a field of cows and their big eyes, gentle nodding and chewing, are the happy movements of a Friesian herd. Cows are under-rated. Harbingers of peace, they are elegant, friendly, and curious. Moving very slowly, I am determined not to spook the crowd nor lose the grip on my covering, whilst maintaining the steady drip feed warmth of sugary milk.

The last thing we want right now is a stampede.

The dryer tumbles through its cycle and eventually I climb down, carefully holding my towel in place and simultaneously reaching into the cavernous depths to draw out a few clothes. Stretching long limbs, for entertainment value, I begin a reverse striptease to the chagrin of the audience. Ever the people pleaser, I smile their way and offer a small bow. No tips or gratuities are offered so, warmly dressed and red faced, edging towards the exit, I look for my next destination.

The internet café is open.

It is time to connect with the world outside. A detached location with which I have had no contact for four, five, or is it six days?

One email attracts my attention. An invitation from Ilaria to visit her in Italy.

We study together in the same Chinese class. She lives in Kensington, an affluent part of London. I live in Tooting, on the opposite end of the affluent continuum.

Her home is close to Milan, a global centre of fashion and the apogee of Italian modern culture. I have no home to call my own and the place where I grew up reached its cultural apogee in the seventies. On a steady decline ever since, and in the top five English hotspots for knife crime and violence, I prefer not to disclose my own social progeny when in the orbit of spectacular beauties. Ilaria is such and her persona consolidates my recent pattern of behaviour.

With a new clarity of purpose for my descent into Italy and a new vision of what the immediate future may hold, I plan my route out of the mountains. This Alpine escapade has been phenomenal but closing the show in another honeytrap or at the very least with some bed and board, a pair of unique bookends bind this adventure. "Honeytrap to Honeytrap – a European exploit" is the book in my rapidly thawing brain, which is functioning again but in maladjusted fashion.

Pulling out my map of the region I can see a single road and a lot of undergrowth. My target destination is Susa, fifty-five kilometres away across the border. That said, if I go "off piste", I can roll through the trees and underbrush on a semi vertical descent. This way I can chop off ten to fifteen kilometres and maintain speed rather than follow around the S bends of the mountain roads. This seems feasible as recent climbing attests, so I ping Ilaria a reply and a gracious acceptance of her invitation to meet in Milan.

Forgetting the cold in my core, I munch through some baguette and cheese from the store, replenish the water in my pack, drink some coffee, and thus warmed up, the race for Susa begins. It is still early. I left my mountain hostel with a hangover at dawn, and it is mid-morning now. If I push hard, I can complete the distance before dark.

My toes hurt. In the laundromat I discovered shredded skin, and raw digits where my wet and dry boots rubbed away the surface. Some gravel, embedded in the flesh of my feet adds a pepper like coat to the grizzled sight of torn tissue.

Forgetting the pain, the complexities of border crossings and possible weather phenomena, and preferring optimism to caution, the next race begins. I like being fit. With no assets, a little money, and limited educational opportunity, fitness and health are my greatest treasures. I maintain them carefully along with books, one or two of which I carry everywhere.

Having just escaped a frosty demise the prospect of warmth is immensely appealing.

The trek ahead is a marathon distance. I have run many distances previously, including a few half marathons across country and on road. Equally, I have hiked thirty kilometres with a pack, in the Welsh mountains. Not as a time trial though, yet that was tough and the blisters were magnificent specimens. This will be an extra ten to twelve kilometres with a heavier pack. A true test. Mentally I switch away from the physical challenge. Optimism is a resilience tool I have honed over the years and it may be Sisu. Nevertheless, avoid the impossible, and no matter how improbable whatever remains must be achievable. Butchering that old Sherlock Holmes phrase with a spring in my step, I chop away the metres which soon become kilometres as the mountainside falls away beneath my feet. Tunes play in my head. Madness mainly, with a little bit of the Jam and some Oasis. Songs that make me happy or remind me of happy times. I have used this tool before. Music is another resilience tool that quells fear, improves mood, and heals hurt. A head full of music I love keeps me moving on autopilot through the trees and over the scree of the mountain countryside. Not quite James Bond cool, I regularly stumble, fall, and end up in a heap on the ground. Humility though is less painful when nobody is looking. With no concept of speed or time, , just the general direction and sense of bearing are goals that sustain me.

Six hours later I crash into Italy. I am not sure where I crossed the border. Blundering out of the underbrush, I sometimes pick up roads out of the mountains then drop back into the trees and slopes heading in a rough south easterly direction. Unlike Switzerland into France though, I see no discernible border or border guards. Entry to Italy is simple. The town of Susa itself is sun baked with stone buildings and a heavy heat. Other than the language on signs, I could still be in France.

In fact, it is only the language on the signs that informs me I am no longer in France. I limp towards the railway station in this quiet, dusty town. Everything hurts. Boots have rubbed my feet raw. Backpack and webbing have rubbed my shoulders and back raw. Hair is full of dirt and forest debris. I have a beard full of grit. As I slow down, adrenaline subsides and the aches and pains grow.

The railway station is empty, apart from a dark train sitting still by the platform. Glancing around at notices and posters, I understand nothing. Several years of Latin studies yield no familiarity with modern Italian. Timetables however are ubiquitous and the train to Milan, leaves shortly. The destination is a couple of hours away. Before boarding the train, I have enough time to ping an email to Ilaria with my arrival time. No time to wait for a response I return to the train car and sit in the cool dark as lactic acid sets in my aching muscles like concrete. I have descended fast from three thousand metres to almost sea level completing a full marathon in these last hours. My hips, knees, and ankles are throbbing from the punishment. Whilst I enjoy supreme fitness, tanned body, and defined muscles, there are also tattered boots, blistered feet, and raw skin to suffer as part of my reward. In just a few days though I have crossed four international borders, peaked several mountains, survived a storm of biblical proportions, one solar eclipse, and a subsequent blizzard that nearly finished me off. Still not quite James Bond, but this epic adventure still feels cool. Life is sweet and, "La Dolce Vita" here in Italy is about to get sweeter.

The train hums, and lights flicker on. It starts to grumble, and an engine somewhere comes to life. I do a final check of surroundings and timings then, feeling the slow rhythmic movement of the undercarriage, fatigue engulfs me, as sleep overtakes me.

MILAN

Later I waken. It is after dark and my body is sore and stiff. Hobbling and inflexible, I flop onto the platform. Scanning the crowds I hobble towards the exits with no consideration that my hosts may not be there. Feet are sore and backpack is hoisted; I ignore the hurt and hope for the best. Scanning and limping, before long I see hands waving and navigate towards the warm welcome of Ilaria and her parents. My disheveled state is conspicuous, but they pay no heed. I tell them about the blizzard, and the final marathon into Susa, simultaneously taking note of the people around me and the family in front of me.

I am sure I stink. Dirty, bearded and burned, I cannot say when I last showered.

They ignore my untidy appearance, and possible smell, ushering me towards the family car which is bigger than any vehicle I have ever owned. Bubbly, they are openly friendly without caution. To be expected from an Italian family this close to Milan, they are all fashionably dressed, sophisticated, and voguish. Ilaria, a story book princess, resonates virtue. Her mother and father look like Sophia Loren and Marlon Brando. The entire family is beautiful. There is a sister too, who they all claim is the most beautiful amongst them.

My word! So much beauty in one gene pool is too much to consider and systematically unfair. Floating in the gloaming of their enchantment, I sit quietly as the car rolls out of Milan towards Bergamo, a red tiled town in Lombardy with cobblestone streets, Venetian walls, and a funicular railway. In the family home I am shown to my own quarters. The internal space includes my own bathroom. Most of my belongings fit into a single backpack. In this generous space like a pea in a whistle, I bounce around on hobbled feet, tumbling over and stripping off my clothes once more. Turning on the hot water, beneath the cascade in a marble tiled shower cubicle, maintenance of self is my top priority. Shredded feet first I find scissors and cut away dead flesh from the soles and around my toes, then soap them clean, and pick dirt from abrasions. Picking out the pepper gravel, as warm abundant water washes over my skin, stinging raw flesh, I harvest small grit from burst blisters and try not to rupture others. Eventually I am clean again. Still sitting beneath the cascade, noticing how water can release pain, I consider my clothes. They are mostly dirty and most certainly not Milan modish. Not much I can do about that right now. I shave my face, and with nothing else to wear, pull on the blizzard-stained shirt and chinos which hang loose on my body. Looking in the mirror, it is only now that I release how much weight I have lost in the mountains. Probably ten or twelve kilos from six or seven hours of climbing and descending each day. Relaxed, feeling my pulse, I can also tell that my heart rate has dropped too. I count around fifty beats per minute.

My flesh stings as it cleans. The cold is finally gone, although I can still feel a residual icy grip on my heart and stomach.

With no fat on my body, burning feet, and a relatively clean composure I limp upstairs.

A large wooden table fills the kitchen upon which a host of delicacies are laid out. The magnitude and wealth of such a display is the like of which I have never seen. Tinned Navy rations at sea, processed foods at home, basic fare as a kid all flash through my mind as the romance of cuisine is laid out in front of me. Switzerland, France, and now Italy have opened windows on to a world I could not even imagine before. You don't know what you don't know after all. Curry and Cantonese are the most available forms of exotic cooking the English enjoy. Anything else, apart from fish and chips, is generally outside of my budget.

Snapping out of the reverie, I land back in the kitchen and notice the dynamic in the room. Sophia Loren fusses as Ilaria works the conversation. She is a proud hostess and honest interpreter. Marlon Brando smoulders handsomely at the head of the table. The patriarch of this kingdom signals for me to sit and doing so, I make a note to self: "Remember your manners, chew your food, be gracious." With stomach rumbling, I am ready to restore some fat to my body.

A basket laden with fresh bread holds the centre. The surrounding terrain is covered. Prosciutto thinly sliced to a transparent pink hue, rich dark salami peppered with translucent specks of white marble, aged pecorino with its unique aroma; fat olives, colourful peppers, thick olive oil, and fresh pesto accompany this culinary composition. I see no butter. Ilaria kindly explains to dip the bread into the olive oil and following suit, I take my first bite. The oil is thick, and the bread is soft, soaking up flavours which feature for the first time in my taste lexicon. Small cups of strong black coffee provide extra pep. This dark and thick elixir is nothing like the brown water served from jars of freeze-dried granules at home. Thimble sized glasses contain limpid liquid. Grappa, a mildly spicy and peppery brandy extracted from fermented grapes, serves as a liquid painkiller to the rapidly subsiding aches and pains of my final marathon.

There is a toast. To what? I am not sure. It is followed by a second toast.

Just to health and friendship, Ilaria explains, but I can barely hear the words as I am totally in love with my surroundings and this unsolicited generosity. More meat, cheese, and bread arrive. Coffee too with grappa pours. Everything is fresh, flavourful, and unlike the processed produce of British supermarkets. The foods are complimentary, blending well with the time of night, they provide sustenance without bulk. It must be close to midnight now, but I eat freely, with cautious manners. Pain means I eat slowly and am seemingly more sophisticated than I normally might be.

As the grappa shots work their magic, stories of Italy flow from the family. A symphony of Italian and English in perfect harmony. Like Winnie the Pooh, I am totally content in this kitchen-based honey trap, gradually returning fat to my body and soul. Mountain memories fade under the gentle, yet persistent, flow of Italian hospitality, and in a moment of blatant transaction, I decide that Italy is wonderful and my new favourite home.

Ilaria and her family are wealthy. Not a noveau-riche wealth which is noisy and blustery. More an understated wealth that may be generational. Sleeping on a thick mattress in a brass framed bedstead, I notice art on the walls, tiles in the kitchen, and real wood furniture. Colours combine with class to create a happy home in this split-level stone city. Imposter syndrome sets in, and I feel awkward again. More at home just surviving in the cold consuming blizzard, the warmth of family is unfamiliar, and the only way to compress my ignorance is by being curious. Food and language are the gateways to culture, so I focus my attention there. Trying to recover lost Latin to comprehend modern Italian whilst simultaneously curbing my desire to eat everything in sight. Olive oil, like wine, has different terrain and is tested for aroma, taste, and appearance. Also, like wine, it lends excitement to a dish, straight from the bottle or as part of the cooking. Regions vary with presentation which impacts price. At home austerity influenced our food budget, where World War rationing had impacted generations of cuisine. Olive Oil, until now, was Popeye's girlfriend. A canister of the liquid sat in the back of a cupboard for many years as nobody knew what it was. Authentic olive oil is like a green gold and, with the happiest of tutors, I became the most diligent of students.

Back in England we mock other nationalities. Our own national propaganda distilled through the tabloid press perpetuates irritation, fear, and sometimes anger at the people "over there." Creating, at times, a sense of victimhood. This is not new. Since Napolean conquered Europe, British media outlets have mocked leaders overseas. Political figures, generals, heroes of sport and entertainment, nobody is spared as they strip off the veneer of civility which exists between nations. Growing up in Dark London's southern boroughs, it is hard to escape the warp and weft of tabloid journalism. In the absence of overseas targets, domestic ones serve equally well. Royal family, football managers, athletes, and T.V. actors are all a salacious grist to grind in the media mill.

I am conflicted.

For here, in the heart of Europe, the standard of living, education, and general kindness is greater than that experienced back home. More than food and wine but also art, music, landscapes, and religion. There is an availability of high culture, it seems, to even those who are low born, low church, or lowly educated. As each day goes by, I learn the paper wrapped nationalistic tendencies of tabloids serve only to foster suspicion or worse. I am no Master of Economics, yet I trust my own eyes and experiences. Knowing that happiness is fleeting, I elect to enjoy the momentary luxury and engage with my environment. The generosity of this family seems boundless. With no other means to reciprocate, I lean in to being the best possible guest by graciously devouring as much food and drink as good manners will allow.

Milan, Verona, and Venice are on the agenda over the next few days. We explore these magnificent cities replete with renaissance statues, medieval architecture, and modern fashions. Sipping coffee in St. Mark's square I try to retain as much new knowledge as possible. Physical fatigue is replaced with mental gymnastics and a groundswell of emotion. Accompanied as I am by beauty and femininity, it is hard work not to be distracted. Stuck between temptation and edification I resist the one to engage with the other, locking on to the imposing frontage of the Basilica San Marco rather than that of my companion. Glistening with gold leaf, the Basilica is a wonderful edifice and testimony to pre-industrial architecture. Tourists snake away from the entrance, patiently waiting in line to explore the saintly interior. Venice, a city built over 127 islands was the capital of a maritime power for most of a millennium. Rising after the fall of Rome, the Republic of Venice was an empire of merchants that sustained for longer than that of the British. The latter spanned four hundred years and seems much less flamboyant than the Venetian equivalent, which grew up under siege from marauding Huns and Goths. The imposing Basilica reflects the dominant mercantile power that extended from the Eastern Mediterranean out beyond the Black Sea with trade routes and commercial posts in Crimea and North Africa. Domed roofs and portico fronts decorated with gold leaf mosaics crown the entrances to the Basilica.

Inspiring and overwhelming, modern British culture feels dull by comparison, seemingly reflected through the lenses of football and national hubris. Maybe hubris is the nemesis of nationalism, a tipping point at which Empire nations start to crumble. Greek, Egyptian, Roman, Viking, and British, all seemed to have reached peak hubris before decline and fall. Will the American empire go the same way? I have no idea. America seems to be a globalization fuelled corporate empire backed by military might, which is not totally dissimilar to its British cousin. The thing is, as I understand it, the U.S.A, claims not to be an empire building nation. The only Americans I have met overseas are extensions of the military which suggests different. There is no point filling my thoughts with unanswerable questions and pointless contradictions. Determined to enjoy the sunshine, coffee, and the company of a beautiful woman, I shut down my thinking with a final rhetorical question: “With the advent of the information age, will America enjoy the record of shortest-lived empire in modern history?”

At which point, Ilaria glides into view and we sail out among the waves of people.

Posing for a photo at the Bridge of Sighs, we walk canals, examine narrow streets, and visit tiny boutiques. Noticing the expertise of craftmanship, the aptitude of artisans, it dawns on me that I enjoy being surrounded by culture and art and architectural beauty. After Venice we drive back past Padua and stop in Verona (the hometown of Shakespeare's great romance), and Ilaria shows me the supposed balcony from which Juliet is tempted by Romeo. Monuments are multiple here and a statue of Dante looks out across the crowds reflecting pensively on his exile from Florence. Verona is a UNESCO heritage city, with provincial capital status and a thousand years of history. A living monument to renaissance with a footprint in the Roman Empire, Verona enjoyed an influx of wealth under Caeser Augustus.

It was a major trade hub.

We have historical wealth like this in Britain too, I have visited plenty of sites and museums. Yet it feels to me that here in Italy the depth and breadth of heritage is up on the surface for all to embrace, and looking around, Italians seem to significantly enjoy their own. Equally Ilaria and her family make their history and culture accessible and enjoyable. Not something I am used to back home. A few days exploring northern Italy, preceded by several days in France, create a sense of enlightenment which moves me to my foundations. It is here that I am becoming the person I needed when I was younger. England by contrast seems muted. I vow to look beyond nationalistic hubris when I return and try to discover more about U.K. heritage.

Heading out of town I forget about home as we drive deeper into the northern Italian countryside. Up towards the mountains, passing through small villages and towns, we climb a steep hill and then stop in a driveway beside the road. A flint and granite villa perches here on the mountainside. A sloped meadow garden, a small orchard, and wooden shuttered windows contribute to the idyllic setting here above the village. I am shown to my room, and I feel like royalty.

Opening the shutters I sit on the window ledge embracing the silence. In a place of peace gazing up at the mountain peaks, ambient sounds resonate at the edge of hearing. Not for the first time, I wonder at the vastness of the world outside of my own.

Slumbering on the edge of drop, the tinkling of bells brings me back to life as a goat herd flows over the ridge cascading down the grassy slope. The shepherd in the rear keeps tabs on stragglers stopping for a chew on the green. The man is scruffy, looks healthy, and sings a happy song. Whatever the complexities of his life, outward appearances suggest rustic romance and simplicity. Life stands still in this meadowed garden in Alpine Lombardy and healing from the hike I contemplate the prospect of a longer stay.

I flirt with the notion of marrying into Ilaria's family. It is a flippant thought but there is no harm dreaming. Imposter syndrome crushes the first flickering of hope as I believe that English social hierarchy does not support upward mobility. For many years I have hidden my upbringing, not least of all the horror stories that wrecked our family. Through Naval College and University, I kept my shame tucked away. Ilaria lives in Kensington, shops in Milan and has family properties in Bergamo and the Italian Alps. She aspires to be an Opera singer, and we talk of Opera singing vocals, arias, and classical performances. The strengths and weaknesses of Domingo, Pavarotti, Callas, and Te Kanawa. The upstart Bocelli who uses a microphone to amplify his voice. The incline and decline of opera over time.

Truth be told, she talks. I listen. Which feels like marriage already.

Totally out of my depth, I wonder at the possibility of a relationship with this beauty. Aspiring singer, flawless skin, large eyes, and waist length hair. A voluptuous figurine I could listen to her all day. But would I be happy living in her shadow. I keep my thoughts to myself. Feeling improper I do my best to keep up with conversation, remaining mostly in listening mode. Better to keep your own mouth closed and have people wonder if you are stupid, then open it and confirm their suspicions.

I keep the vision alive though.

Dreams are life's stretch goals and without them nothing can be achieved. They may sometimes seem foolish, but dreams bring the inspiration to be more and do more. In the nighttime silences the stars are so bright I cannot sleep. Looking up into the sky I create new dreams and say a small prayer of thanks to whoever is guiding my decisions and opening the doors to other worlds. There is no going back to the life before. Dark London is far behind me, disappearing in the rearview mirror. Nightmares still occur though as neural scars take the longest of time to heal. Even here, in the still night of the most idyllic of havens, bad dreams rupture sleep and cold sweat beads on my skin. In the daytime I soak up the dolce vita knowing a life like this may be out of reach. Nevertheless, daydreams are harmless and cost nothing. I dare to ponder a life in northern Italy wrapped comfortably in the rarefied air of high culture, cosy in Lombardy.

When the sun shines through the morning dawn, now in clean clothes, with cleaner skin and feeling healthy, I squash down dark memories and enjoy this family. Grandma lives up in the mountains too. She is here over the weekend and joins her daughter and granddaughter to generate more hospitality which, in true Italian style, means even more home cooked food.

I remember the two rules of society. Never upset mum, nor piss off grandma.

Downstairs in the kitchen nonna is rolling pizza dough by hand. Coffee is bubbling its rich dark fluid on the stove. Real, thick black coffee with an aroma so deep it goes from tongue to toes in a nano second. Ilaria has offered up more education. Coffee culture. There is no Starbucks here. I like it black and hot. Simple. The stronger the better. But there is more, and I learn that coffee comes in many forms. Cappuccino, espresso, and latte, and when it is appropriate to drink one rather than the other, and at what time of day. The nuance escapes me to be fair. I love the tastes and textures of each. Freedom of choice means I want some of all of them and am regularly told off by Ilaria when I pick one out of turn.

Feeling closer to this family, they invite me to stay for the remainder of the Summer.

Unexpected!

It reignites my dream. Stumbling over words of gratitude, I try to hide my embarrassment. Of what? I have no idea. Comfort exists in the bosom of luxury. Yet the confidence to reach up and take it is missing. Am I sending out signals? Misreading theirs? What happens at the end of three weeks? Once again, the prospect of a romance floats in the air. Is it a real sensation? Or is it merely a response to food, family, and the allure of a life unknown? I question everything. Another byproduct of life in Dark London, where so many trust contracts have been broken.

As the struggle continues in my head, I return to the sanctuary of food. In England we eat food, in France, they taste food. Here in Italy, people create food. A magical blend of colours, textures, and aromas exist here; a palette of tastes and teasing temptations that breathe life into your senses and sensations. Grandma is still rolling pizza dough, simultaneously adding wood to the pizza oven. Before long she is breaking out polenta and mozzarella, hand making pasta with Sophia, and prepping the family for a feast.

The world needs more grandmas.

They are mostly good, stuffed with wisdom and knowledge.

Also, they suffer no shit and distill centuries of secrets to daughters and granddaughters. They have seen and survived the menaces of mankind armed with nothing more than sharp comments and a solid stick. Grandmas are iconic and can control the unruliest of men.

Today is Formula One race day, and with a guest in the house only the best will do in terms of village hospitality. Grandma is firmly in charge. Offering no real value to the team, feeling like a voyeur, I find a tree to sit under with a book to read. Marlon, the man of the house is confined to quarters. Watching Ferrari win the Formula One is not the harshest of punishments and with the men removed from kitchen the feel of culinary magic is in the air.

Three generations of womankind work this kitchen, only the most foolish man would enter that space. This is not misogyny, this is smart. Food worthy of the best restaurant is prepared with love, passion, disagreement, and a perpetual chatter. Correcting, discussing, and debating the right quantities of flour, water, egg, and other ingredients is required to make the best textured pizza, pasta, or polenta-based dishes. The list is long: lamb, mozzarella, truffles, mushrooms, butter, olive oil, rosemary, pepper, sausage, cheese, figs, olives and more constituents than the capacity of my comprehension allows. Mesmerizing, fascinating and a little bit frightening, three generations of Italian culinary know-how blend into a symphony of art and science to create the most eye-wateringly resplendent meal.

As the symphony plays out, Marlon watches Ferrari.

I read under the trees.

Beneath the boughs I realize how much I love these moments of tranquil expectation. Like living on the mountain slopes in France, I learn to wait for something good to happen. Being silent, accepting solitude, I replace the convenient world with one of patience. You can't hurry art and learning to be content in my own company is a refined skill. It allows for moments of contemplation that have not existed before. The art of reflection is portable and transformative, costs nothing, goes everywhere, and opens your mind to solutions and opportunities out of reach to the frenzied spirit.

Lunch arrives.

At a table on the flagstone terrace overlooking the village, talking and eating together this family is wholesome, not broken. Three generations dine in ensemble, enjoy each other, and contribute to their collective well-being. It is special, and to my mind, a real stretch goal. My grandparents are all deceased. My parents are divorced. My mother lives far away and my father, in his second marriage, is reckless with relationships. My siblings are scattered, and we rarely sit together in harmony.

Familial cohesion is something other people have; the feelings are overwhelming.

Shaking out of reverie, a baked yellow globe rests in front of me. Taking a piece, the taste sensation blows my mind, drooling is imminent. Ilaria sparkles with Italian pride, as enjoyment of their food is the biggest and easiest compliment I can make.

It is not difficult.

This is polenta. Baked and wrapped around a mozzarella. Or is it ricotta? Or mozzarella di bufala? Or ricotta di bufala? Goodness knows. Either way, the baked texture of warm grain infused with melting creamy white cheese is a virgin food experience like nothing I can remember. So simple, yet an unreal combination. There is of course wine and grappa and vibrating like a tuning fork on a piano, I forage deeper into this epicurean dream.

Hiking through the Alps, the various climates have torched through the fat on my body. The lean muscular look appeals to my vanity. Here in the gentle embrace of food kindness I wonder how long it would take for me to go from lean and mean to ball shaped. Ilaria, Sophia, and Grandma are the cornerstones of this Italian honey trap, and I am in conflict between Bacchanalia and Beefcake. The struggle is real. A struggle between the love of authentic food with an existing desire to be a steely world traveller.

Romance springs eternal but adventure is my game. The soft embrace of a kind family is a route to fat, dumb, and happy. I am not sure I am ready for that, even though my own world is one of chaos and dysfunction. Ilaria's world is beautiful. As the women chatter, Marlon says little. In fact, he does not say much at all, even in direct conversation. For most of a week, the family patriarch has spoken quietly, a handful of times. He is not bombastic, just quietly goes about his business and looks after his family. Could I be like him? I consider the possibility of a loving relationship. Ilaria is graceful and gracious, and I know from London life that she has plenty of admirers. That said, nobody has visited her family here. I am the only one who accepted her offer and the reception is real. Feeling emboldened, I vow to approach her the next day. I can stay here until semester begins and we can return to London together.

At church in the morning, I join the family. This is high church, a first for me. A Catholic service, in Latin. Another first. Stepping into the vestibule, the congregation crosses themselves with blessed water from the font. I mimic without meaning. They find their seats on the pews, seemingly in rows designated for families. I squeeze on to the rear most pew. The most influential families are up front. I try to keep a low profile. The priest enters reciting cantations and swinging an incense burner. Uncomfortable, I feel like a fraud and the deeper the priest gets into his service, the more fraudulent I feel. Nature is my temple and spiritually, I am happiest in the wilds. Will the church find me out? Nobody pays me the slightest notice but the sense that everyone knows I am foreign and not Catholic deepens my discomfort.

Glancing over the congregation, I see the beautiful family and think about their daughter. Impropriety fills my mind. The devil on my shoulder chuckles. As the Latin service continues, I miss the gaps in sermon where a response is required. The congregation is in unison. I am not. This is a house of God. A hot house too, jam packed full of people from the village dressed in their best. It gets hotter as thoughts of hot food and a hot woman weave their way through the sermon. Shifting on the bench, I hope nobody can read my mind. Church Latin is impregnable and after an hour, what else am I going to think about. The discomfort is palpable. Trying to avoid the holy, I think about the honey. The honey gets hotter, and the recollection of honey traps is a humbling pattern of behaviour that emerges in this house. "Your sins will find you out." What? Where did that come from? To my knowledge I have committed no sins. In recent days at least. A Latin cantation reaches my ears and I am sure the Priest knows what I am thinking. He is admonishing the stranger in their midst. The feeling is daft and very real. Does the thought of sin really constitute sin? Philosophically that is up for discussion. Food and femininity are natural. How can they be sinful? Creeping superstitions tells me I should not be here spoiling the tranquillity of this family. Looking up at the ceiling, Old Testament retribution becomes a possibility. Trapped in a conundrum of my owning making, stillness and calm thinking seem to be the best disciplines.

Back to the honey. It is never far away. An amorous liaison is enticing. But what is love? A tortuous twine that binds two souls, it fires a passion that powers the earth and creates a burn that is hotter than hell. The prospect of passion is fixating, as is the heat of the burn. My own emotional burns are more than skin deep; they are scored into neural pathways and etched into bone. To avoid the latter, I often forgo the former. A dangerous liaison here could ruin an experience. Not least of all, it could bring down divine retribution. And potentially piss off Grandma. That's a bridge too far. The conundrum is complex and perpetuates impostor syndrome.

I know it is time to leave.

We part on good terms. Ilaria, Sophia, and Marlon return me to Milan, and the railway station swallows me up once more. They are oblivious to my inner wranglings and in their wonderful fashion have implored me to stay. Eat more food. Drink more wine. Be family. I want to cry a little. And they all look so good, smell wonderful. I want to cry some more. There are kisses, hugs, and expressive chatter.

Kindness hurts. Words are hard. Farewells are harder still.

This family have shown me everything, inspired dreams, and created the memories of a lifetime.

And the food. Will I ever know such cuisine again? Grandma fussed at how skinny I am. I should eat more. Without a doubt, within three weeks, I would be as big as a house. An excuse to return to work is the rationale within which I hide. Overnight though, the fear of rejection or disconnection has strengthened this rationale.

The path, for now, is a life less amorous.

A train bound for Nice brings an end to an adventure of natural phenomena, physical endeavour, and honey traps. Ilaria and her family are gone, and so are those dreams.

BOUNTY HUNTER

Nice is a sunny city with yellow, pink and orange frontages spicing up the old town. The train from Milan has crossed the border into France without stopping. My passport sits in the depths of my backpack, weatherbeaten yet untouched after four border crossings. Wondering how to fill my time, I am reluctant to consider any return to London. My life here has been a comparative luxury: affordable quality in terms of sustenance, an extended foreign holiday and, not least of all, the luxuries of kindness and generosity. I am unsure why I fear the latter. Beyond my own dysfunction and damaged family conditions, my own evolving intelligence has yet to grapple with the nuances of trust and family. Italy, just a few hours behind me, was alien and triggered an inner emotional crisis. Failed institutions have created the vacuum of loneliness. Filling that void requires both the restitution of trust and the sacrifice of independence.

Not ready for the former, I instinctively hold on to the latter.

Sipping coffee in an internet café, checking correspondence is at the bottom of my list of priorities. My bank account is diminished though; the necessity of revenue forces my choices. I click open my emails.

The French Riviera is an adopted home of so many English aristocracy. The city promenades along the edge of the Mediterranean Sea, aptly named the Cote d'Azur. Here cerulean waters sparkle under bright sunshine. The second largest city in the Alpes – Maritime region nestles at the foot of the mountains. Offering spectacular views in the north, I can imagine Geneva in the distance and scan the peaks moving south southeast. Picking out the mountain tops so recently crossed on foot I rotate further towards the descent into Italy, reminisce briefly then face south. Out to sea beyond the horizon are the islands of Sardinia and Corsica. Here in Old Nice, near the Cathedrale Saint-Reparate, I find breakfast. Coffee and croissant offer tasteful simplicity and a stark contrast to the opulence of Italian fare.

The sun warms my face.

The Promenade des Anglais, (Promenade of the English), borders the beach in a unique form of entente cordiale. The nineteenth century walkway constructed by aristocratic Anglo visitors is ironic. The English mistrust of things foreign leaves me wondering at this irony. I cannot imagine any stretch of British coastline being named the French Esplanade. Newspapers would tear out their paper hearts at the ignominious creep of European influence. Housewives would clutch pearls as suited husbands tut at the erosion of sovereignty. All the while, the same folks would overlook their love of skiing, wine snobbery and second home purchases.

Upward mobility may appear evasive to me, but down here on Maslow's bottom rung, the reigning hypocrisy in a classist society proves theory often kowtows to practice, particularly for a subset of society that would prefer to suspend downward mobility. It seems that the people who tell you how to behave are better arbiters than advocates of the standards they proselytize. Glancing at my emails, a new bounty presents itself, illustrating this very issue. The subject is a banker, Mr. Harris is what I shall call him, with allegedly sticky fingers. Lots of sticky in fact. About one million pounds worth of unapproved funding have vanished from the coffers of his employer in the City of London.

My mission, if I choose to accept it, is to find Mr. Harris, identify him and tag him. The bounty is good and subsidizes London life. Skills learned in darker places pay for my education today. The combined wisdom of the OG and the OP, along with the real-world experiences of being hunted by hyenas and gorillas, gives me a unique set of skills as I move from prey to predator. In the white-collar jungle where we live I have the advantage, as their senses are often dulled by their love of the luxurious.

Harris is a fraud rhino, and their characteristics are mostly defensive. Hiding in plain sight, they use a camouflage that renders them almost identical to fellow citizens. With a similar hide, features and diet to their fellow creatures, the fraud rhino preys on weaknesses in the rhizomatic ecosystem to further extend their own status. A special kind of predator, they quietly feed off those around them, almost unnoticeable, exploiting loopholes and draining funds. If smart, they can remain undetected for years. Now and again, one gets too greedy and unbalances the ecosystem, creating a wave of retribution. In such a case, the rhino will bunker down in a defensive fortress of their own making.

And so, I will track, trace and tag this wild rhino until such time that the long arm of British law can reach out and seize him.

He is somewhere here, in the wilds of western France.

These jobs give me purpose as well as bounty. A sense of doing good in the world. I nearly died on the hill of truth and integrity at the hands of unscrupulous people and so, those values are scored into my psyche. White collar crime, deemed victimless, is very cruel. Witnessing people physically crumble when their meagre savings are gone, taken, or misappropriated is heart rending. Tagging the fraud rhinos suggests some hope of compensation or protection for the vulnerable. It is my small contribution to society.

The operations and pay are frequent enough to give me a lifestyle beyond that of standard students. They also provide for a freedom of movement and satisfy somewhat the need for adventures. Facilitating an exploration of the great metropolis, this work on occasion affords trips to the world outside of London. Working mostly alone, when I do have partners they are colourful characters. A French Legionnaire and a Special Forces Major are two examples that spring to mind. Highly professional with generally unattainable skills and knowledge, they freely share their experience to get the work done. They are open, honest and forthright. I walk away from team jobs mostly improved with new skills, new knowledge and better equipped to deal with the world at large. At the very least, I am more capable of defending myself from the chattering classes, uniformed gorillas, and greasy hyenas.

New assignments arrive via email, phone or, infrequently, in person. The fraud rhinos are mostly male. Like the creative and optimistic Pooh Bear, they are obsessed with honey and can appear affable; but unlike the naïve and friendly "bear of very little brain," they are more sinister and calculating and are semi permanently stuck in someone else's honey. Ordinarily secure in affluent London post codes with private security, the fraud rhinos outside of London, are tucked away in stockbroker homes behind the genteel façade of red bricks and green fields. Surrey, Hampshire, West Sussex in the South. Royal Berkshire, Buckinghamshire or Hertfordshire in the North.

Contracts are timed agile projects. The clock is ticking even before I get the paperwork. Discretion is essential. It may take thirty days to track and tag a rhino and apart from a handful of contacts, knowledge is restricted to the contract facilitator and the paying client. Fraud, I learn, brings shame. Corporate officers do not enjoy being exposed nor having their pockets picked. It makes them feel vulnerable which is not good for outward appearances or shareholder confidences. The fraud rhino trail is visible once you know what you are looking for. They all have a footprint and a pattern of behaviour. The spoor may be old, but the dots still connect, and a live target can be found promptly. Using the entire time allowance, I like to make sure that the targets are authentic before moving in. This means I often get close to the rhino himself. There is an assumption that white collar "crims" are harmless. This is another rationale for fraud being a victimless crime. From a distance these money movers seem tame; up close they are unpredictable and can be dangerous if they feel threatened.

The fraud rhino is well hidden behind a veneer of respectability. They launder the contents of pension funds, extort lump sums, or help themselves to other peoples' money perpetuating hardship on a large scale, remaining elusive to avoid accountability. Their actions rarely hurt the C suite executive nor seems to put a dent in their salaries, particularly if insurance pays the bills. Which means sightings are rare, particularly as the fraud rhino looks down upon the people they hurt, which also means they blend well with their surroundings. Glancing askew at people without privilege or opportunity who are deemed stupid for not having money, the fraud rhino hurts the people without a voice and resembles very closely some of their counterparts. They prey on people without legal representation and hurt people who toil hard, who save pounds and pennies over years of dreaming for a better time. The aspiration of the victim, a softer future with some small comfort, gets burned in a blink by people for whom there is never enough money.

The fraud rhino has a softer present, and larger comforts yet still wants to deny others the opportunity for a better future.

Harris is a fraud rhino.

A dirty dealer.

Old lady, single parent, children or cherub are of no consideration to the fraud rhino. Dirty dealers take from whomever. When they decide to take, they just take. Many get away until their haul is big enough to blacken the eye of corporate overlords. When they hurt their own though, it gets nasty as there is nothing more visceral when the fraud rhino collides with the corporate rhino.

The work is mundane until the rhino is up close and snorts with rage, causing a cold prickle of fear. The sinister Indian princeling in North London threatened my end of days as his servants quaking around him were testimony to his power. The rage boiled Irishman in South London, executing his threat to end my existence, his anger a clear testimony to the limits of his honesty as he pursued me in his Range Rover. The New Zealander in England's green pastures hiding behind bullet headed security, the tamed gorillas with whom he deigns to bring violence upon my person. The skulking Englishman in West London wishes cancer upon me. His disdain is testimony to his arrogance. With no sense of his own wrongdoing, his actions were the least violent, yet his words were the most harmful. The American was different. With total peace of mind, this Wall Street banker carved a rhino shaped wake through the rippling city crowds. My partner on this case, a former forensic investigator, and I were good at surveillance operations. Like a pair of stealthy panthers, we tracked him across London and back again. Outside of the edge of his peripheral vision he was totally unaware of his surveyors, bathing in his arrogance of anonymity and the confidence of his status.

On the surface none of these men seemed to need the extra money. They all had more wealth and trappings than I could ever hope for. Smart suited business folks with nice clothes, nice houses and nice cars. Upstanding members of the community with excellent credit scores they were also illustrative of the failings in our fragile society. Undermining the institutions within which they worked, if there was no possibility of upward mobility for me, at least I could make a small contribution to their repair and refinement. From good schools and the right kind of family, some of these rhinos were members of the highest ranks of society.

All with status.

All with sticky fingers.

All with a bullseye on their body. One million pounds on average.

That's a lot of cheddar.

Mr. Harris is out West, near Toulouse. With mission in mind, the door closes on my own form of honey pot. My fingers are not sticky, and my sins are miniscule relative to the actions of these men. Sighing at the thoughts of what might have been, a comforting realization dawns. My recent experiences can never be sullied, nor can my dreams be tainted by the tarnish of reality.

Time to move.

A new train ride is in my future. At the Nice railway station, I study timetables and access points around Toulouse. Heading west along the southern coast of France, through Cannes, Antibes and Aix I notice the beauty of this land. Returning thoughts of a wonderful family in northern Italy are distracting. Their dolce vita provides a blueprint for my own better life which gets overlaid with a French influence. Folding that blueprint away, we are all business now and scanning the downloaded correspondence I learn that my rhino has been seen in and around an isolated villa, in a tiny hamlet. Isolated from London he maybe. The landscape here is large, but the villages are small and in the bucolic countryside, tracking the beast will be no great drama. Tagging the rhino offers a good bounty and I squash down any concerns of dangers to be encountered. The financial buffer will afford some good living and new books back in Westminster.

Disembarking in Toulouse, I lock up my gear to travel light.

Money, a small pack and one change of clothes are all that I keep on my person. Riding local transport deep into the rural countryside of Haute Garonne, the bus stops in a small town ten kilometres distance from Mr. Harris' hamlet. There are taxis here, accommodations and several exit opportunities back to Toulouse. Tourists are plentiful and it is easy to masquerade as an out of towner. I speak reasonable French a mainstay of my high school and now university education. The local dialect however has a nasal quality hard to imitate. As far as the locals are concerned, I am from the north, beyond Paris, or even another European country. Whichever version of the truth springs to mind, it is readily spoken to vendor, receptionist or assistant. Touring the town I hire a room, visit a café and learn the surroundings. Doing normal tourist things, it is easy to lose myself here. Then, hiring a bicycle I pedal through country lanes. Harris' hamlet about ten kilometres away is an easy ride. Fields and fields of tournesols (a descriptive name for the helianthus genus that turns with the sun), are so stunningly beautiful I stop and draw breath. Stretching into acres of sunflowers, each more than two metres high, they cloak the surface of the earth right out to the horizon. In my life I have seen single sunflowers in a vase. Here, golden-yellow blooms on a bright blue sky roll away as far as the eye can see. The Midi-Pyrenees awash with a plenitude of colours brings France once again to the top of favourite places to be. Whatever happens now, this terrain will stay in my thoughts forever. Brown, weatherbeaten, lean and alone, I still feel replete and have good cover for the task in hand. Light years from resembling the standard Englishman, for now at least, I am totally anonymous and can be whomever I choose to be. I feel like I am living in a parallel universe and the sensation is liberating. Thoughts of crossing back over the Channel are cast from my mind.

Go slow, be thorough, then eat well and be at peace. Out here, that is my mantra.

The kilometres click by. The rhino is deep in French farmland, sunk deep in his own mud bath, well hidden from the watchful eyes of the locals. An irony of being on the run, so to speak, is the number of unanswered questions it poses. Where do you go? When do you stop? How do you sustain a living? How do you blend into your surroundings? Absent from your natural environment, the more isolated you become, the more you are exposed as a foreign object. No matter the complexity of disguise, you will nevertheless stand out and be obvious. Stopping regularly to orientate my map maintaining my own guise of "cyclo-tourisme" I navigate closer and closer to the known homestead of the rhino. After several weeks in southern Europe, my skin is baked brown, a deep walnut colour, and my hair is sun bleached. My language skills are passable and whilst Swiss French was a struggle, the immersion into these three countries, Switzerland, Italy and France, has fired up old synapses. I speak and understand much more than previously realized, thanks in part to being totally removed from an English-speaking environment. Some locals think I sound Parisien. I allow them that assumption. City folks are as welcome here as they are anywhere. Tolerated at best, rural Parisiens seem to have the same reputation as Londoners exploring their own country. Some folks are more engaging. More curious they ask questions which I use as an opportunity to evolve language skills. Creating a story that I hail from a northeastern suburb, this flimsy deception will hold water long enough for me to complete the mission. If someone guesses I am English, so be it. In small towns and rural locations, everyone knows your business before you do anyway. Whatever the outcome it is best to appear transient.

A tree lined track leads uphill to a small overhang. Propping the bike against a tree, I trek the last few yards into the brush. Reconnaissance saves lives so squatting down in the undergrowth, and virtually invisible, I use this as a comfortable vantage point at the outer edge of the hamlet. A farmhouse below looks like the villa. An orchard runs adjacent to the main road and parallel to a long drive up to the front door. Beyond the single story building land stretches away to a tree lined horizon. The map coordinates tally with the address given so I stake out the residence hoping to catch a glimpse of the rhino. There is no traffic here. The roads are empty. There are no people around. Some farm vehicles roll through fields in the distance. Time ticks on. And doubt sets in.

Is he here? Am I in the right location? How long will I have to wait?

We have no knowledge of Harris' movements or current lifestyle. Sitting quietly, scanning the terrain, I take photos. Time on the clock creeps forward and I hope that the rhino is nearby. It is unlikely he can return to England with a warrant out for his arrest. Nevertheless, he could be anywhere in Europe, and the duration of wait is unclear. This initial recce gives me the lay of the land and knowledge of any approaches. It could be hours or days before the rhino shows himself. I settle down and enjoy the tranquil scene.

Silence reigns.

A natural silence like that discovered in the Alps.

Not the foreboding silence of danger in Dark London, this is the silence of peace and clarity.

This is the silence of happiness.

At ease in the countryside, I lie prone wrapped in bucolic bliss. If the rhino is here, I have some empathy with his temptation. Far from the age-fast stresses of "City Life", there are choices out here. In London, my future is limited.

Get a job.

Get a mortgage.

Get debt to service.

Get sick.

Grow old.

Die.

It is the same formula for many and the only formula for most of those with whom I grew up. Served with several years of excessive violence and the abuses of corrupted officials, this is thin gruel indeed. The institutions I believed in failed me and even in service, the black thumb of corrupted power reached out. The mark is indelible, and I feel its stain on my skin. France changes that though. Here there is choice and liberty. Out here I am me, not the hard man I became. Everything and anything seem available. Food, drink, clothing, language – freedom of expression – art, culture, music and people are all different. The colours are warmer, and the nature is new. Heart, body, mind, and soul all need maintenance and here in France, they are intact and in a recharging state of flow. Even speaking in a different language helps me to be a different person. In French I learn anew how to speak, how to connect, and how to heal.

This is why I empathize with Mr. Harris. Whatever his underlying rationale to commit a grand larceny, it has secured a bubble existence within which he is enjoying the rich cultural heritage and the fresh food of Aquitaine. The rose City of Toulouse is a short ride away, rich with boutique shopping, art, and history. The stadium hosts rugby and football teams. Tucked up here, baguettes de pain, bouteilles de vin and a whole new world are available beneath the slopes of the Pyrenees Mountains.

I wonder about Harris. What kind of rhino is? The act of tagging is quite easy after identification. It really is just a question of serving legal papers. This may not appear dangerous to some, but the lessons of previous experiences have taught me that exits are important. Get in, get out, move on. It is a matter of seconds, maybe a half minute at most, between tagging the rhino and the roar of pain that precedes their next action. Whilst many are meek, collateral damage is possible, and with large sums involved, large behaviours are probable. Graciousness is unlikely. A knot forms in my stomach, and I consider my options. On foot across country is not realistic, nor is the bike. If Harris is violent, I need to get away fast and be untraceable. Back in London, I will have to swear an affidavit to confirm my actions so, I want to keep the business clean or else I run the risk of perjury.

An affidavit is the conclusion of business and means payment for me, it is important to do the job well.

There is movement below. A car stopping at the top of the drive disgorges a woman who calls towards the front door. Her voice carries on the wind, but it is hard to determine the language. Spouse, lover, another? I have no idea. There is no mention of a third party in my notes. The greeting suggests familiarity which gives me hope. That said, out here in the jungle, males can be more prone to violent behaviour, particularly when they have a mate around. The presence of the mate springs hope of discovery, which is diminished slightly as she carries the bags of groceries into the rhino's den.

The rhino remains invisible.

With occupation of the property confirmed it is time to move.

Returning to the bike, I head back to town stopping first in the hamlet. A local man with dark weather-beaten skin and the fat fingers of a farmer stands in the street. I ask him politely about the house over the hill.

"Do you know who lives there?"

My French is Parisian, the language of academia. His French is local, the language of a farmer.

"Ding dong, bing bong, singalong" I have absolutely no idea what he's saying. The melody is beautiful, but his lips barely move. A cigarette hangs from the corner of his mouth bobbing with the rhythm. Comprehension is challenged as I have no idea what he says, nor do I know if he understands me. Words sail through the air competing for space like the songs of two birds in the same tree. Blindly optimistic, I explain there is important news to deliver the Englishman in these parts. Country folk know everyone's business so if the rhino is here, the farmer will know.

He responds.

Straining my ears for anything familiar it is with comedic hopelessness that I try to understand him.

A new cigarette has appeared at the corner of his mouth.

Rural French, like rural Welsh or Gaelic is totally unfathomable. It is impossible to understand so I spit out words devoid of syntax. "M. Harris? Anglais? Ici?" The farmer continues his nasal song accompanied by shrugs and guttural utterances. He is in no hurry. This is the country. Patience is essential.

The cigarette is eternal.

Five minutes later I am ready to pop. This is useless and I have no idea how to get out of the conversation. Staying engaged I make one final effort. "Oui, merci, oui, d'accord" random words fall from my lips like the ash from his smokes. I wait for a chance to insert my simple question : « La maison, là-bas, c'est maison Harris n'est-ce pas ? » The house over there, is it M. Harris' home?

Bracing for more nasal singsong, the farmer pauses. Staring at me anew, he is clearly wondering at my business. I shrug, raise my eyebrows, trying hard to be casually Gallic. The smoke of his cigarette trails into eternity. He shrugs too, looking at me like I am hard of intellect. Blowing like a whale he slowly emits the words I am dying to hear "Ouai, Ouai, monsieur l'Anglais, le rosbif, il est la." Yes, yes mister, the English man, the roast beef, he's there.

The relief is real. The first point of confirmation. Gold dust.

"Merci monsieur!" I simultaneously bow, smile and salute. Casually climbing on the bike, I try not to appear excited. Giving the farmer a simple wave, I hope he forgets our brief encounter. Pedaling away, I wobble down the road in the direction of town, arriving in the mid-morning seeking out the Hotel de Ville. The town hall is open from about nine to eleven, when it breaks for lunch. This is the country; lunch could last forever. I am lucky that the town hall is even open. No doubt business happens elsewhere in the community. Over wine.

Inside, the lady at the counter is buxom, with glossy lips and glasses. Effortless chic in the French way, she is also nonchalant, scans my person and with a soft "Oui Monsieur," offers the services of the house. The town hall is not where tourists hang, nobody drops in unannounced and it is here that my footprint in town will be the deepest. With some effort I stumble through a few phrases of formal French, supported effortlessly with the demeanour of a somewhat flirtatious buffoon. She sparkles as I bring some light entertainment to the day. A mélange of simple bonhomie and curiosity, I am seeking a copy of the deeds of the villa in the hamlet. Representing the interested parties of a private transaction, they want to confirm ownership discreetly. Of course, I have money to pay for any inconveniences. The Hotel de Ville is a repository for all information and, unhurriedly, my buxom lady friend is obliging and tempting. She pulls the plans of the house, a map of the region, and ownership details. For a few billets I purchase copies and store them in my pack. With business done and a second point of confirmation for the identity of Harris, "perhaps Monsieur would like 'partager une verre' – share a glass of wine'" and so, we exchange pleasantries agreeing an appropriate time for dinner. The prospect of enjoying "la vie en rose" is an appealing end to a sordid matter.

Outside the town hall, two silver grey cars under yellow taxi cubes are parked in the square. The drivers look relaxed. I flag the first one. Joe le Taxi, for that is what I name him perks up and scanning the map I thrust under his nose, drives at chill speed towards the hamlet.

This pre-game routine is critical; it is important to be mentally clear of all distractions. Joe le Taxi is in no hurry, he is on local time. At slow speed I draw down data. Roads, traffic, hedgerows, lanes, field enclosures, people. All information is useful knowledge in case of emergency. Who knows what that might look like out here but lived experience reinforces the discipline. Surrounded by farmland with an orchard out front and a high bluff to the east, there is only one entry point to the rhino's lair. At this moment there is one lady, possibly his mate, and an unknown resident who may or may not be the rhino. At the very least, I can get a confirmation of the rhino's whereabouts. The car is local, yet on these traffic free roads we stand out proudly. Joe creeps up the driveway; I tell him to turn the car around and keep the engine running, and to wait for me down the drive. I need him pointing the right way and hope he does not see any bother.

Exiting the car, I walk in the tree line up the sloped drive. Madame's car rests at the top, facing in towards the villa. Good news. The distance from the door to Joe le Taxi is maybe fifty metres. Calming my thoughts, I walk with purposeful nonchalance towards the front door. Madame comes out. I wave, walking calmly to close the remaining twenty metres.

"Coo – coo 'allo!" I speak to her in French, and wave at her smiling. Arms open, body language positive I hate this part. Knowing from experience that people most hurt by the actions of the rhino are often those closest to them. Spouses and partners are part of the collateral damage in the shit storm of this service. Whilst I have no love for the greed and hypocrisies of the chattering classes, it genuinely hurts my heart when the reality of the situation collides with the truth of the unsuspecting.

"Livraison, madame. Livraison!"

Delivery madame. Speaking French, feigning Gallic, I behave in appropriate fashion.

"Livraison, madame. 'Arris. Monsieur 'Arris – ouai ouai ?!? Il est là n'est-ce pas ? »

Mr. Harris is here? Yes, yes? Eyebrows raised she looks perplexed, she is a classic "pearl-clutcher," hand flat on her neck and arm across her chest, hers is a very English action.

"Oh, I don't know. What is it? Oh, I really don't know. I'm so sorry. Can you come back?"

Rummaging in my bag I pull out papers and offer them to her.

"Livraison madame. Today. Monsieur 'Arris? Oui ? Livraison, livraison. » Like my own conversation with the village farmer, she strains at the edge of comprehension. Hearing simple words, some lights come on. I test the waters some more, straining credibility with an Anglo – French word blend.

"Livrasion madame. Er, delivery en anglais, Meester 'Arris? Oui? Yes?

"Oh. Mr. Harris! My husband. Just a moment please. Ralph, Ralph" she calls turning into the doorway. The madame seems nice. The knot in my stomach tightens at the prospect of her next reaction and that of the fraud rhino. Harris is clearly home – point of confirmation number three has been delivered and now it is a question of execution and exit.

Like all good performances, the execution is merely a display of excellence. The highs and lows of theatre, a sports match, or a symphony are really the smallest percentage of output. The show is merely the final product of initiation and planning, followed by a close and a review. This is no different. Here I am mid performance, the adrenaline of expectation mingling with the anticipation of emotion. How will the audience respond to the score?

Looking down the driveway, Joe le Taxi is there, a puff of smoke from the window signals a cigarette break. The fare is good, he's happy to wait. The gravel crunches behind me. Turning slowly the rhino appears in enormous glory. He fills the doorway. Harris is a big specimen. Not like the OG, who was a bear of a man, nor like some of the Afrikaners I played rugby with. He has the largesse of wealth, and large chest and stomach hidden beneath a layer of designer clothes, like many of London's stockbroker community. Wearing the uniform of that community today, the rhino dons a checked shirt with jeans and boots. The very image of English country gentlemen the only missing articles are a Land Rover, a Barbour jacket, and a shotgun for the clay shoot. Luxurious hair, hawkish face and a ruddy complexion envelop his demeanour. Poised, he is arrogant.

"Can I help you?" He snorts through his nose in my direction.

"Oui m'sieur, oui, oui. Merci. Livraison pour le m'sieur 'Arris. » Deliberately returning to French, I hope to create confusion. The arrogant are notoriously impatient. He wrinkles his brow. The rhino has not yet learned French. Loud English spoken slowly is no doubt his modus operandi. « Ah. M. 'Arris. C'est Rof or Raph 'Arris je pense ?" I ask, in the most deplorable faux French. An impersonation that sounds God awful, even to my own ears.

Tutting the tsk of an important man he snorts.

"Yes, yes, what is it? Come along now. That's me, I'm Harris."

Bingo! A fourth point of confirmation straight from the rhino's mouth. Not necessary but it's always good to hit the bonus jackpot.

"Eh bien ! Mon ami. Je suis content maintenant." I begin then return to English. "Well, here's some legal papers for you including a court date in London."

Tagging is simple. When you have done your pre-work that is.

I hand over a sheaf of legal documents, no signature necessary, the threat of perjury irons out that wrinkle. Finding and serving this guy in France though, is a grey area especially with no support nor safety net. Still, four points of confirmation on a fraud rhino in the wild means a good payday and the job is done. Time to exit before the milk turns sour.

Tagging is simple, execution is excellent, a planned exit is essential.

Steely hardness is not a natural state of being, but a characteristic I have developed to survive. Physical fitness is my armour but in secret I prefer gentler past times. Kindness though is mistaken for weakness, so protection becomes the essence of self-preservation.

Here in front of the rhino I am a hard man and will protect myself if necessary. I trigger my exit.

"Merci M'sieur. Allez les bleus ! On y va !" Returning to French, I spew out random phrases, seeding more confusion, about turn and head down the drive. Casually. Harris has heard a bit of cohesive English sandwiched between some French jibber jabber. Enough to stall him for a few moments, roughly the lifespan of a fruit fly.

The silence is pregnant as the rage builds.

Flashbacks of previously enraged fraud rhinos encourage me to pick up speed.

Joe le Taxi is in range.

The anger of the rhino is imminent.

Beware the indignation of the righteous.

Like a screaming kettle, the roar manifests; it is different in each rhino but generally involves some form of snorting, a wail, insults or threats and incoherent shouting. In the worst cases physical violence is a possibility. Wondering at his disposition I glance back over my shoulder. Harris is reaching inside the door jamb. Time slows. Madame is pearl clutching. The rhino is turning with a long iron in his grasp. Unexpected. Golf club or shotgun, the preferred armaments of the middle-class white rhino, is to be determined.

Exits are essential.

This one is about to get complex.

Coasting downhill, Joe le Taxi is enjoying another smoke break. Out of the car. At ease with the world.

"Allez Joe! Allez, allez!" I call out to him. Time to earn your fare my friend.

The rhino is snorting behind me, and an ominous click suggests that the long iron is not a golf club. The ultimate accessory for the Barbour wearing country gent has two barrels and a polished wooden stock. Harris like his kinsmen in the Surrey and Hampshire sets is a member of a tooled-up class. Gangs in Range Rovers and Jaguars who roam the countryside terrifying birds of feather and clay, drinking fizz, or a blood red claret. Fun times back then, until he became a robber of the robber barons.

The ominous click is Harris breaking the gun. Rummaging for shells in his pockets he will be shoveling those down the twelve gauge barrels. It dawns on me in the moment that his next actions will be justified by his rage. What are the laws on trespassing here? Will I bleed out on the rhino's turf, whilst he explains my presence as an intruder and a threat to safety? Even with Joe present, the rhino is a man of deception. He can make up a story to benefit the local constabulary.

This is stressful.

"Allez Joe, allez allez...." Come on Joe, let's go. Start the car.

Joe, of course, has no earthly understanding of my predicament.

For a start, his name is not even Joe. What is his name? I have no idea. He sees me hustling down the drive, obscuring his view of the rhino who is no doubt on fire right now. Loading does not take long, even for the fattest most irritated gent. I need to get out of range before he is ready to pull. Joe, at the climax of cigarette appreciation has reached the apex of Gallic calm. Or maybe a nadir. I am not entirely sure.

Apex feels like an achievement, and nadir seems to be more of a failing. That degree of calm in the current circumstances is surely something to aspire to. A gunshot breaches the sky and snaps me back to reality. Harris has misfired in his rage. He is snorting and even more mad as he misses his target.

Shooting the messenger, like avoiding accountability, are standard practice for management types. Looking back Madame is still pearl clutching. The rhino, manhandling twin barrels, digs for shells in his Barbour pockets. A back full of buckshot is in my future. Or maybe birdshot. Briefly I consider shot pattern, distribution, range and weighting. Ugh! Useless! Safety is the car.

"Allez Joe, wake up man! Come on! Start the bloody car." Joe raised an eyebrow at the first gunshot, trance broken, his smoke break is over. Cold sweat runs down my back while he casually opens the back door, falls into his driver's seat, patting his pockets for keys.

Tunnel vision slows everything. Moving at glacial speed, my single point of focus is the open back door.

. . . Ralph is silent. Madame is hushed. The weight of anticipation is heavy.

. . . the gun is lifting as the car engine turns over.

. . . the engine fires, will the gun?

. . . the open door is at my fingertips.

. . . the shotgun is level now with Harris looking down both barrels.

The heat of the sun contrasts with the cold of the sweat. Like the solar eclipse in the mountains, birdsong ceases, crickets stop clicking and ambient noise is reduced to silence. I pray for a bad shot and a smooth exit.

. . . final breath, brace for impact or dive for the back seat. Option A or option B.

We are all business now as life is reduced to two choices; seconds are reduced to milliseconds and existence hangs in the balance. Joe guns the engine.

The rhino snorts again as his finger curls around the trigger. This is no time to di...

SITTING IN THE ROSE CITY, sipping a cold rose, I count my blessings. Slowly chewing the magret de canard on my plate, I glance at French rugby jerseys hanging on the walls. Rugby is on T.V. This is my France. A place of passion and purpose, liberty and choice. Maybe one day a land of living and love. We shall see.

Rueing an abandoned dinner date with the Gallic chick, I reflect briefly on the fraud rhino. These beasts roam freely in the wild yet with a veneer of civility they are disguised by people around them. Sniffing the air around me, like an old bear, memories of Toulouse are the final chapter in an epic adventure. From Geneva, across the Alps and through Italy I am still stuck on Maslow's bottom rung. Bound for London, a train will return me to Paris, the City of Lights, where I will climb the Eiffel Tower.

For now, though, la vie est belle. Life is beautiful.

Trans-Siberian

YEAR OF THE DRAGON

Dragons are the mightiest animals and Dragon people prefer to be leaders of groups. Not afraid of challenges, they make every effort to achieve their goals. Active and brave, they are also aggressive, domineering, with a high demand for work. They always like to be boss and want to control everything. Dragon people it is said, are fond of the limelight.

DARK LONDON

ARE WE GOING TO DIE? Possibly. If I make the wrong choice, then possibility becomes probability.

We're talking degrees and millimetres here, not feet and inches. A bit too much oversteer or a tap on the brakes is enough to end this adventure.

What are my choices?

It is after midnight, the early autumn night obscures my vision which is slowly recovering from the headlight glare of the night bus we just passed. The Porsche is moving fast, about Mach three and is fishtailing in the pointed curve of the diamond shaped roundabout we just entered.

I am driving.

Try to stop, and hit the brakes then I lose a bet, a large cash bonus and maybe control of the car. Alternatively, I can trust the engineering and let the "Vorsprung durch Technik" prove its worth. I am not good at trust; I do not like vulnerability. This makes the choice harder. But this is a different car. I've made similar decisions in the Audi A3 and Audi TT. They did not have the speed and responsive acceleration of the Porsche. Both are German though, so I rationalize that the latter must surely be an upgrade of engineering excellence. Pumped full of adrenaline, with less than a few seconds to execute, a leap of faith is imminent, along with a leap to ludicrous speed.

Tapping the brakes feels safe, there are no safety nets though and that triggered the fishtail.

"Ludicrous speed" says the devil on my shoulder, tempting me to smash the gas and see what happens.

"Trust the Germans." Says the angel, on the other shoulder, a counsel of caution and wisdom. There is no downside. Use the technology and make the horsepower work for you.

There is no room for hubris here. I have faced death before. And the threat of death. This is just a new installment. All movements are critical and sweat beads on my forehead as the drag of the spoiler towards the extreme end of a parabola fights the draw down of gravity and the power train of the engine.

I only know two Germans. One, a Porsche fanatic from the West. The other, a survivor of the Stasi regime from the East. East Germans made the Trabant, a compressed cardboard car with sewing machine engineering. West Germans made the Porsche.

No *"racing cardboard"* in this motor.

With my left foot buried in the footwell, far away from the brake pedal and Pavlovian reactions, I hold tight to the steering wheel and feather the gas pedal; execution is all about excellence and split-second decision making.

Putting my trust in technology, we'll soon find out the true extent of Porsche performance engineering.

THE OLD POLICEMAN LEANS IN. He's smaller than me. Physically only. Not intellectually. He holds a pint in each hand, one for him and one for me. Placing them gently on the table he has a subtlety rarely seen in officers of the law. At a pub in Greenwich Market, a stone's throw from the National Maritime Museum we are spitting distance from the Cutty Sark. The three masted tea clipper is one of the last and fastest ships of its time; serving the trade routes between China and Britain, tea was the cargo then. Today in dry dock, the cargo is a seafaring history of Empire for the parents and children clambering among the ropes, the capstan and the stories of yesterday.

The OP is kind, worldly and keeps bees as a hobby. Retired from policing, the revenue made from honey tops up a pension made by Government. With few distinguishing features and slight of build, OP really is the grey man. A slight curvature in his teeth hints to wear and tear from pipe smoking. Calm bespectacled eyes resonate with the strength of knowledge.

OP, like all good grey men, has appeared from nowhere. Out of the past he has arrived at our doorstep at the height of our troubles. Sent by Fate, I like to believe; the truth of this is yet to be discovered. Like the OG, he is authentic. This old man of law is a new man of letters, PhD to be precise.

A Doctor of History.

He is a survivor and another old bear who can smell trouble in the air. Keeping bees means he can make his own honey and stay out of trouble.

Former Police Inspector and Royal Navy mine clearance diver, the OP sips his pint. A mentor, like the OG, he's the newest addition to my fragile support network which comprises two people. I like his stories, they bring calm to my turmoil, and the benefit of lived experience to my questions. He knows the region and how the world works.

> "You'll be alright Angus. You can live well outside of the house, with proven courage, you're trusted to be truthful. Stay square and you'll come through."

This has a familiar ring. He fears nobody, except maybe the

Russians. There is nowhere else for me to get help. Unsupported, navigating a new world where traditions cave in and help comes from surprising quarters, I choose to believe him.

Authentic he speaks truth to reality.

A rare commodity.

> "You know, we used to run cover during the Troubles, see? They were tough times. Freedom comes at a price. Release them early they would, out onto the steps of the prison, see? We'd have them bagged and tagged on the way to the mainland minutes before their boyos showed up."

The OP sips his beer before moving on.

> "Tough times the Troubles. Freedom for those boys lasted fifteen minutes, before they were held again at Her Majesty's leisure. Politics is a nasty business."

He shares stories of a southeast London full of characters, gangsters and survivors like himself. History books don't discuss the crimes he speaks of. Nobody addresses crimes that involve high profile figures, least of all those where the executives of companies have been relieved of millions by the tattooed and the street smart of the region.

The OP shares information that overlaps with that of the OG. They do not know each other. Common knowledge is the glue that binds them. Separately and independently, they verify the authenticity of the other. This is comforting, not least of all because it gives me hope that there are genuine people out there.

> "The problem is," he continues, "loyalty and knowledge come at a price. Eventually you know too much and before you know it, the people on your team are no longer on your team. In my case, they sent me to East Germany, before the Wall came down, to bring back a defector. Easy task really, except he was already dead. They knew he was dead, the other side had shot him a week before, so I was bagged

> and tagged into a Stasi cell. I was collateral damage really. Expendable."

I believe him. The OP has always been kind to me. Unsure of his progeny, he has shown me a photo of police college. One badge number from my own father, they joined up together and were friends for some time. In a jungle riddled with traps, some set by gorillas, others by hyenas, the path of life is unclear now. Like all jungles, there is need for a guide, and I believe that Fate has conjured up the OP to help clear the way.

He knows too much to be fake. Too many cross-referenced details connect, join the same dots and lead down the same roads that the OG or my father have walked. I keep silent in these moments, not daring to speak, unsure how to process the picture.

> "I sat in that cell for a week. Waiting for my own execution after a beating by the Germans. No time to say goodbye or close accounts back home. Just knowing that on a cold morning here they'll take me out and put a bullet in me. Waiting for the Russians to show up and close my account. Disappointing you know, when you think you're working for the good guys. When the Russian walked in, he was KGB. Big fella, gangster type, looked like a bare-knuckle boxer. He wanted to know if I played chess. We played for a few days. Like playing with death it was, every move an extension of life as the Jackals outside waited their turn to put a bullet in me. None would though, not until the KGB man was finished. Not until the Russians had their say."

The OP shows me respect, mainly because I fight my own battles. He's seen the struggle and knows the effort it takes to get out, get educated and get away. Unique research on the French Revolution and the American War of Independence have influenced his success. Studying in Paris he uncovered first edition handwritten letters from Jefferson to Franklin, gathering dust in library archives, they had been left untranslated. He speaks French fluently, thanks to a library assistant who helped his research. He also speaks German.

"We played chess every day and before long, I noticed KGB would tap his finger on the Queen at regular intervals in our conversation. Each tap corresponding with a word in our chat, we coded a conversation uninterpreted by Stasi eyes and ears. 'Say nothing' he says 'No reasons, no requests, no responses. Just nothing and we will send you back at the end of the week. Your man is dead. We know that. London knows that. Berlin knows it too. We don't want them to know that we know what you now know."

The Russian mind is complicated.

"We can bury the issue in the grey area of Stasi incompetence.' We played chess every day and at the end of the week they released me. The Germans gave me a hell of a beating. You can imagine the faces in London when I turned up for work on Monday."

OP delivers. He's more empathetic than the OG, but his lessons are no less impactful. I notice when his umbrella opens for protection and know when I must weather the storm alone. He shows up when guidance is needed, and over a beer or two at a predetermined pub near the maritime museum helps me find the right path on the map that will take me out of danger.

He understands that politics is a messy business. London, Belfast, Dublin, Berlin and Moscow are all unusual stops on his beat. Lived experience has taught him when to speak and when to listen. When to see without looking and when to walk away without engaging.

He also knows how to manage the police. Particularly the gorillas, the bad guys of the force.

Politics is business and all business is quid pro quo.

Not just the exchange of money for goods and services, but also the exchange of life for death.

This is life in the jungle. Berlin, Moscow, Dublin, or London, it does not matter, for here in Greenwich he explains the rules of the jungle and the extent of the quid pro quo.

Thanks to the OP, the rules of the game become clearer.

. . .

London is complex and the law of the jungle is sometimes confused with the lore of the jungle.

There are many houses here and sometimes it is difficult to distinguish man from the animals.

HELSINKI

Finland is a place of peace. I love it here. Summertime in Helsinki is great. The days are long, and sunset is no more than a dip beneath the horizon around midnight. Coming out of the sauna at night, cooling in the air with a cold drink, the magnificent midnight sun is still visible at the edge of the sky. For half of the year, the sun is dominant, days are long and the sky is bright. For the other half of the year, the moon reigns supreme and the snowy lands lie beneath a blanket of silvery light.

This is a rare visit, and we enjoy precious time together.

A Finnish stoic and economic migrant, mum suffered at the hands of British law. Losing custody of her children in a visceral divorce battle, in a world where mothers are almost automatically given duty of care, mum endured a depth of pain I can never understand. I can only imagine the mud that was slung and the loneliness she must have felt as a foreigner in her adopted nation.

We have this in common, yet I struggle to articulate my world. She needs no further pain and I am ashamed to speak out loud what I have to do to survive.

The only crime she committed was being incompatible with my father. And for this she has served her own personal life sentence.

Ever dignified, mum maintains connectivity from a distance, remembering birthdays and special occasions, recalling special interests and administering care in small thoughtfully processed packages. This is a kind of Finnish fortitude, a trait of Sisu I believe and a foundation of this centuries old resilience.

I understand pain more than I understand joy. Physical, emotional, and mental. These are all by-products of growing up in London. For many, not for everybody. Bored with Fate and the unanswered questions over seemingly endless bouts of suffering, I am mining my own reserves and discovering the benefits of Finnish genes. Through nature I explore the wealth of spirituality and the riches of people.

Externally, the signs are there. I love fast driving, long distance running, and natural light. Walking out of a blizzard in the French Alps in defiance of the snow and its creeping cold were part of my initial discovery of Sisu. Like an emerging butterfly I adopt the spirituality of Finland and am content, shedding the superficiality of England. Time spent with mum is precious, uncommon and in typical Finnish fashion quiet.

Small talk is for others.

For the Finns, why use a sentence when a few words will suffice.

In Seurasaari wild birds eat peanuts from my hand as red squirrels climb my legs to share the same fare. Sitting quietly, even butterflies land on my body, rest a while then move to their next destination. Lightweight creatures, they bring no burden. They are fascinating, colourful and bring joy as the hover, find a place to land then fold their wings together like hands in prayer. In the stillness, the minuscule movements of butterfly antennae and wings are visible as they catch a break on the gentle breeze.

These are magical moments, almost like a Disney cartoon, and not something I have experienced in Britain. The Finns embrace nature. "Every person's right" is a law that means all citizens have privileged access to the wilderness across the country. People can pick berries, hike trails, and enjoy the lakes and rivers without fear of trespass. This is different to Britain where property developers seem to reign supreme.

On the ground, in Seurasaari, tall ancient pines are mottled with the beams of a summer sunshine and this island lake, just fifteen minutes' drive from Helsinki Central Station could be at the ends of the earth.

Sandwiched between complex neighbours, the Swedish out West and the Russians in the East, Finland is a young country.

In November 1917, Finland declared secession from the Russian State and by December of that same year was fully independent under the right of self-determination. Just over twenty years later, the Soviet Union under Stalin invaded their Nordic neighbour with battalions of soldiers and armoured divisions. Lightly armed Finnish soldiers showed Stalin the cost of occupation and the value of independence during the Winter War of 1939 – 1940. Stalin cited security as the reason for territorial expansion to counter Nazi Germany and make Leningrad more secure. The big Soviet leader declared little Finland their biggest threat kicking off his invasion under a false flag operation by shelling a border post at Mainila.

Russian interference in Finnish independence triggered a civil war, the Winter War and then the Continuation War, after which Russia was instrumental in the cause of the Lapland War.

Finland lacked logistics support, communications equipment, and heavy armaments. Significantly outnumbered with an army of only one hundred thousand men they were, however, excellent winter fighters. Particularly in the densely wooded forests of the South. The red army made attacks all along the Karelian isthmus border up to Suomussalmi where they tried to cut the country in half. Finnish ski troops, in the face of armour, artillery and full air supremacy, killed more than three hundred thousand Russian military men. Simo Hayha alone, nick-named "The White Death" was credited with five hundred kills. Like ghosts in the night, the Finns would fight a guerilla campaign in their own country. From the Arctic, through the midlands and down into the southern regions, they fought by day and by night, in temperatures as low as minus 40 degrees Celsius. Counter attacking with a courage that attracted foreign volunteers from other countries including Sweden and Britain, the Finnish Army prevailed. The Red Army increased their force to twenty-five divisions, some six hundred thousand men to smash through the Mannerheim line but the cost in resources forced a peace treaty to be signed. The Finns felt they had to fight or disappear as a nation, losing twenty-five thousand killed. For the Russians, exercising a land grab, the cost was higher. More than one hundred and fifty thousand dead or missing and over two hundred thousand sick and wounded, not including the loss of armaments, was the final bill. Creating the image of Russia as a paper tiger, the Winter

War partly inspired Hitler's eastward invasion and advance to the gates of Stalingrad.

Today in Toolo, a suburb of Helsinki, the enjoyment of Finnish culture over Russian intimidation has created a beautiful city. The Sibelius monument here reverberates with the four winds from the ocean air. A unique structure of welded steel organ pipes, the landmark embodies the spirit of his music; less known than his Germanic counterparts, Sibelius' work is nevertheless emotional and an expression of Finnish spirit. A large bust of Sibelius himself is a suitably bombastic addenda to the monument, with a fiery quote illuminating his purpose:

> "Pay no attention to what critics say. A statue was never erected in honour of a critic."

This resonates for me as Dark London continues to fade in the rear-view mirror, and a lighter greyer version emerges. Helsinki in Summer is the heart of happiness in a country of peace. In London, I work at night avoiding the daytime crush of people and the churning crowds of human hamsters running in place on their wheel of life. The nighttime of London brings solitude, and alternative opportunities for exploration of the city with a thousand-year history. Over here in Helsinki there is no crush. Opportunities for exploration are under a bright sunshine dappled green by the trees on sparkling blue waters. Finland is a little slice of heaven at the edge of the sky.

Despite my love of this country, I will be leaving Finland soon.

From here we are heading east to the port City of Qingdao. Situated in Northeast China we will cross a Russia under the iron rule of Vladimir Putin. The "we" is Steff and me. He is my constant companion. From East Germany, he grew up under the weight of Stasi control, and the heel of Soviet power in the German Democratic Republic. As West Germany blossomed into an industrial powerhouse and West Berlin grew into a desirable city for business and the arts, East Germany stagnated. The Stasi, an organ of this Police State, was an extension of their Soviet Russian overlords. Surveillance and suspicion their trademark. Stifling economic growth, incarcerating enemies of the State and gunning down citizens who tried to reach the West are their legacy. Steff, however, is a reedy intellect, with very few possessions. In London for further education, he appears to enjoy Western decadence through extreme candy consumption. His pockets, crammed with jellybeans and wine gums, are a myriad of colours often reflected in his skin. There is nothing athletic in his form, and he apparently lives without nutrients for no vegetables or fruits ever seem to enter his mouth. Steff scratches a lot. Allergies, eczema or micro-doses of sugar are the usual subjects, I guess, as he abrades his skin.

My own flesh itches in sympathy when we are close; In the hope of breaking his sugar-based regime, I want to force feed Steff some peas and carrots, roast him some potatoes or poach him an egg. Anything to stop the itchy twitch that I feel when he scratches.

Yet, he appears to be semi - permanently happy.

Cautiously I have accepted his offer of companionship on the Trans-Siberian railway. This journey could be wild, and I am unsure of his attributes, nor am I aware of any lasting scars from life under authoritarian State where he grew up. That said, Steff is friendly, kind, intelligent and speaks Russian. Fundamentally, he is a good person and completely harmless.

Mum has brokered tickets for the Mongolian train through a Finnish agent. She makes no judgements. Finnish businessmen cross into Russia all the time and return unscathed. That said, the wilds are vast, unknown to many and spread northeast through Siberia out to the northwestern edge of the Pacific Ocean. As ever, I carry some sense of guilt borne of breaking away from traditional norms and broken social constructs

Mum has many friends, mothers of sons, who like many Finnish women combine stoicism with gregariousness and jocularity. With little constraint they question my sanity.

"Why are you going to Russia?"

"What on earth are you doing?"

"How could you be doing this?"

"Think of your poor mother?"

"Are you mad?"

"Oh, my good god!" Etc. etc. etc.

The struggle with my conscience is real. I am not sure if they are serious or joking. After the Alpine blizzard adventure, which I have kept quiet until now, I know that my own sense of adventure presents a skewed logic when viewed through the lens of "normal people".

In the face of Finnish maternalism, the devil and the angel on my shoulders are uncommonly taciturn. I am on my own with this onslaught.

Mum's group of friends are adjacent to the generation scarred by recent Russian aggressions. Their questions are sound. Nevertheless, the opportunity for adventure is too much to resist. The prospect of a flight to Beijing and thence to Shandong, booked in London at more than twice the price of this locomotive dragon, is mundane. Finland, Russia, China by train sounds much more romantic and what better way to enter the Middle Kingdom than in the carriage of a noble monster.

In truth, what lies beyond the border is a mystery.

This gives some cause for concern.

Stories of Communism with the chatter and patter of Finnish matriarchs renders me unnerved. Steff's physical presence is evidence supporting their concerns. Their memories are linked to conflict and atrocity. But the new man in charge, in Russia, Mr. Putin, is apparently an internationalist first, a Communist second. I squash uncomfortable sensations and stay on plan, after all what's the worst that can happen?

It is just a summer train ride.

The timetable is fixed, visas are secured, and the journey will be completed in a week. Communism is a failed ideology, and Russia has opened its arms to the West. Putin is a reformer apparently and shrugging off the naysayer sentiments, we prepare for departure.

I will miss Finland though for it is a beautiful country, a spiritual home and a place of peace.

As the magnificence sun blazes, we head for Helsinki main railway station.

DARK LONDON

There are no safety nets.

On Maslow's bottom rung we are scurrying to satisfy base needs. The physiological level in this hierarchy means air, food, water, shelter and sleep are my main points of focus. Like a dog chasing its tail, I am not sure how to break the cycle nor ascend to the next level. I have merely a toehold on the next level, which is sustained health and personal security. Peak fitness sees me physically in good shape and this remains my armour as emotional and financial security are not even on the horizon.

Trapped in this world, – I get to muse upon the frailty of broken institutions, too often, I catch myself wandering down this rabbit hole of dysfunction and sometimes corruption. Mine was an absolute belief that these institutions were pure. A belief drummed into me from the youngest age. Respect the police, your teachers, the doctors. These are the pillars of community in whom we must invest. The police I learned to fear. With teachers I was often in trouble. As for doctors, we should heed their wisdom and medicines without question, even though they peddle as many drugs as the street level dealers.

That world is gone and shattered beyond repair.

At least, for the time being.

In this new world, I make my own adventures and live or die by my own endeavours. At times on the edge of an abyss, I flip a coin on jumping forward or stepping back. This is a form of education after all and can be no more or less painful than the past. Thanks to the corruption and brutality though, new relationships are treated with caution, friendships are hard to cement, intimacy and love are kept at arm's length. The third rung on Maslow's hierarchy is a stretch goal at best.

Whimsical hopes subject to a capricious Fate mean that a world of love and belonging can never be reality.

Tonight, like many people in my stratosphere, I serve the rich.

A Porsche 911 Turbo will be my charger. The sleek and silvery steed squatting in the midnight of Knightsbridge, a stone's throw from London's Hyde Park Barracks, home of the mounted Cavalry

Regiment. Waiting in the shadows, observing the car, I tune into my surroundings. This is not bounty hunting, but some of the behaviours are similar and stalking wealthy neighbourhoods at night requires some degree of caution.

In these hours after dark a private club nearby plays host to the wealthy of Chelsea mixing with officers of the Household Cavalry. Modern troopers with a private income to maintain their uniforms and their horses rub shoulders with modern men of leisure. The Household Cavalry are prestigious warriors and the first protectorate of the British Royal Family. Present at every major conflict since 1660, their list of honours is lengthy. Few soldiers, or civilians for that matter, can afford to live in this money magnet corner of London. Yet, in the early morning dawn the regiment can be seen exercising their horses through three hundred and fifty acres of tree lined Hyde Park. Between Kensington Palace and Marble Arch the drumming hooves of stallions creates a stir amongst the chattering classes that echoes back through time and the reign of Kings. After dark though, classy officers and citizens engage like fashionable peacocks in a human dance of modern chivalry. Men named Charles, George, and Edward, like so many monarchs before them, wander the bistros and boutique lounges, enjoying the best of everything from London's top shelf.

The chill darkness betrays no movement. The streets and culdesacs are clean. Boutique stores a few blocks away are un-shuttered. All the street lamps are lit, none flicker, none blink, and dark corners are just that. With no hidden surprises, I relax a little. On the safe streets of Kensington and Chelsea, the confluence of city money and nouveau riche wealth wash up against Arab royalty, Russian oligarchy, and English aristocracy. They all have homes nearby, doubling as tax deductible, registered corporate assets. A rarefied air circulates here. The Georgian red brick headquarters of Tate and Lyle, sugar barons since the nineteenth century, stands to attention across the square. All around are status homes. Not the kind of home you live in, rather the kind you host in. Updated every season. This is where parties happen and the level of your lucre is expressed via the medium of designer furniture, refrigerators full of bubbles, and new kitchens every year. Kitchens here are fashion statements. Not the kind of kitchen you cook in either; rather the kind preferred by in vogue celebrity chefs – Ramsay, Oliver, Lawson, Pierre-White – money cannot buy knowledge, but it can bring stars to your house and a Michelin to your kitchen.

The only commonality that binds these people to those in the boroughs is cocaine. Chelsea cut coke lines more notes than treasury ink. It is rumoured that one ton of coca residue is peed into the river Thames every day.

No wonder the banks and businesses charge us so many fees.

Not only are we paying taxes and tariffs, but we're also paying the rehab fees and the dealers of the rich and famous.

The Porsche is safe and glistens, waiting impatiently to be driven, not relishing the stillness. Public police rarely cruise through here. There is no need. Private security is abundant and so tightly wound they could eat coal and shit diamonds. In fact, I am probably on camera in multiple homesteads right now. In my dark uniform stood still in the shadows I can imagine the furrow in the frown of the fellas on night duty.

Assuming they are awake.

A tall man walks towards the car. Garbed in the clothes of the wealthy he strides with confidence and poise.

My client.

I drive.

He pays.

This is a contract hire business for the rich and famous; it's a clever business.

They go out and get greasy in clothes and cars whose price tags have more zeroes than a Broker's bonus. Once they've had their fun, vetted drivers like me are on site to take them home. They might be drunk as a skunk in its bunk, but we tuck them up safely leaving the car in the drive and the keys in the mailbox. The owner of the business makes a lot of money. The owners of the vehicles are safe in the knowledge that no matter how wild they party, they arrive chez eux with assets intact and no police interference.

The drivers are a good bunch.

Former military, respectable and discreet, we are what many people call “characters”, arguably a group of “ne’er do wells”, we nevertheless are honest and get the job done. “Bandy” is one. A moonlighting soldier musician from one of the Household Regiment. He practices tunes on his trumpet, rehearsing for the upcoming funeral of a senior Royal. We all know who is dying, the world at large does not. We are sworn to secrecy. The tabloid press is yet to be informed of the soon to be deceased.

The Saffas here, or South Africans, are wild men from the Cape. Former conscripts of the South African Defence Force, they have experienced two twilight zones: the Angolan border war or the shanty towns of the African Cape. Patrolling without protection in the late apartheid era, they have completed national service in violent townships carrying arms without bullets. Either that or they were the remnants of combatants who fought an asymmetric campaign against a Russian funded “Peoples Liberation Army” in the thrall of Communist sponsorship.

For the young men patrolling the shanty towns, Politicians decided their role no long needed live ammunition. Which made the streets of Dark London a much safer place to live for them.

These young men riding open sided Land Rovers through the rugged roads and broken boroughs, mostly unprotected, were perpetual targets for sling shot ball bearings and random petrol bombs. Their lived experiences render my own challengers insignificant. Work in London pays pounds sterling multiplying their buying power to purchase farmsteads back home in rand. For them a short stint in the “Big Smoke” buys an estate without mortgage in the motherland. Sometimes they disappear, engaged in special projects we don’t ask about, and, in one case, medical experiments to accelerate their earnings. I like South Africans. They’re good people, grounded in life with a sense of humour. Everything is “lekker” when they’re around. The solitary Namibian is similar. He tells tales of German and American trophy hunters, paying thousands to hunt in the wilds beyond Windhoek. Men of wealth purchasing hero holidays with local guides who help them find the right targets and clear up the mess when they miss.

Like my other vocation, this job pays well, tips well, and helps cover the costs of a university education in the combined districts of Westminster and Marylebone. It also provides dopamine without danger.

Mostly.

Tonight's client is a lawyer. The kind of guy who, on the one hand, represents the fraud rhinos for a good percentage of their ill-gotten gains. On the other hand, he protects the institutions and organizations that stockpile money and accrue wealth without compassion.

The cut of his suit suggests Savile Row tailor. The cut of his poise suggests Oxbridge or public school educated. Clean and pristine I guess he is possibly "old money". From my notes I know we are heading southwest to a townhouse residence in Putney, adjacent to the River Thames. A prime location for the annual Oxford Cambridge boat race. An easy run home this one. City and West End lawyers have offices close by, so he has clearly enjoyed a night out straight from work. A short hop for a bit of posh, Knightsbridge is not just a money magnet, it is also a fanny magnet. The cocktail mix of money, influence, and power here attracts the beautiful to the rich and vice versa.

Empty handed though, our lawyer friend has had no luck tonight. Perhaps he lost out to a Cavalry officer or maybe even a minor Royal. The "midnight plus change" pick up time is suggestive and corroborates my thinking. If business was good, the Bolly would be flowing, and this would be a two-a.m. collection.

Stepping out of the shadows I give him a friendly wave. A peace of mind salutation. Appearing from the darkness, he flinches at my bulk but recovers quickly. People often flinch when I walk in, make swift judgements, lazy assumptions, and pointed comments. It bothers me. I have lived this experience for the longest time. At this moment in time, I have sailed two oceans, one sea and a couple of gulfs, crossed the Alps on foot, and learned three languages. These are my achievements and make me the hero in my own journey. I respect people who achieve anything outside of their comfort zone and try to ignore the critics: those people to whom life has given plenty and from whom Fate has taken little.

Low born I work for any gain and fuel my purpose with dreams of a better tomorrow. Naively I believe hard work gets you ahead in life. As the judgements of others are boring I discard many opinions and am yet to learn the power of relationships.

Growth comes with forward momentum.

If you are not moving, you're dying.

Being big brings "front loaded" opinions, often from "Karens" who look down their noses and confuse discomfort with danger.

Generally, being big means you are slow, stupid, aggressive, clumsy, fat, lazy, frightening, and intimidating. Sometimes all the above. I may be some of these things, but not by choice. It also means you are a target for two subsets of society. One that is viscerally motivated, using violent means to show off to their buddies, mischievous monkeys looking for a fight, often "mob handed" wanting to bring down the big guy.

The other subset is politically motivated, with a gender war or status clash always bubbling beneath the surface, their own anxieties justify their rationale for targeting men of my persuasion. Frightened people can be cruel and hide their cruelty behind righteousness.

Beware the indignation of the righteous, for they are the most savage of judges.

The combat of rugby provides a haven from this jungle through which I tread carefully. Nevertheless, it is impossible to avoid trouble. Non-obeisance, non-conformity, or non-observance of real and arbitrary regulations brings pain. With regular frequency I find myself in hot water just for existing – or so it seems. Recently I discovered that the keepers of rules and the guardians of accountability are fallible and often unable to live up to the expectations they desire of others.

Growing up left-handed has not helped. Labelled stupid or incompetent, there is no manual for being "sinister." No handbook or operating guidelines. The world is ruled by right-handed people. To me, most things are either inverted or work backwards. It slows me down and feeds the judgement. Football, school, and the foundations of life have often been painful as I try to master a right-handed lifestyle which is counterintuitive. Conversely, over time, this endeavour has evolved a personal brand of empathy and significant problem-solving skills. By perpetually recalibrating my own movements to adapt to the whims of society, it means I learn fast to keep up with a right-handed world. The grains of Sisu are founded in these struggles.

Lying prone on the range one day, red hot 5.56mm casings eject across the bridge of my nose. Nobody notices I am firing left-handed, including me. It is natural. The hot casings are not. Shifting the rifle to my right side, I stop, adjust my thinking, and in a few short moments continue shooting right-handed, hitting the target and keeping the instructors happy. Problem solved. Not for the first time I recalibrate in the moment to meet a required mechanism. No point asking for help, that makes you look weak. There is no support. So, I internalize these joyous moments and celebrate inwardly the many times where I deploy a lifelong skill and serve as my own pain reliever.

To fully realize the beauty of this condition I live with it as a subconscious function of life and foster the behaviour as a wellspring of optimism.

Thanks to mum, I could draw and create craft, appreciate light, and develop artistic capabilities. Finns are empathetic educators, and she was a natural.

In later times rugby leveled the playing field of evolution. Military service delivered confidence and competency, provided structured disciplines and recognized good humour that rounded out some of life's sharp corners. The instructors didn't make it easy. They merely clarified standards so that everyone had the opportunity to achieve. They did not shift the goal posts. They brought everyone up to a common baseline. A rising tide lifting all ships.

These were fond memories.

Still, life has changed, and being a hard man is as counterintuitive as being right-handed. But it is necessary as there are no silver spoons for this Prince Charming: work, learn, work, exercise, sleep, then rinse and repeat is my current frequency. Stuck down here on Maslow's bottom rung, I can hope that one day a door will open to a higher level.

I snap back to the moment.

Lenny the lawyer, for that is what I name him, unlocks the car and hands over the keys. We exchange pleasantries and judging from his manners I implicitly confirm he is old money. Accustomed to wealth and status, old money clients are often nicer than the nouveau riche; they are polite despite the distance over society. They have nothing to prove by unnecessary dominance or ostentation borne of new wealth and are often respectful of, and sometimes curious about, the world outside that which they inhabit.

The nouveau riche, however, look at you like you just dropped two bags of garbage in their front yard.

Climbing into the passenger seat Lenny locks his harness and waits patiently.

I climb in the driver's side, adjust the seat, the mirrors, check the type of gear shift and push the starter before asking Lenny about his day.

He is relaxed. All is good in the hood. Which will make for a better drive.

The Porsche purrs and German technology hums.

The engine speaks with a desire to be driven. This car is not designed to be stationary and with a final check of the control panels I am ready to roll.

Then Lenny pipes up.

"How fast?" Lenny's aquiline features barely move. I look over inquisitively wondering if the bubbles he's been drinking are fueling the talking. "How fast can you drive this car?" inquires the beak of the regal eagle.

"As fast as you like" says I "but there are speed limits hereby and police beyond Knightsbridge."

"Can you get me home in twenty?" he challenges.

"Not legally."

Lenny responds.

"You know, I have had this car for less than three months, and the tyres are just broken in. It's a dream purchase and a dream drive. Right now, my Porsche is primed to go fast. Less than one thousand miles on the clock it is a great feat of engineering. An articulation of German vehicular perfection. Seventy thousand pounds down, it hugs streets, is driving heaven, and most importantly a badge of hope for attracting the ladies.

But Lenny did not score tonight.

"Three months ago, I was merely a lawyer.

Today, I am a lawyer with a Porsche, which makes me a bigger wanker than I was before."

To the police on the highway and the señoritas in the saloon, that is very much a truism.

He sighs at the pointlessness of life.

I like Lenny.

Authentic candour is unexpected.

I think we can be friends.

There are people in the world who seem to have everything and want more of the same. Property, possessions, prosperity, they are rarely happy and sometimes, like fraud rhinos, blur the lines between the lore and laws of the jungle.

We assume, implicitly, they are aloof and out of touch, for many are.

Lenny portrays a level of self-awareness. He is intelligent and grounded. He is educated with some sense of enlightenment, chuckling at his own predicament with an obvious sense of irony. These are first world problems.

Previous clients, whilst entertaining have often been lacking in authenticity. The famous film star, drunk in Chelsea, riding to Fulham. Upstanding, polite and obsessively anonymous, he denied his identity all the way home from the back of a Mercedes. The City of London broker, new Jaguar, was showing off his wealth, making it rain for charity in West London. Homeward bound, he and his buddies were snorting cocaine all the way to the desired W1 residence. The football hotshot was languishing behind tinted Range Rover windows from West End nightclub to his estate in Essex. Or was he?

The car is empty.

A foil for the paparazzi, I drive "him" steadily back to base. An empty car for an empty journey.

Male clients are often loud, brash, and full of blended knowledge and half-truths that they show off with their buddies. In Audi TTs, Maseratis, BMWs and Mercedes they fly through the streets of London. The Honda VTEC two-seater is a jet-engined penis extension street racer whose solitary passenger is the businessman owner, Charlie the cokehead. Amped up on speed he loves it when we roar down the Chelsea embankment. Crossing the Chelsea bridge at seventy m.p.h. barely touching two thousand RPM, the supercharger kicks in around three thousand wedging us into bucket seats. The needle touches eighty and we brace for impact. The south bank of the River Thames rushes up, and the east end of Battersea Park creates a vomit inducing backdrop. Weaving our way through the nighttime, we land Charlie in Brixton as the darkened denizens of local nightclubs start to pump up the volume.

Nevertheless, like Lenny, he has no girlfriend.

Women clients are different.

The car is not the star. Safety is their priority. Traveling in groups, they are sassy and brassy and mostly friendly. Tipsy, some have had a toot, but they look out for each other and go home together. Parties of three or four, they are seldom solitary, and sometimes two abreast as they lock arms for mutual support after a night of indulgence. Their dopamine rush is during nights out in the gladiatorial arenas of Brixton, Clapham, on the edge of the Elephant or down near the Palace. They visit trendy venues in dangerous destinations. I find their cars early and meet them at the exits.

One, two, and three a.m. pickups.

The lateness of the hour is an indicator of the expected liquidity of movement and possible requirement for rescue.

After all, the darker the hour, the more chance of danger.

I like this life after dark. The study of people is the gift that never stops giving, and the streets of London are great classrooms.

Naturally introverted, the club experience is not pleasurable for me. Previously with friends it was almost painful. The sounds and lights pulsed electric currents through my limbs. The exhausting crush of bodies and intensity of emotion would suck the air from my lungs. Emerging into the night I would gulp for air like a free diver breaching the waves.

Clubs are fire hazards, but the real hazard is people. Different clubs, like pubs, in different territories produce different music and cultural experiences. Loyalties spill over and as the profit margins grow, so does the opportunity for a hostile takeover. Brits love a drink and a fight on any given Friday and can still settle a score on any other Saturday. Sometimes I was the score, and several times found myself crushed in a doorway facing down menace precariously perched on the perimeter of a pain about to be meted out by violent fashionistas.

The meteoric rise of London night clubs through the 80s and 90s was vertical. Darkened doorways no longer led to smoky jazz haunts with live players and a couple of cocktails; they opened on to huge music halls where creative art met technology, pumping out sound and pulsating light. Sensory overload for the masses who hand over their cash in the millions, bump and grind in the hot box, drink industrial volumes of booze, and, when nobody is looking, top up with their favourite narcotic.

London night clubs are a study in people letting loose after the grind of the week. Friday and Saturday nights are a form of musical stock exchange, where cash and credit buy futures and options in listed and non-listed companies – entertainment, pharmaceutical, and beverage industries thrive here as globalization and deregulated financial markets turned London into the hottest City in the wettest country. So good is the business, the model scales up nicely in Sheffield, Manchester, Liverpool and north of the border in Scotland's Glasgow and Edinburgh.

At the appointed pick-up time, drunken adults can be funny, sometimes dramatic and often a bit of a handful. Whatever their wear and tear it is my job to get them home intact. I drive some of the best cars on the market, rally performance motors wrapped in the skin of production line vehicles. Taking regular leaps of faith in modern engineering, I often drive at ludicrous speed, flouting the law with an underlying feeling, and a sense of purpose, in a form of asset protection.

It is a matter of personal honour to get my charges safely home.

Tipping is variable and not specific to gender, social status, or perceived wealth.

Tipping is personal, individual, and not always rational.

No matter how good the drive, there is no correlation between the value of tip and quality of service. The best ride could end empty handed yet the most mediocre of plain vanilla may yield ten- or twenty-pounds sterling. At the end of a shift, I could walk away with nothing more than an exchange of pleasantries or more than fifty pounds in extra currency.

Humans are erratic.

"So," says Lenny, "tonight is a one-time only special deal. I need some vicarious excitement. Get me home in twenty minutes and I'll tip you a ton" That's one hundred pounds to you and me. For twenty minutes work. Not including my hourly rate.

"I'll do it in fifteen, if you are sure." Says I. "But I need protection."

Lenny shrugs.

"I have decided to sell the car and spend the money elsewhere. You drive, you navigate, and in the event of an interaction with the Law, I shall provide counsel. In return for safe delivery in twenty minutes or less, at my home address, safe, scintillated, and free from scratches, I shall give you one hundred pounds of Her Majesty's finest."

Deal.

Lenny is authentic. A true gentleman I choose to believe. My leap of faith starts here.

People strive to exist in their own context. Look beneath the superficiality of trappings, and you discover the real man or woman. Some folks are of course invested in their own dogma, others in their own ostentation; Lenny though, is a product of his birth. He is treading the mill of his society, but our worlds have intermeshed temporarily, and we are friends pro-tem.

Striving for continuous improvement, hoping for upward mobility, I push every experience to the limit. It is how I learn. To achieve upward mobility there needs to be a downward mobility which I cannot create. I can merely be ready if the opportunity arises. Every dawn delivers new opportunities and adventures, if I believed otherwise then prospecting for upward mobility risks becoming a self-licking ice cream cone.

For Lenny, law is life.

In his world he is running to stand still. In the upper ranks of society, maintaining the status quo, he is unlikely to face downward mobility. Even at the end of the Empire he will never be short of money.

Authenticity is what we have in common.

"Ok boss. Hold on to your harness and be careful what you wish for."

Outwardly confident, I am chomping at the bit to see what the Porsche can deliver. The force is strong in German engineering. My faith in the Germans is based on hours of World Rally Championship viewing. I am a good driver not a trained performance driver, but recent driving experiences have proven that production line vehicles handle well. Working with the Saffas has given me a new perspective on how much energy you can get out of a single engine and how much performance you can squeeze out of one vehicle. German and Japanese cars are streets ahead in technological performance. Apart from several flawed attempts at left foot braking, which were unmitigated disasters resulting in head to window confrontations, these cars over mitigate for the risks I would not otherwise take.

Engineering is in danger of restoring my faith in human nature. Behind the wheel of a street tuned Audi, Porsche, Subaru, or Honda I can live a man child dream of "I want to be a racing driver."

As a result of my counterintuitive upbringing I may have an eidetic memory, the ability to recall and retain detail with high precision. This may be a matter of survival too, or it may be instinct. Whatever it is , visuals of roads to Putney scroll through my mind at an overwhelming speed. No point reading a map, I can feel the journey. Feathering the accelerator, nighttime crowds, choke points, police patrols, and bus lanes all spin through my mind. Knightsbridge, Kensington, Chelsea, their streets and avenues slumbering after dark, are safely wrapped in the cloaks of comfort; Battersea Bridge gets me to the fast lanes of York Road, a broad boulevard with bus lanes and the diamond shape roundabout south of Wandsworth bridge that slingshots past the Hurlingham Club towards the gentrified gentility of Putney.

I visualize success and am already folding the bank notes in my pocket as the Porsche tries to free itself from the clutches of the kerb. Twenty minutes is generous. Fifteen minutes is a challenge. Let's go!

Time to give Lenny a good show.

A night out in Knightsbridge means he has easily spent five times one hundred pounds, especially if he is competing with the "Cavalry Ruperts." They're a breed apart. Lenny deserves to finish Friday and start Saturday on a high and I aim to please. He can afford an extra hundred.

I smash the gas.

The Porsche leaps off the line.

The sports gear box helps.

Shifting fast through changes without the necessity of clutching and declutching we charge down Trevor Place into Trevor Square. If I make Battersea Bridge in seven minutes, we're in good shape. Right on Brompton Road by Harrods there's too many traffic lights and too much uniformed police, so we sling a left onto Hans Road then right onto Walton Place onto Walton Street.

I know these streets, but I drive by instinct. It takes too long to read the signs.

Lenny's heart rate is up. I can hear his breathing.

My heart rate drops. The tunnel of focus closes in.

Left foot wedged into the footwell of the car, that hoof is redundant, and the benefits of fast gear shifts are sometimes thwarted as I tap the floor seeking out the missing pedal. Inadvertent left foot braking would be disastrous, career ending, and painful. The sweat of concentration appears as I try to consciously not perform normally subconscious actions. An unintended consequence as we rush at speed through the streets of London.

In the darkness there are only the Porsche controls, tarmac, and the immediate geography rushing out of the darkness. The low-lit cabin allows for optimal visibility. The limit break of the streets and avenues are almost imperceptible at speed, and I trust the car to hug the tarmac when I corner blind turns.

Gazillionaire town houses hitch up their pants and pull in their stomachs as the Porsche careens wildly down their way, now growling like a panther, now roaring like a lion we split the difference between gears prowling the second and third, dips in fourth gear losing precious seconds as revs and turbo drop out then re-emerges as we find the rhythm of the race.

The Porsche 911 thrives at lower gears in this urban setting as the speed barely stresses the German miracle.

North of fourth there's a fifth and sixth gear somewhere, but this is not the autobahn. In third gear we can top sixty and seventy, maybe eighty, and keep the turbo ticking, respond to any eventuality, and secure one hundred pounds sterling as a cash tip.

Fourth, fifth, and sixth gears are the siren songs of face loss, temptations to be resisted at all costs.

Dopamine pumping, eyes dilated, my senses are heightened. I could see a grey cat in a dark suit up a black tree right now. I can smell the energy from Lenny who's either fizzing with frisson or praying to his priest. Either way he's holding the seat beneath him. Personal car and care are in the hands of a stranger. He could have backed out a while ago and chose not to. I admire his courage and feel deep down that the authenticity of humanity perhaps has some currency.

No plod.

No posh.

No hiccups.

Like cavalry chargers we hurtle through London, west-south-west of the Household Regimental barracks, knowing full well that speed wins and in the few seconds it takes for bystanders to register our presence, the peerless Porsche is gone like a ghost in the darkness.

My shoulders are twitching. Music bumps in my head as adrenaline rushes my brain. The car cabin is total silence but for the crackle of intensity. The Porsche is tried and trusted now but one wrong flip and we will be a front-page feature. Narrow roads, cars both sides, townhouses and Georgian era properties peel back from the fiery torch of our headlights. So many one-way streets here, so many hidden entrances there, pick the wrong one and we get a forced detour, or worse, a definitive dead end. Overlay the unlucky appearance of the boys in blue, and the nighttime constabulary will be taking down our particulars.

That could be painful.

Instinct now beats out memory. I can feel the direction of Battersea Bridge.

The trick in London is to know your destination, understand it as the centre of a web, pick a landmark close to the centre and roll and rotate the map in your mind as you close towards the middle. Visualize the map and you can close out obstacles to progress. Bollards, cameras, gated communities and surprise stops. Very soon you shrink your options to a handful of highways and thereon speed and skill will bring you home.

Easy peasy.

Spinning the wheel, the low-slung car grips the autumn tarmac, growling through Walton, right on Draycott, and hard left down Ixworth. At warp factor five we are near the back of Chelsea Stadium.

I can smell the river.

I can taste the money.

I can sense Lenny.

I hold my breath.

Somewhere east of here is Sloane Square. That's too far. Heading west the Porsche pulls a tight left onto Beaufort Street and, gunning the engine, turbo kicking, Lenny breathes out. Battersea Bridge is within our grasp. We are about to exit the tender embrace of Chelsea and Kensington for the south bank boroughs of Battersea, Wandsworth, then Putney.

Game time.

Foot down, the needle climbs to fifty, fifty-five, sixty, sixty-five, now seventy. Seventy-one, seventy-two, seventy-three. No plod, no trouble. Can I tip eighty miles per hour on the Chelsea Embankment. Not sure. Either way, we are now so deep into this escapade that, if the milk goes sour, we're going to need Lenny to walk the walk on his promise.

Battersea Bridge is there.

Visible.

I hit the bridge apron at seventy-five and we accelerate, tipping eighty and cross the Thames in a handful of seconds. Lenny is breathing hard. Out of the corner of my eye I can see sweat on his brow. Inhaling through my nose I pull air deep into my lungs and down into my stomach. No margin of error here and no room for second thoughts.

Boom, we're across the river.

Less than seven minutes by the Porsche clock.

The race is on.

We spin hard right onto Battersea Church Road, Vicarage Road towards the short dual carriageway of York Road. It's there, I know.

I feel it.

I have run these routes many times, but this is a true test of what you know against a backdrop of probability mathematics. This is also not a sanitized racetrack free of debris.

This is a live London borough and a real showdown.

York Road at this time of night is fast and, accelerating towards the Wandsworth roundabout, the Porsche is unleashed, sprinting down the straight carriageway. Like a wild cat in full chase lunging forward we enjoy a rare moment in fourth gear. Lenny has relaxed. Me too for that matter. Uninterrupted seconds of pure speed and fewer than 3 miles remaining, that's a few short minutes at this rate.

One ton of folding money is crinkling away at the base of my motivations.

Smiling inwardly, I know that Lenny has had his thrill; the Porsche has proved its mettle, and I can add another badge to my book of prestige motors.

We could probably slow now and still win.

But what's the point? Better to go out on a high.

A night bus is the only traffic ahead. A lugubrious red elephant slowly rolling in the same direction. A gentle downward tug on the steering wheel brings us around the outside of the bus and gunning the accelerator we rush into the space alongside...

...directly into the lane of another doleful red beast. A sibling red elephant running parallel and uniquely in our direction. Unexpected.

Lenny shudders and grips the seat hard.

In the glare of headlights, I can barely see the gap but know it to be there. Blinded by the other bus, the next few moments are instinctive. York Road is straight here and so is the bus route.

Stopping or slowing will end in an unholy mess of metal and more.

"Breathe in," I mutter. Taking a deep breath through my nose, I hold the car steady, drop a gear, feel the surge of power and the Porsche jumps.

Is it too late?

I can barely see the gap, I close one eye against the glare of lights, hold my breath, tap the steering wheel down slightly and feel the machine. The Porsche lives up to its racing heritage rushing into the shrinking gap between the front of the two night-buses at mach 3. Sweating, I ease out half a breath, trying to slow my heart rate as adrenaline pumps into my body.

Opening the other eye, and closing the first one, restores some night vision.

A gentle nudge on the wheel and the car aligns with the road, tires hold tight to the tarmac, and I risk a full breath.

Exhale. Glance at Lenny.

Gripping the seat, he is still as a statue. Staring hard through the windscreen.

Bam!

Shit!

The diamond shape roundabout on the south bank of Wandsworth Bridge is on us.

Inhale.

Both eyes are open now.

There is no way I can stop the car safely. I tap the brake. Wrong move. The Porsche starts to fishtail, the spoiler in the rear-view mirror moving left and right as the car tries to regain traction in the curve of the road. I have no idea of our speed.

Focus.

Do.

Not.

Breath.

Left foot buried in the footwell, right foot eases off the gas pedal. Steering wheel holds at an obtuse angle, encouraging the car towards the exit. I hold the steering wheel in both hands, the car is pulling left, I need to bring it right, around the bend of the roundabout and into the exit. The spoiler on the back is moving out further to the left, the engine is keening, starting to whine as the tires grip the road and the rear wheels spin and grip, looking for traction.

Thank you, antilock braking.

The car shudders.

The engine and wheels easing right, fighting with gravity and momentum, which is pushing left. Every movement is micro. I lean into the bend, braced against my harness, willing the turn.

Trusting the engineering.

Thank you, Germans.

The car is pulling, I can smell the rubber gripping the road, my stomach pulls down into a knot; I bite my lip, determined not to become a statistic; the small stab of pain keeps me focused on the moment.

Are we going to make it?

The spoiler and the back of the Porsche have swung through equilibrium and reached the extreme point of the pendulum. We wait in the split seconds of anticipation for our final moments as the car spins out across the other lanes into the barriers, trees and paving stones that mark the edge of the road.

We sit, trapped in time, breathless beneath the Recaro seat harnesses.

And in those final moments of breathlessness, the speed drops enough for gravity to get a grip, for the Porsche to find a true sense of direction and for the tires to hold the road. The spoiler regains equilibrium and the big cat lunges forward into the Swandon Way exit, direction south-south-west and the final half mile.

Lenny coughs.

An erudite kind of cough that one expects to hear from a learned mouth. The kind of cough employed in Court to get the attention of the Judge.

An "excuse me" before the embarkation of a massive monologue.

Ignoring the invite to speak, it is all I can do to calm my nerves and keep my hands steady. Biting the inside of my lip, outwardly I am calm. No emotion, no disturbance in the force. Just another day at the office.

Shit, that was close!

We complete the journey in silence coasting through the rest of the brick clad landscape, watching the car clock gently tick over. As we growl uphill to the gated gravel driveway marking the perimeter of Lenny's home, he coughs again. I breath deep, in through my nose, calm and at fourteen minutes and thirty-seven seconds glance over to his side of the car.

"Here you go sir! Home we are, safe and sound."

Opening the door, I climb out and hand over the keys. I touch the front of the Porsche gently, a loving caress of this sleek beast in the cool early morning air of genteel Putney.

"Well," says Lenny. Aquiline features somewhat wrinkled and slightly textured he reaches inside his jacket. "Looks like I owe you some money."

Pulling out a wad of cash, he offers me five crisp twenties with a sparkle in his eye.

"Well done!" he says. "Best time I've had in ages. What a thrill. Thought we would come a cropper at one point. Marvelous driving. Bloody marvelous."

The memories of failed fortunes in the Cavalry clubs of delicious 'donnas and ostentatious officers fades along with his silhouette into the darkened recesses of the front door. Upright, straight, and legal once more Lenny heads to bed.

Lenny is authentic. In a weird way I feel validated in my trust. Counting the bonus turning away from the house I hear some final words of bonding before the night swallows us up.

"Marvelous, bloody marvelous!"

HELSINKI

Alongside a platform at Helsinki station, the Russian train to Moscow is a dirty old monster staffed by uniformed attendants. Blondes and bleached blondes wear militia like uniforms beneath large hats representing both Mother Russia and the State Railway (the OAO Rossiyskie zhelezny dorogi).

Across the platforms, sleek Finnish locomotives offer stark contrast to these dirty old Russian monsters. Likewise, the Finnish people in brightly coloured summer wear with happy countenances are distinctly dissimilar from the Russian train officials. I can feel the burn of multiple stares. The Finnish matriarchal society, owners of "we told you so" glances are righteously positioned to confirm their own bias.

Mum is here of course. My brother and his children too. A few days spent together as a family has been a rare occurrence. Together in a place of peace it makes this farewell hard to accomplish. Moved, I hope it is not goodbye. I have not shared my trans – Alpine escapade nor some of the other crazy behaviours. The adventures are epic, but I feel a weird sense of guilt for not conforming to social norms. Right now, though, I am as close to family as I have been for many years. It makes this next part of my journey feel like a real step into the abyss. Shaking off the tremors, the Russian train whistle blasts and, discarding fears of what lies ahead, the late afternoon sun witnesses the departing civilization of Helsinki station and the waves of the platform party. I miss them terribly. The kids are tiny, and I do not know when I will see any family again. As the distance grows the sadness of dislocation increases.

I generally dislike travel.

Daily commutes and airplane journeys are mostly unpleasant.

Airports and railway stations are dirty, crowded places manifesting the worst emotions.

The peculiar sense of ownership found in Western society is concentrated around airline seats, highway lanes, and road junctions. The smaller the space and the tighter the time frame, the more aggressive the battle for available real estate. Squirrels do not fight over empty acorns, birds do not squabble over vacant husks, but the human need to exert dominance over diminishing spaces of minimal value is unparalleled.

Extended train journeys are different. Canned humanity in trundling, rolling stock offer a shared feast of rumbling observations with passengers more genteelly disposed to their neighbours and less inclined to the anxieties of autos and airplanes. Train journeys are accessible adventures and a disentanglement of history. It is for these reasons I love a train adventure. Time unravels along with the world around you.

Russian trains, like their Chinese counterparts, are products from another time. A Communist era alternative to the "auto lovin' West," rails replace roads and carriages replace cars. As we "trumble" into the night, I consider my travel companion. Steff, one of the two Germans

I know, is parochial, eternally curious, and academic. Undernourished, skinny, and short-sighted he can speak Russian and has no other obvious competencies. He is nevertheless friendly. I judge him harshly because of his nonathletic appearance. Bodily free of nutrients and muscle mass, he is a physical illustration of life under "The Regime". He will never adorn a propaganda poster. Staring out at the world from behind steel rimmed spectacles he was keen for this journey. In fairness I was happy for some companionship and respect his courage as we step into the unknown. We can be friends. The remaining carriage space supports a sparse population of travelers. Paying little heed to who's who in the zoo, I slip into slumber with the encroaching sunset.

Sometime later the clunk and clutter of a stopping train awaken me. The darkness outside supports the statement of my watch, which says 11:30 pm. The train says nothing.

The silence is deafening and has a familiar tang.

Like an old bear sniffing the air outside his cave I know trouble is in the wind. Outside lights, muttered voices, and an absence of train staff is suggestive. Of what? I do not know. The darkness outside is unhelpful. Are we in Finland or Russia?

Steff wakes from his slumber as a new uniform walks in. Not the bleached blond matriarch in charge of the samovar and cleaning duties. This one is a different militia.

Big hat, stern face, the body of a young officer fills the outfit. Twenty something years of age, the authoritarian surveys the carriage. Young men with power are some of the worst kind of gorilla, like the Burberry clad policeman. This gorilla is surrounded by a pack of hyenas, who like Steff, are young, malnourished, and reedy. They are the lower echelon of "The Regime". These hyenas are dangerous.

Comedic in loose fitting uniforms they are accessorized like the fraud rhino, with a long iron. The assault rifle looks familiar. The beloved Kalashnikov I believe, armament of bad guys in movies around the globe. The big-hatted gorilla stares, the hyenas sniff and shuffle around.

Here comes the shakedown.

Sitting quietly, I do nothing to draw their attention. After all, this could just be how Russians do passport control.

At the embassy in London, the Russians offered a menu of visa options. Business, tourist, etc. all with processing options. Upon inquiry, the only available option was the most expensive. Whatever you chose had to be expedited for an extra hundred pounds or so. Otherwise, three to six months with no guarantee of completion was your next best option. Helsinki was my logical option. The Finns know how to manage the Russians. Within a couple of days and at an appropriate price, train tickets with visas have been sorted by a Finnish broker.

"Passports." Big Hat spits the word and holds his hand out. We hand them over obligingly. Others here have crossed the border before, so I follow their lead. Big Hat disembarks and, in the silence, I reflect on the chorus line of Finnish matriarchs. Sssh! I try to quieten them.

Sometime later, Big Hat returns. The eyes of the malnourished hyenas are wide, with extra sparkle. They are excitable and I know what's inbound, a Dark London style shakedown. Steff is still, like a rabbit with all senses alive. Wired to bounce out of danger, he makes no eye contact, staring into the middle distance.

> "You have entered our country illegally and must pay a fine or you will be arrested."

The statement is made in Russian.

A Norwegian lady emerges from the darkness and translates for those of us in need. Smouldering with indignation she looks good. Sounding experienced she pushes back, switching between English and Russian. Big Hat looks twitchy and clearly is not enjoying the challenge. Not in front of his hyenas, not by a woman.

Everyone is still now. The atmosphere is pregnant with anticipation.

Low grade bullies are rarely linguists; body language speaks volumes though and the Russian troupe are no exception. Their modus operandi is very human: liberty in exchange for money. Dollars, euros, and pounds, they will accept all denominations. Cash of course.

Fixated on the word "illegally" I want to lean into the situation. But the hyenas are fidgeting. Excited by a cash bonus, they scan the carriage, eyes over gun muzzles. Unchecked uniformed authority with any form of weapon, be it stick or sidearm, is rarely open to dialogue. This I have learned the hard way and Big Hat holds all the cards right now.

Who is he?

Who are they?

Border guards, a militia force, or something else altogether.

Stories from the OG and the OP infiltrate my thinking. They have survivors' wisdom and so I remain quiet, non-threatening, waiting for an opening. Big Hat has seized our passports under false pretenses and is demanding we buy them back.

Acquiescence is not ideal, but the stage is well set. Big Hat has a window of opportunity here in Putin's Russia. At ten minutes to midnight, the train is early, and the visa dates are for the next day, which it would be if the train had been allowed to continue to Moscow. Big Hat however sees a gap in the market and exploits the arbitrage with menace. This looks like a well-rehearsed act, I wonder how often it happens. Clearly not enough to create a scandal. Too many questions remain unanswered as the smell of sweat, gun oil, and musty uniforms permeate the closed carriage environment.

"Добро пожаловать в Россию, к черту вас!"

("Welcome to Russia, fuck you!") I presume this is his motto.

Bullies are cowards though. Push back is possible and as the seconds stretch into minutes the conveyor of nervous tension rolls. Steff is still in rabbit camouflage. The hyenas track the business end of their AKs around the car, the other folks are quiet. Norway is the only one standing.

Are we going to die? It is a possibility, but I am not convinced.

A bloody mess on a darkened train somewhere near the Karelian Isthmus is a bit of a stretch. These are opportunistic border guards, nothing more. Ready to engage Steff, he speaks Russian, I reckon we can find a way out. That said, guns are guns. Twitchy youth, and itchy trigger fingers are unpredictable. I am not in a hurry to die, and less of a hurry to hand over my money. As shake downs go, this is clever.

There must be a flaw though. Stay calm and the loophole will show itself.

Bureaucracy, that is where the flaw will be revealed. Bureaucracy enjoys a world class level of infamy. The strength of bureaucracy is in its inflexibility as is its weakness. Does Big Hat really have all the cards? Superficially yes. Logistically though, this is a complex operation. This is a business train; it brings revenue directly and indirectly to the country. A bloodbath would end that, and then the foreign outcry. And then what about the paperwork? Big Hat and the hyenas are playing with a forensic disaster. Time will equalize the odds and I relax guardedly.

The OG and the OP nod their approvals of my wisdom.

Their tacit approvals are comforting. And then the words "*Not frightened of anything, except the Russians*" seep through. Ugh! What a mess! Time trickles like molasses. The Russians are not pressing their advantage. The feeling is nuanced but it is obvious. Nobody is handing over currency, everyone is still. Bullies are cowards, we are at a stalemate. Big Hat is still cold, not angry; yet.

The standoff is real. Norway is still standing. Facing the Russians. She is the first to speak:

"I want your name, ID number, and unit number" she states confidently.

Unexpected.

She has made the first move. That takes courage.

"I also want the names and numbers of your men, a signed written receipt with a formal stamp. When we arrive in Moscow, I will report you to the Norwegian embassy."

Bureaucracy – there it is. The strength and the weakness. Norway is offering an exchange. Money for information and no matter how glacial the process, she will report it through the system.

I am paralyzed by size. Not in my inability to move, but more in the knowledge that a certain type of person likes to inflict violence on big men, as part of their show of strength. Bullies in uniform with an armed entourage are a classic example. Also, I do not speak Russian. Which feels important at this moment.

Norway bristles with a beguiling defiance. The men that I know would either escalate, foolishly, or just cough up, meekly. Norway however has found a different path, the lessons of mothers and grandmothers from across the world are in full flood here. She is holding these men accountable. The hedgehog of courage pricking the tension of the stalemate. Big Hat holds the cards, Norway holds the moral high ground.

Like a game of chess, it is time for the next move. It is Russia's turn. Big Hat blinks, face deadpan, a small flexion in his features indicates distaste. Is bureaucracy enough to tame the gorilla? In the West we enjoy freedoms. The freedom to be opinionated, challenging, discursive, expressive, and mostly without repercussion. In the East, beyond the edges of Europe, it is different. Consequences are real and can be immediate. Big Hat operating independently is showing unwelcome initiative. Particularly if there is no cut for the man upstairs. In Russia, the man with the biggest fists wins. How big are Big Hat's fists? Are there bigger fists above him?

I hold my breath.

Big Hat moves.

No words. No gun. No action.

Leaning into the closest hyena he whispers a command and the pack shuffles towards the door. With all the icy cold of Russia in his eyes, Big Hat stares at Norway and slowly comes about, glaring at all the other nationalities in the room: Finland, Sweden, Germany, Britain, we all enjoy the glare, unfriendly as a Siberian winter. The freeze of the silence bites my bones.

Big Hat steps back, turns, and exits the carriage.

We breathe again.

Warmth returns to the room as the electric tingle of adrenaline heats my soul. Norway explains her position. She knows Russia, does business with Russian men. Strength is respected. It is not encouraged. She can drink their drink, eat their food, and play their bureaucratic chess games. In the light of this new knowledge, her recent stance seems more like a calculated tactic than a careless gamble. Knowledge is strength. Wisdom is knowing how to use that strength. Norway has knowledge, wisdom, and strength. As ever I am smitten by a smart, strong woman. The intensity of a unique shared experience heightens the smit, and then the fuse blows as I remember...

Big Hat still has our passports.

In typical Nordic fashion, nobody talks much. I look around the room. Stoic silence sustains.

Everybody is waiting for whatever happens next. This is strange. London is noisy, chaotic, with colour clashes and emotional overloads. Lots of shouty people populate the capital. Here I am stuck between the rock of Nordic silence and the hard place of a need for action.

Electricity hums.

It is the train's warm up song, an indicator of movement, and it breaks the tension. Still no Big Hat though, nor our passports. So where are we going? The hands of time wrap around midnight's mass and in the cold choke of bureaucracy we are now legitimately on Russian soil. There are footsteps. The militia uniform emerges from the darkness and enters the carriage.

No Big Hat. No hyenas. The bleached blonde matriarch of train order brings a warmer officialdom. Her gloved hands hold a stack of passports and betraying no sense of what went before, she returns each book to its rightful owner. I open mine. There is no damage. A red stamp, Cyrillic text is a new addition to the pages implying a more formal welcome to the Motherland. The train starts a slow roll.

The moment is surreal. The theatre has ended, as the drama dissipates, everyone rolls back into their seats. Nobody speaks. Did it really happen? I look at Steff who grew up under Russian repression and Stasi actions. Betrayals, incarcerations, forced education, economic hardship are the reported outcomes of Communism, an ironic ideology for the masses managed by the overlords of the chattering classes. A handful of elite elites for whom absolute power brooks no repudiation.

Rolling into midnight's darkness, the danger is over for now. The other passengers return to peaceful slumber. Removing my shoes, I follow the trend, not thinking too much about what lies in store. It is just a train ride after all. What could possibly go wrong ...?

MOSCOW

Dirt, dust, and a sense of low-level menace greet us at Moscow Central Station. The interior is characterized with a press of people, prone drunks, and an underground railway network. In fairness this could be any railway station in London or Paris. Bolshevik art deco propaganda in the metro distinguishes our destination. The scale and detail are impressive. The underground train is punctual and clean and shortly we arrive unmolested at the cobbled Red Square fringed with its iconic buildings. Steff warns me that we should avoid the police. We can be stopped and searched at their convenience. Without approved identification we can be arrested, alternatively they could relieve us of our passports and incarcerate us. After our recent experience I do not doubt him. Stay away from uniforms. Whatever the outside world believes, Russia is still a functional dictatorship, and Moscow is the engine of autocracy.

In Red Square, the onion domes of St. Basil's cathedral, a 16th century architectural icon, look askance at the 19th century GUM shopping mall. The *Gosudarstvennyy universalnyy magazin (GUM) or State Department Store* looms large. It is a few minutes' walk from the infamous Kremlin. The fortified complex built in the 12th Century spans history and has survived the rise of Communism. The Kremlin is the centre of extreme power in the Russian political landscape. Imposing and muscular, it is the architectural embodiment of "the man with the biggest fists." In the heart of Red Square, Lenin lies dormant. Embalmed forever on public display in his mausoleum, he has a forever view of the broad avenue down which Russia's military machines mobilize alongside the infiltration of Western decadence. Uniformed duty guards are conscripts in dress uniform. Eyed by tourists, they are Russian versions of Buckingham Palace guards. Across the street, GUM houses boutique shops. Prada, Burberry, and Gucci, are all available to modern Bolshevik heroes buying gifts for their partners and lovers. Lenin, founding leader of the Bolshevik revolution, lies within easy embrace of Western luxury. The irony is real. In the absence of religion or opposition, over time Russian leaders have elevated themselves to iconic status. Mr. Putin is no exception.

Our budget does not justify a visit to GUM, so we head over to see the dead man himself. Curiosity piques as we approach the glass tomb. Unlike Elvis and Hitler maybe, Lenin is dead. A man of modest stature, size is clearly no indicator of revolutionary competency. We shuffle around the glass absorbing details without reverence consciously avoiding eye contact with the guards. I presume it is Lenin. He looks like a waxwork model. This is a man who spearheaded a revolution that toppled a monarchy ending the Russian empire. The leader of a bloody revolution that implemented a new ideology, the youngest system of rule in modern history. Not democratic, nor republic, but a flattened hierarchy of rule for the people by the people.

Maybe.

Reactionary Communism, a violent response to the rule of Emperors, Czars, and Monarchs, inspired the rise of Mao in China, and thanks to the Vietnam War, Ho Chi Minh. The reverence is real. All of them are embalmed and publicly staged. The ideology for the many, which crushed religion, wealthy landowners, the ruling classes, and continued onwards in death and glory struggle. The new Communist regimes methodically burned books, rewrote history, and exterminated citizens who most resembled a past which had to be extinguished. No lessons learned, just a total wipeout. Lenin gave way to Stalin, whose greatest foreign export was the Chinese Communist Party under Mao, and collectively their crowning achievement is the wholesale slaughter of more than one hundred million people. Ideology is bloody, and politics are weapons of a bloody proletariat. This world has been closed to outsiders for many decades yet feels like the seat for many adventures.

Public displays of entombed leaders seem weird. The cult of personality discomforting. Knowing well the flaws of the human condition, human based iconography does not cut the mustard. Personality cults are riddled with danger, and an intentional embalming process is up there with child beauty pageants or the taxidermy of hunting trophies. Is it just a Communist thing? Why not have a World Series of dead Presidents, Premiers, and Prime Ministers? A World Cup of embalmed reverence as the icons of history - Lincoln, De Gaulle, Churchill, Lenin, Mao, and Minh are paraded in a global pissing contest of public adoration. Like Mexico's "Dia de la Muerte." We could also throw in a few Popes, some African dictators, fireworks, and food for a happy occasion. It is just what the calendar needs, another holiday.

International Dead Presidents Day.

Beers, BBQs, and a celebration of human icons across continents would be a great reminder of who did what to whom, improve cultural awareness, and hopefully give politicians pause before starting the next war. It would probably be cheaper too.

As these thoughts wash over me in the heart of the autocrat's capital we move away from Lenin's tomb. I am uncomfortable here. Unlike other cities around the world, Moscow feels repressive, the rules learned elsewhere do not apply in this jungle, which feels more like a graveyard of culture than a cradle of civilization. A sense of watchfulness is in the air. Like the ambient silence of a new danger the sensation hangs heavy waiting for a trigger action. Our departure time is in a few hours so, nudging my constant companion, we head off to find the Trans – Siberian train. The "Mongolian train" that will take us away from here, to the fabled land that is China. Even poorer and dirtier than the diesel-clad Russian and Chinese monsters, the Old Mongolian Beast is the least famous of the Trans-Siberian railway fleet.

The humid summer heat here is oppressive as is the vastness of the crowds. Steff navigated us here by taxi, a blue Lada with springy faux leather seats and dodgy steering. At the station, embarkation is a crazy affair as a heaving sea of families beneath a flotilla of luggage, pallets of packages, and cases of merchandise sail all over the platforms. The seething, hissing, and bubbling emotions are crushed upon the sea of humanity the like of which I have never seen. People bump and wobble in a confluence of currents edging towards any carriage entrance, hoisting their belongings through the hot dusty Moscow air. The sun beats down, baking the bodies, highlighting here and there some pale foreign heads in the ochre of colour.

Grateful as I am for him getting us here, Steff is spindly and looks ready to be broken in the crush. Using my bulk, I push through the crowd defining a gradual path as he tries to interpret numbers and letters on each car. We eventually find our compartment. A hard sleeper and an oasis of empty, cool and peaceful space. Two bunks line each wall, a lower and upper. It is relative luxury for the journey ahead as other cabins are brimming with humanity, shoes, leather goods, umbrellas, dry goods, and even car parts. They look like mini warehouses for the temporary tenants, who in turn appear to be more than travellers. Settling in, Steff speaks to the neighbours. They are traders and smugglers bringing goods from Moscow to sell across the country. The train is their home, and the platforms are their markets. Our eastern trajectory passes through Nizhny Novgorod in European Russia, Yekaterinburg in the Urals, Novosibirsk on the Western Siberian plain, Krasnoyarsk in Arctic Siberia, Irkutsk and then Lake Baikal. Exotic nomenclature conjures up visions of endearing wooden villages populated by "womble" type characters wearing colourful threads, affording ready markets for the Mongolian smugglers.

What on earth have we gotten into? There are traders and smugglers everywhere. At first blush I am concerned by this new discovery, but we mean them no harm, and the locals seem unconcerned by our presence.

Anyway, what could go wrong? It is just a train journey after all.

Luggage stowed, I remove my boots, massage my feet, then pull a book from my backpack. Reclining on the couch I hear the crowds bustling and settling, readying for departure. Our space is clean and undisturbed. Steff watches the crowd. It feels safer here than the Russian train, or even Red Square, as the noises gradually diminish the old diesel monster that is our train achieves a settled quiet, blows its whistle, and starts to roll.

In the heart of Russia, we have left the relative safety of Europe on a train taking us ever deeper into a great unknown.

MOTHER RUSSIA

Our berth is rectangle shaped, a hard sleeper with four bunks. A soft sleeper, for there are a few in another car, have two bunks with bedding and VIP status. A small table sits beneath a large picture window opposite the door to the corridor. The long passage connects all the compartments which are replicated throughout the train. A bathroom at one end smells of industrial cleaning fluid. It stings my eyes and seems strong enough to remove skin. I am cautious about making contact and footprints on the toilet seat suggest that someone else has enjoyed similar sentiments.

A samovar at the other end of the passageway incessantly boils water and is a welcome luxury. Primarily I brew tea which is drunk black in the Russian style. But having a clean water source serves many other uses. Particularly as there is no bathroom for washing. Traveling light, I carry dried fruit and nuts for sustenance. A small amount of cheese and tea leaves embellish the stash. Bundles of small denomination dollars are secreted around my body and in my pack. Some clothes, a book, water bottle, and toothbrush make up the rest of my belongings. Official documentation is hidden. Strangely at peace, we roll away from Moscow. The hot, humid, and dusty city is oppressive physically and mentally. I am glad to be away from a capital city where autocracy is rising. Our neighbours are quiet. Everyone is comfortable in their temporary nests and the journey starts peacefully.

The world outside our window gives full exposure to the rolling Russian countryside and as the afternoon pulls into the evening, the silence drifts into nighttime, and the endless landscape disappears into darkness. Sleep comes easily and so do the nightmares. Men in uniform, abusers of power, and wielders of pain are prominent. Moments of violence too. The interaction with the Russian border guards unleashed old demons. Awake in the night, covered in sweat, I reflect on recent history, slow my breathing, and calm my racing heart. Education through exploration is a purposeful adventure that brings its own risks and rewards. Yet the arbitrary acts of men with a little bit of authority have left deep wounds which are slow to heal. Uniformed wielders of micro power can inflict a pain beyond their level of authority. Consciously, quietly, my response to trauma is to leave the source of pain behind. Mental health issues are never spoken to. Kindness is a sign of weakness, so moving on is the best cure.

The light of dawn streams in through our picture window revealing a forever landscape reaching to the ends of the earth. The train keeps rolling and the old monster keeps puffing. Everything is normal. A new temporary normal in the world of smuggling.

A professional lady is perched amongst a multitude of boxes. She appears to be the solitary occupant of her own space.

We make eye contact.

She speaks. Mostly Russian.

Steff translates.

From Ulan Bataar, she is Mongolian and a doctor. Apologetic, she cannot offer us tea, the boxes are an inconvenience. We share our own and she offers her story. The veneer of Communism is stripped bare out here, where everything is up for sale. The facade of ideology is revealed by the clear failure to provide at a local level, so market trading thrives. Everything is for sale, from iconography to tea sets, demand dictates price and in the case of the lady doctor blood plasma is her product. Moscow is her vendor and Mongolia is her market. She has seen a gap in that market and pays an annual visit to her Russian peers. Life in Moscow is expensive for anybody below the rank of Commissar or Oligarch. The poorly paid Muscovy Medics, happy for some hard currency, particularly U.S. dollars, will trade anything to improve their lives. Business is good for the lady doctor, yet it is unclear from where she gained enough dollars to start up. More than thirty boxes occupy her hard sleeper, where she is the sole occupant in this cabin for four. Even with travel, logistics, and facilitation payments to border guards she will make enough profit to live for one year. A mid-year break with after sales yields to hospitals means she can return to work as a doctor, survive the winter and repeat the cycle next year.

Putin's Russia is a black-market exchange where, beneath the noses of the oligarchs, everything is up for sale. The gorilla militia around the Kremlin offer a veneer of authority. Those closest to the capital are the protectors of the wealthy and the last remnants of an ideology "for the people." In the rest of the country human need drives commodity values like everywhere else in the world. Out here though, in the Wild East, open smuggling is the mechanism of mercantilism. Red Square is a luxurious showroom of a dysfunctional nation state evolving into an oligarchy owned feudal state. Over tea, the lady doctor shines a light on the rot which Steff translates in a matter-of-fact tone.

Hungry we walk up to the restaurant car, and Steff asks the waitress for her recommendations off the menu. We place an order based on her chosen favourites and without appropriate language skills I observe the theatre in silence. The words are alien, and I grasp tenuously at Cyrillic syllables, musical notes that flutter out of earshot like butterflies.

"These foods are not available" the hostess is a boss.

"You just recommended them" smiles Steff. Ever aware of his surroundings he has donned rabbit camouflage once more, senses heightened, movements minimal.

"Yes" says the Matriarch with an edge of exasperation at our stupidity. "You asked me what I recommended, not what is available."

This is a new form of service. We try again.

"What is available?"

"Well...." She is clearly thinking, a good sign. "Everything!"

Great. My stomach rumbles appreciatively.

"That is, if you work on the train. Nothing! If you are traveling on the train."

The bureaucracy of ideology is a special form of poetry which she speaks with practiced meter. The disappointment of hunger though is supplemented by the reward of repercussions. One week on a ration of tea, nuts, cheese, and water will get boring quickly. Within the confines of the train, where the only form of exercise is walking the corridors perhaps it is not too bad. Functional Communism at least keeps the train rolling. Feed the workers not the consumers. There is hope yet for the proletariat.

About to leave, she utters some final magic.

"We have vodka."

From nowhere our hostess conjures up bottles of the clear liquid. At four dollars a bottle the exchange happens swiftly. As the hard currency disappears into her uniform, we head out of the restaurant car to share our discovery.

The train rolls a steady course through the Russian countryside. Outside the summer colours of green, yellow, light browns on a blue-sky backdrop extend to the edge of the sky. Inside is quiet, still, and for the second day there is little interaction of passengers as the etiquette of society brooks no response to the consumption of vodka which has yet to fully filter through the behavioural membrane of this international community. Meanwhile, Finland is calling. The harmony of spiritual peace, never previously enjoyed, is a powerful force and given the chance, I would turn back now. On these journeys of discovery I have glimpsed happiness, tasted peace, and enjoyed tranquillity. Fitting the pieces together I notice myself moving further away from desired destinations of stability and normalcy. Forward is the only direction as completion is the only solution. The dull ache of longing subsides along with the rolling Russian terrain and I switch gears, determined to make the most of this experience. Life is not a dress rehearsal and if this is my last endeavour, then let's fill it with colour.

With precision accuracy the train rolls into scheduled stops once or twice daily. A fluid farmers market bringing goods and services to the small concrete towns of angular buildings populated by the Russian proletariat. Traders step down to hawk their wares and milk their customers. Under the hot summer sun, a Mongolian man, a living mannequin in a long leather jacket holding pink parasol, opens his store. He sells leather goods and umbrellas and with an engaged, effervescent spirit, barters with Babushkas and blokes, exchanging products for roubles. Or in the absence of roubles, any other product.

His buddy sells car parts. A mucky looking mechanic with smears of grease on his complexion and clothing, I wonder at the act. These traders are clever. They look like what they sell. Authentic apparitions bringing new news, screws, and clues from the fashionable metropolis and beating heart of modern technological advances.

Flashes of gold teeth, amongst real and metal teeth, in wrinkled, smooth-skinned, and weather-beaten faces, chatter in local dialects as free-market intensity is driven by a short buying window. The deals and squeals yield profit and product under the watchful eye of Lenin, who exists in stone statue form on a podium at every station. Homes, shops, garages, and bars are stocked for winter thanks to this train. The Mongolians control the exchange, the regulations, and the worth of each commodity as rarity breeds value. Economics 101 is enacted here in the schoolyard of the Asiatic Steppes. A school for earthy traders. This not the electronic exchanges where the suits and stripey blazers of city bankers are waving papers, shouting prices, and yelling options in a pit of blazing screens and digital data; business here is conducted under bobbing headscarves and hats over unkempt hair, in the worn clothes of people fighting to survive. The outback of Russia is a world without comforts. No bitumen-coloured espressos or lathery cappuccinos here, just an intensity of trade for car parts, clothes, and cosmetics. Demand defining values, roubles on the run, and dollars driving dialogue.

I play my part.

Small denomination U.S. dollars buy cucumbers, tomatoes, the odd potato, and some fibre for my diet. Furrowed faces of old ladies' wrinkle with smiles as they fold greenbacks into the creases of their costumes. The short-lived happiness of these transactions means I willingly pay over the odds. I thought I was poor and low born. The Russian populace is on another level. They fight to survive. There's nothing out here beyond government control and some subsistence farming. The odd factory maybe but I have seen no smokestacks nor heavy trucks, nor other signs of industry. Betrayed by their leadership I hope my meagre contributions of a few extra dollars might relieve some pain or buy some extra warmth in winter.

Other foreign travelers sail through the crowds in a bobbing sea of heads. Exchanging culture and creating their own experiences, there are just a few of us and I am yet to discover their motivations. Two Dutch women, a cellist and a violinist on a music exchange; a large American, bulky beneath his flat cap speaks Russian; a brace of Swedish doctors partial to vodka and depressing stories about China have a soft sleeper cabin in another carriage - they visit long enough to drink and depress the room, then return to relative comfort; the third brace, Australian backpackers with ubiquitous energy make a lot of noise – "mate, mate, mate" – in nasal tones. One curly haired, one not, I call them Bubble and Squeak. The Mongolians leave us in peace. We provide light entertainment and, with no negative impact on trade, are merely oddities to be curious about.

The lady doctor rarely leaves her cabin. Protecting her precious plasma cargo, she is confined to quarters for the duration of the trip. The American similarly protects a precious cargo. His primary threats are in Moscow. Here, he strolls through the crowds for amusement without engaging in trade. In the small-town wilderness, there is no necessity for a low profile, so he can enjoy the air and some respite from the confines of his cabin.

I have never met an American before. Not a real one outside of the T.V. He is bigger than me. Not taller, broader. Although his size is suggestive of nationality, he is not noisy or brash and he speaks Russian. Which makes his nationality less obvious, until, with the aid of vodka and a friendly face, I flush out his story.

Boston John, for that is what I name him, is a Yankee, of Slavic descent. Which is confusing. I thought all Americans were Irish, or Italian, or Native Indian. That's what the media tells us. Whiskey drinkin', cigar smokin', pasta munchin', gun slingers, and Apaches. Boston John is a unit. A bilingual bear of a man with an appreciation for vodka and conversation. I am enthralled as the door opens to a new learning opportunity.

"Let me show you something" he reaches under his bunk, pulling out a case.

The triangular Balalaika entombed within is a traditional long neck stringed instrument played like a guitar. The sounds of the Balalaika have been heard across the centuries, the Steppes, and beyond. This one, formerly housed in the Moscow State Museum, has been liberated, like the blood plasma with the help of some fresh greens, in a secret exchange between Boston John and a poorly paid professor.

Professors, like the doctors of Moscow, are reduced to selling their assets. Scraping a living on the paltry breadcrumbs handed down by Putin and the Oligarchs, the loving remnants of Russia's yesterday are steadily exported on the black market by the poor guardians of history.

The train is amazing. This old diesel monster is cover for a school of economics overlaid with lessons in Russian politics and culture. I learn here that trade is the life blood of humanity and survives the repression of ideology. If you squash trade, it will manifest outside of your control. If you deny growth, it will occur in the blind spots of your influence. Totalitarianism is not total. It is a rigid fragility reliant on menace and undermined by mercantile mechanics and the tools of trade. The single act of artifact smuggling removes the responsibility of cultural preservation to another land. Boston John the facilitator of this liberation from oppression is bringing the Balalaika to Russian emigres populating the north-eastern USA.

"So why the train trip?" I ask him. Vodka, the Great Russian Lubricant has made us warm friends and fuels my curiosity for more information.

"Well, the Russian government knows artifacts are being sold." he explains. "Rather than provide better pay and living conditions, remove the oppression of control, and reduce the problem, their focus is on prevention by detection. This makes flights to the U.S. and Europe a trickier prospect.

Look around though. Nobody pays the slightest attention to the Mongolian train. There is no coalition nor coordination with the Mongolian and Chinese authorities, so I return to the West by heading to the East.

A healthy profit after auction more than makes up for the time, travel, and trouble."

Boston John makes more than one trip a year, erratically and often by request. He has created his own network of customers and handles his own supply chain logistics. Low frequency, high margin operations underpin the ethos of his business.

Like the lady doctor, Boston John has found a way to earn a living beyond societal constraints and the "culture of no," preferring to explore the grey areas of possibility. He is a smuggler exploiting Russians, stripping down their cultural heritage. In my world of conflicted values and broken institutions, I admire this kind of pioneering entrepreneurialism. The opportunity, adventure, and breaking with traditions give me hope for my own cause. It feels like a lifetime has been lived in the two days since leaving Helsinki. My head is spinning with the impact of experience, the frailty of civilization, and the vastness of Russia's elastic landscape. In the long hours between station stops I push out record numbers of dips between the bunks in my cabin. Physical exercise is my base and the confinement of carriages leaves me alone with my own thoughts for too long. I need to fatigue myself somehow. Otherwise, I eat nuts, drink tea, and enjoy the vegetable purchases from the wrinkled babushkas. Black tea gets boring and bitter so I drink it Russian style when jam is available. Other times, adding vodka blunts the sharp edge of the tannins. Reading and long walks up and down the carriages add a variety which I learned on long sea crossings.

It would be too easy to drink vodka from dusk 'til' dawn then sleep through the day.

Bubble and Squeak, the Australians, do that.

Their infectious energy, however, leads to spontaneous vodka parties and card games. Cards, like food and language are a gateway to culture. Sometimes you can learn more about a people over a few hands of cards than through months of study and conversation.

In the card parties, everyone shares. The Dutch have peanut butter as their luxury, which they eat with celery sticks. The Swedes, when they show up, bring more vodka - Absolut of course, from Sweden. The Australians have purloined bottles of Seven Up from somewhere to mix cheap fizzy cocktails. The Mongolian traders and the serious smugglers stay away. Boundaries are set; we share cabins for our noisy games; we close out at the start of rowdy behaviour; whoever calls time first is respected. Card games and drinking are stopped before any bad life choices are made. This is home to all of us and community respect is a guiding moral code. The Samovars work incessantly, and I am fascinated at how these are a cornerstone of life here. Boiling water is a luxury to treasure, unheard of back home where wastage and convenience are facts of life. Fundamentally the samovar is a life saver which not only hydrates but keeps at bay infection and disease. Fixated, I visit the samovar multiple times a day, give thanks to hot clean water, and try to work out the mechanics without considering too deeply where the water comes from in the first place.

By comparison, I visit the bathroom once a day out of necessity rather than desire. The caustic industrial cleaning product burns my eyes, throat, and skin. Following the predilection of others, I squat precariously on the toilet seat to achieve number two. Number one pit stops are easy, standing up in a rolling train. Number two pit stops are a stretch goal. Timing is essential and it is wise not to eat anything unfamiliar or be in any state of emergency when it is time to visit the bathroom. Poop planning is essential. Pants down, you are faced with hopping backwards up onto the toilet seat or, failing that, pants off climbing up and executing a one-hundred-and-eighty-degree turn. Which presents its own issues.

What do I hold on to?

Can I put my pants down anywhere?

Will the chlorine product burn a hole in the material?

Am I going to die in a freak toilet accident?

I wonder if anyone has touched skin to toilet seat and who might be wandering the train with chlorine burns on their arse cheeks. Perched now on the edge of sanity, gripping with toes through the thick soles of my boots, one must lean into the movement. Reaching out towards the bulkhead for stability, you hope the train holds steady long enough to finish. Pointing down into the dark abyss of the train toilet any tremor will result in undesired outcomes: connecting with the seat mid ablution, dropping partially into the abyss, or worse flying forward and bouncing your brain against the steel bulkhead. A toilet-based concussion risk. The struggle is real in this Hobson's choice of options where a loss of dignity is the only real outcome. Once a day, I bounce around the bathroom, mitigating damage and finally, upright, reclothed with a re-rendering of dignity, I return to normal. Within the moral code of community respect, nobody speaks to their bathroom adventures and thus I remain ignorant to any useful suggestions. As I shuffle back to my cabin, I empathize with the women folk who get no reprieve. Number one and number two pit stops are all conducted sitting down. Or maybe it's an ensemble movement. As the samovar heaves into view, the luxury of boiled water for washing overtakes the curiosity to explore this subject any further and, with a sigh of relief, the bathroom reprieve resets for one more day.

When nighttime comes, the bunk is comfortable, even without bedding. On the upper tier there is a semblance of privacy; it is a quiet place to read, a safe place to sleep, and warm in the summer heat. Nightmares come after dark, always the same themes: violence, forced removal of liberty, and the narcissistic behaviours of authority. The

Russian border guards were a shocking experience. They are not alone. People like this exist everywhere. Ideological rule followers with one or two degrees of power, leveraging their authority to bring righteous pain. Stories from the OG and the OP spice up the dreams. Their experiences overlay my own and in the maelstrom of corruption and violent justice, I wake up sweating, sometimes shouting. On one occasion, in the half-light, I see uniformed dark shapes enter our cabin. In the morning, shamed by my fear we have been joined by a Mongolian family. The father, in uniform, is a train policeman, with his wife and two small children.

They are kind. Friendly too, they share tea and bread. Steff plays liaison officer. The policeman has the unenviable task of managing law and order on the train. The role is for show, the train is ordered, and the traders are the rule of law. Unlike his Russian counterparts, he carries no armaments and bears no menace. Their presence in our cabin breaks the monotony and in return for tea and bread, we share stories from other worlds. Entertaining the children we teach them words in English and German. Much to their amusement they practice words out loud, clumsy in pronunciation yet enthusiastic in their execution. The family are gentle, and we bond quickly, sharing a small space and ironically a simple sense of security.

A large ewe bursts through the crowd of traders. She is shoved unceremoniously aboard the carriage by two men. Like house movers shifting a great woolly piano, she is manipulated to the top of the stairs and suddenly gone. It is the middle of the day on the platform of a random stop. Behind the crowds the concrete town is visible. Lenin stands proudly on his podium, one arm outstretched, open palm facing up, the other hand clutching his coat lapel. Looking down upon the people he must be proud of the advances made by successive Communist leaders. The scars of totalitarian authority are visible all around. The people are poor, the shops are empty, and the buildings are derelict. Under strict autocratic control there is no motivation for improvement; under the watchful gaze of Commissars there is no hope for betterment. For the people, by the people has been reduced to absolute obedience.

The station population is ambivalent to authority.

The foreign enclave is absent in this moment as the ewe busts out of the crowd. Is the vodka in my bloodstream playing tricks on my mind? Heading inside I discover the beast penned in her new home, a coupling gangway between carriages. Unaffected by the ascent she chews on a bag of fodder that has been laid down considerately. Descending again, I return to the platform for the final moments of trading, ever enthralled by the hustle of the market. My companions return to the carriage in their pairs. Amused by my shaggy sheep story I show them the pen. The sheep has gone. A trick of the train they say. A vodka vision they say. A mere blague they cajole. For there is no ewe, no bleating, no chewing, no wool, no fodder. The gangway pen is void of sheep. My companions disperse along with my credibility and the mystery of the disappearing animal occupies my mind. Out here in the Russian wilderness, where daily markets and walks in the corridor are the peaks of excitement, this vanishing act is a big deal and a great distraction.

The smugglers are masters at making their profitable products disappear. Stashed in ceiling cavities, behind wall panels, under bunks and beneath floorboards, the evidence of trade can be swiftly hidden within concealed cabin spaces. But a fully grown sheep? That's admirable and a different level of magic. With the barriers of language and the invisibility of evidence my investigation is quickly scuppered.

Some hours later as we consider our basic rations, a strange aroma permeates the compartment. Meat is in the air. Cooked meat. I have not eaten meat for days. Maybe weeks. Finland was perhaps the last place I enjoyed sausage or perhaps London. Memory fails me on this subject as the world of supermarkets seems so long ago. Meat is scarce here in Russia's backwater. Supermarkets are rarer still, non-existent in fact. Walking the passageways I can see that Mongolian families are enjoying a feast. My stomach rumbles as spirit burners in each cabin bubble with their own stash of herbs and spices. Mongolian casserole thick with gravy, carrots, onions, and turnips bubbles away throughout the train. My stomach groans louder. Several days of nuts, tea, vegetables, and vodka pales alongside some meat stew. The shiny happy faces of the small groups of diners increases my sense of yearning edged with envy. Returning to my own cabin the policeman and his family are breaking bread with the neighbours having a wail of a time. Steff sits with them, greasy and shiny. Realization dawns. The community at large is eating the ewe, collectively involved in mutton murder. Aroma, gravy, meat, and casserole are everywhere.

But how?

Is it really the same animal?

In a few short minutes a fully grown sheep disappeared without a trace. No blood, no fleece, no bones. Nothing. And yet, the evidence is cooking up all around us. There is no room to sit down in the cramped confines and without room at the inn I forgo the opportunity to join in the meat fest. Moving up the carriage, I join Boston John to hear more stories of artifact smuggling. He has whiskey, the Irish variety, and we sit comfortably in his room for four where he speaks, and I listen.

Like the OG and the OP, he educates me on the real world and as I lap up the knowledge the Russian hinterland rolls by. The vast wilderness hides gulags where the final curtain falls on staged-managed vanishing acts and the disappearance of State labelled dissidents and then ne'er-do-wells of society. The Kolyma Highway is out here too. A mud and dirt road only accessible in warmer months it was built by prison labourers from the harshest gulags. They worked with hand tools, were shot for lack of enterprise, and regularly frozen in minus 50-degree temperatures. The road is cold in many senses. If John is caught smuggling, I wonder at his penalty. Will he serve time in the gulag? It does not appear to cross his mind. Autocracy might be absolute but apparently there are loopholes in the system. John and everyone else on this train are evidence of that.

The Kolyma highway spans 2,000 kilometres from Yakutsk to Magadan, like a scar in the terrain, it represents two decades of brutality. Constructed between 1932 and 1953, it is a constant reminder of the reach of the power of ideological forces. At a cost of one death per metre hundreds of thousands of bodies are buried out here beneath the "Road of Bones". With a shudder I contemplate the prospect of incarceration for simply diverse thinking or for just being challenging. I return to the whiskey, and Boston John's stories. In the adjacent cabins hardy, colourful, and enjoyably entertaining Mongolians dine together. Themselves the meat in the sandwich of Chinese and

Russian Communism, they are a nomadic warrior nation, almost unstoppable in carving the largest land empire in the world. In the context of cold Russian history, the train feels warm and being amongst Mongolians seems the safest place in the world. It must be day three now, or perhaps day four but time flows like treacle. There is no beginning or end to the long hours. There is just the cycle of life from sunrise to sunset as we cross the Volga, the Urals, the Steppes, and the Arctic plains. Mere titles for the limitless geography of river, mountain, grassland and wasteland. Out through the picture window, the hypnotic green and brown landscape melts beyond the horizon into the sky. Russia is continuous. The scars of Russian history are endless.

Then a shining bright blue jewel crashes through the window.

Green, brown, and yellow ochre is gone in an instant as a blue rift in the landscape crowned by mountains enters the scene. Lake Baikal heaves into view. Surrounded by elevations up to 2,000 metres high, the oldest lake in existence brings a wave of excitement through the train. Lake Baikal is vast, breaks the monotony of the Russian landscape, and is a basin for one fifth of the Earth's freshwater. Like prisoners given a yard break we are allowed 15 minutes to hustle down to the shore and return before the train rolls on. I have not touched or tasted freshwater for days and on edge it is not clear what to do. Drink, bathe, pee, make tea? The magnificent expanse of water is intimidating and inspiring under the tick tock of a counting clock. Cold to touch the fresh water invigorates the senses, creates a desire to swim, and seems like a magical apparition in the land locked state. Symbolic bathing seems the best option and, squinting at blue reflected sunlight, I splash water on my face and hands, reveling in the cool and fresh feeling. The slow shuffle back to the carriage is a marvel of sensation. Not knowing when we will next experience freshwater, I marvel at the luxury of something taken for granted back in the Western hemisphere.

The train whistle sounds. She is ready to roll again. Southbound now as we take a right turn for our next destination.

Ulan Bataar, Mongolia's capital city by the Tuul River on a windswept plateau.

THE MONGOLIAN STEPPE

The perpetual landscape of the steppe outside Ulan Bataar rolls to the horizon. At all points of the compass the land meets the sky as far as the eye can see. I squat with our host, beside his Mongolian Ger, the round tent dwelling home to his family. Supported by two poles in the middle, and a wooden crown with spokes sloping gently under the roof, this Mongolian family home comprises an ageing nomad, his spouse, and two other generations. Their son, his spouse and a grandchild live here too.

The old man and Steff speak quietly in Russian.

He is wealthy with a large flock of sheep, a less large herd of horses, some foals, and a handful of dogs. The ger is warm inside. Colourful woven rugs are laid over large wooden cases; divan beds elevated off the hardened earth ground are further testimony to his wealth. His face is boyish and has a mischievous look. His mannerisms remind me of the train traders. "Ger man" is generous and offers us victuals. Airag, a horse milk fermented in a large vat, is passed around. A good guest, Steff accepts. The vat is a fifty-gallon drum with a sealed lid. A plastic eyesore in the tapestried interior of the ger. It is opened at regular intervals and stirred to promote further fermentation. Curds resting on top of the liquid, are scooped out and served as a snack.

Ger man and his son could be any age. Walnut brown weather-beaten skin on lean muscular bodies, they drink airag in half litre vessels. Steff passes me the drinking vessel. The flavours are alien and acid. Following suit, I take a mouthful and, under the watchful gaze of our hosts, try not to gag. The liquid is vile. Water is rare out here and casting back to Lake Baikal more than forty-eight hours ago, I realize water is the most precious of commodities. Airag appears to be the main source of hydration.

Drink it I must.

Externally calm, the struggle inside is real as the bitter liquid and curds grumble down my gullet. Food and drink are scarce in the nomad's world. Breaking bread together is a ritual to be respected. We are preparing to ride across country and negotiate prices for their horses. They are tethered horses and the wooden saddles on the ground adjacent suggest this will be a tough ride. The horses twitch their ears and sniff the air. Our odour is alien. The son stands and dresses the horse. Wooden saddle with short stirrups are designed for standing which he illustrates with ease. "Ger son" will be our guide and only sits down when the horse stands still. The resilience of the Mongolian people is clear. We have learned that they are friendly and out here on the steppe they are generous with their belongings.

Other than Steff there are two Germans around. Out of earshot and aloof, Steff nevertheless made friends with them while back in town and they join us on this expedition. Their clothes are well-made and their soft skin reflecting a comfortable life. From West Berlin they are on a romantic adventure and have flown in from Beijing. Younger than me they are a different breed to Steff whose language skills have helped us navigate some tight situations.

Somewhere north of here, beyond the horizon is the Russia – Mongolia border.

It was there that our train decelerated into a large hangar and local engineers replaced the undercarriage. An amazing marvel of mechanical mystery as the wheels, suspension, and supporting structures are all replaced. Hoisted into the air to be recalibrated for a new gauge of railway we waited for several hours as the old diesel monster was refueled and refitted. Our traveling companions were also transformed. Mongolian smugglers, laden with cash, have reduced their stock to negligible levels and hidden their profits. Disembarking the train, the now honest traders file in to pay their dues at the Customs house.

As the engineers work the train, the value of goods and services are debated and determined. For five days the smugglers made bank on the railway. For five hours the traders are humble in the customs house, reporting meagre earnings. Over tea and talk they reduce facilitation payments to acceptable sums and distribute happiness among the border guards. Like their Russian counterparts, the Mongolian uniforms are blue with big hats. Unlike the Russians guns and threats are not part of the theatre. Communications are civil, paper money is folded and traded for paper passes. An extracted process perhaps but over the full five-hour window agreements seem to satisfy all parties. The lady doctor and Boston John make their pledges too, and the last we see of them is in the capital city where success is within their grasp.

In this train shed I learn that we are not the only ones distrusting of the Russians. Steff enlightens me on Sino – Russian relations. Over time, Chairman Mao the primary benefactor of Russian aid to China, became wary of Moscow's intentions and paranoid about an invasion. A red-on-red conflict was the stuff of nightmares. Thousands of Russian troops aboard long trains like ours, rolling over the borders in a massive land grab, kept the Chinese Communists awake at night. Claiming territory in Tibet and India in the west, China was also sensitive to Russian intentions along the northern border. At the time, with the Russian superpower challenging the might of America, influencing Cuba, despoiling African nations, and courting South American dictators, as well as warring in Afghanistan, Mao had justifiable concerns and a short memory of who sponsored his rise to power.

The paranoia of cult leaders is the poison in their power. It drip feeds through the Party system and before long the human condition reacted and relationships cooled. When former lovers argue one side will inevitably take back the keys to the house and deny favours to the other party. China under Mao, in a final symbolic gesture of humanity over ideology, changed the national railway gauge system, simultaneously creating thousands of jobs for The People and locking out their former paramour.

In the world of cults, the power of paranoia is far reaching.

And what of the Mongolians?

Landlocked between the colliding Communists, the Mongolians architects of the largest ever land empire preserve their centuries old history and culture. Quietly shouldering the schizophrenic relationship of their two complex neighbours they go about their own business. As a thousand decades of ethnic evolution bubble away on the Steppe the only common ties between new world ideologies of Russian and Chinese communism are bloody revolution and ethnic cleansing.

Stoically managing the rise and fall of Empires, the Mongolians endure and remain a cultural constant.

The train is ready as Steff's story ends and on new wheels we cross the border. In a short time we reach the concrete urbanity of Ulan Bataar. The city is unique. A Soviet style affair where wild dogs roam and utility-mains pipes are located above ground. The image is dystopian. A statue of Genghis Khan stands proud in stony silence on the central city plaza. Despite his achievements on the global scale, unlike Lenin there is only one statue of Khan, which seems to reinforce his significance. Adjacent to the square we find a simple hotel and discover Mongolian BBQ, which trendsetters are yet to bring to Western cities. The food is fresh and delicious, stark contrast to the buffet car on the old diesel monster and affords some yearned for nutrients and vitamins.

Concrete apartment blocks with ceramic tiles line the streets and add to the dystopian feel. Our television broadcasts The Simpsons in dubbed Russian baritone. One dull voice for all characters is a real lack of effort and the defining quality of State controlled influences. Seeking new adventure, Steff discovers an advert for a tourist trip. And soon our white van bumps out onto the grasslands of the Steppe. Sceptical of our soft friends, I am not keen on the Berliners. Steff however seeks their companionship and so it is that the four of us find ourselves in the Mongolian outback.

The space is overwhelming.

The silence is deafening.

The anticipation is electric.

OUTBACK

Ger man and his son shush and soothe the horses. The beasts are beautiful, mildly skittish, and unnerved by trace scents of London, Berlin, Moscow, and Helsinki. A lover of animals and all things in the natural world, I approach my horse slowly. This is his world not mine and being careful not to spook him, I stirrup step up onto the wooden saddle. "Horse" for that is what I name him remains still. Testing for splinters with arse cheeks, the wood is hard but smooth.

Ger son adjust his stirrups and reins then stands up. I imitate his actions. The Berliners have opted for blankets on their saddles. A palliative solution to discomfort. I cannot see how that changes the density of wood.

That said, this is a simple tourist ride. It is uneventful fun for us and a profitable exercise for our hosts. A bit of faux comfort keeps the customers happy.

What could possibly go wrong?

Long limbed Ger son is tall. At ease in the saddle, he has spent hundreds of hours since birth riding and rounding up. Refusing the blanket I mimic his style. I have ridden horses a handful of times, mostly during summer vacations with family. What I lack in skills I make up for in strength and balance. Physical exercise has been my constant and, despite rugby bulking, I have worked hard to stay lean and supple. Yoga and aikido and some gymnastics mean I can flip forward, roll backwards, as well as run, swim, jump, and climb. I may not be a natural horseman like Ger son, but I have empathy with animals and can balance well on the Mongolian steed. After days on the train, thigh muscles will burn but this is small discomfort compared to a solid wooden saddle.

We head out across a pockmarked landscape home to many marmots. Large, furry, and fat, they are inedible. Rabies is at home here on the range. Roaming freely, the marmots dig openings that are invisible at full speed. The horses know their business exploring at a steady pace. Walking, sometimes cantering, never galloping, we move away from the sanctity of our ger which disappears under the endless sky. Caring little for direction, thigh muscles burning, I have full faith in my trusty steed. A leap of faith perhaps but no greater risk than a train crossing Russia, nor a carriage full of smugglers.

The grasslands are empty of all civilization. No farms, no stores, no roads. No bushes, no water, no trees. Industry is absent and the nomadic life is preserved. Airag and curds are supplemented by root vegetables and infrequent mutton. Growing seasons are limited. Hardiness is essential. Winters are deadly. Nothing survives temperatures that plummet to forty degrees below freezing.

Two hours out from base, there are no waypoints here. Navigation is celestial as there is nothing to fix on. The sun determines our situation which informs us of our total reliance on horse GPS and Ger son's sense of direction. Our ger could be anywhere. The Berliners are whining a bit, butt hurt I suspect, and missing frothy coffees. This is a tough environment, the toughest. Whining changes nothing, nor will it make you feel better. In fact, it is irritating, and I stay out of range for anger prevention. Steff is stoic. A bespectacled scarecrow astride his beast, his horse is driving the rider. Mine too probably, but I like to believe I am holding the reins. Respecting Steff's resilience I say nothing. He is totally trustworthy, brave in an understated way. Not one to escalate issues, he uses intellect to solve problems. Equally curious he uses conversation to create relations. We are a long way from any civilization, and I learn from his methods.

Rabbit camouflage has benefits.

Quiet stillness removes tension.

That said his latest decision is special. This is no tourist trap with fixed gers on a concrete base and comfortable beds. Or tame ponies for short horse rides next door. We are in a dude ranch on steroids. The Wild East is the harshest of landscapes, where rabid animals thrive, and life is capricious.

The skin on my thighs rubs raw. My jeans afford little protection against the movement of the saddle. Even standing up I cannot escape the ever-present wooden seat. Stubbornly shutting out the pain, I close on the others. Someone shouted and the horses are still. Ears twitching, bowing their heads they grab at tufts of grass. The Berliners look uncomfortable. Horse bound for more than two hours I am guessing even the padded saddles are hurting. Steff turns to me and explains. Ger son heard dogs barking. There is nothing all the way out to the horizon yet Ger son points towards the emptiness. At the edge of vision squats a lonely white shape almost invisible at long range, a homestead like our own.

A howl goes up.

That can't be good.

With a tail wind our scents have carried. The alien odours have reached another territory long before we have even noticed the small refuge. Shielding my eyes, dialing into the distance, I see no horses, goats, or signs of life. This is not a happy hood. It is a poorer and wilder existence.

Another howl goes up.

From this distance it is hard to see the condition of the dwelling but, with no assets on display I am sure it is less than comfortable. The dogs now are barking up a storm, I hear them snarling their warnings. Horse is blowing, his ears are twitching, catching the noises and trying to sense the direction. These animals are survivors, semi-wild themselves, they know the terrain and the behaviours of other beasts. They are nothing like the stallions as seen on T.V. Unpolished, they are trained for wild living not for jumping at the gymkhana. Thank goodness the dogs are tied up.

Or are they?

Leaning into the scene, the dogs look bigger. An optical illusion maybe.

Scanning the ground there are dust clouds around their feet.

I look around. Ger son has turned his horse and is moving away. Steff and the Berliners are following suit.

Time to go then.

The dogs are bigger and getting closer. Closing the gap between us and their homestead, their intent is clear and loud. We are intruders, or food, or both. They are moving fast, roughly the speed of sound. Not good. These are not fluffy Doodles or angry Alsatians; the beasts are bear size hooligans protecting their territory from allcomers.

We are allcomers.

Alien life forms that smell funny. They are angry at our trespass.

Horse is skittish, and I turn him around wondering what to do next.

"Run like the wind my friend" I tell Horse. No further encouragement is required and revving up the Horsepower, finally showing who was always in charge. Pulling his body around we accelerate towards the horizon. In the distance, Ger son rides his steed with balance and poise. Standing more than six feet tall, he is a bit shorter than me. Leaner too. I can probably achieve balance, poise on the other hand is out of my league. Ignoring the pain of raw flesh on wood I squat over the saddle, lean forward, and settle into the rhythm of momentum.

Every ounce of focus is dedicated to balance. Pitching and rolling we make good ground.

Ger son is out front. Steff is close behind him followed by the Berliners who, already in pain, are audibly sobbing. My thighs are burning, gripping the saddle, as Horse finds his head. Bringing up the rear there is no room for heroics, just speed and hope. Horse is no Porsche; built for comfort not for speed he is also a frightened animal being chased by angry beasts. Fear fuels flight as the big black bear sized fur balls close the gap. The sweat on my back feels cold. The sweat from Horse heats my front. The lather on his back an illustration of effort.

Horse is carrying the heaviest load, and it crosses my mind that his chances of survival improve if he throws me off; wondering if it has crossed his mind, I whisper admiration and friendly homilies. Horse speaks Mongolian, in English I offer him an endless supply of carrots. One of us is faking. Horse stays the course.

Glancing back, Winnie and Paddington, for that is what I named the bear shaped dogs, are closing the gap. They are huge. Teeth dripping slobber from gaping jaws, they are seriously mad. Like toddlers woken from a nap, they ooze fierce intensity. I think about rabies. Back in London the jabs are expensive, multiple, with no guarantee of success. Like the epi pens we were given in Bio Chem warfare training, they may or may not work. You only know after the fact.

Come on Horse.

Marmot holes pockmark the landscape, yet Horse keeps building a head of steam. We may not be walking but moments of galloping are interspersed with canter. One trip means end of life for Horse, so speed is undulating. The tempo is stressful.

Winnie and Paddington, close enough for their breathing and snarls to be audible, are a single leap and bite away from Horse's rump. Weirdly I think about the law of diminishing returns. At some point the energy investment must return some profit. That would be safety. Or, we reach a critical point, where the juice is no longer worth the squeeze. The opposite of safety.

Am I going to die? It's possible.

With the odds stacked against us, possible arguably becomes probable.

Horse's energy is directed and focused. Heading home is his safe space. A bit of divine intervention would expedite that. Lack of divine intervention and we are faced with burnout, trip hazards, or death by Paddington Bear and Winnie the Pooh. That's no laughing matter. The odds are long. Longer still if we go down, a fist fight with the two bear dogs will not end well. With no stick, crop, or similar object for defense, this will get bloody fast.

Winnie and Paddington have stopped growling. That can't be good. I can hear the beat of their massive paws drum alongside Horse's hooves. They are close enough to lunge. Biding their time, they will leap any moment now.

My own leap is one of faith. Balanced and low I whisper:

"Stay the course, Horse! You got this."

Left-handed, I hold the reins loose in that fist. Not sure what to do with my right hand I grip the wood of the saddle crushing my fingers as we pitch and roll. This is not dressage. This is survival National Geographic style. Adrenaline pumping, the rush makes me smile, for out here on the edge of death I feel totally alive. The humdrum of London life is forgotten as these animals compete for dominance here in the Wild East.

We are closing the gap on the Berliners. With a lower pain threshold, they are moving slow, holding tightly to their reins and faux security. Winnie and Paddington are hot. Horse is hot. My thighs are burning as muscles scream and flesh chafes. Ger son and Steff are half a kilometre ahead, one lap of the track, maybe less. Ger son for sure will have a knife, maybe a whip. That said he shows no sign of stopping.

"Come on Horse"

The distance narrows and the devil on my shoulder whispers "Widen the angle, open up the Berliners, give the dogs some choices."

Tempting. Winnie and Paddington would love a slower target.

The angel on the other shoulder is indignant. "Unnecessary movements will bring down Horse" she tuts. "Have faith" she says, for that is all she can offer.

The Berliners are stupid. They split away from the group, oblivious to the wisdom of staying with the pack. Does being stupid merit pain? I don't think so, nobody has the monopoly on stupidity. Leaning in, we make a final push for Ger son, a native warrior of this land. Gut instinct tells me he has some trick up his sleeve. Mad dogs are surely in his wheelhouse.

As the cocktails of adrenaline and fear narrow our field of view Horse continues the flight over scarred terrain, peaking against all wisdom, on an upward curve towards the speed of sound...

... in a race for or,

...well, that is it really. Race or fight. Ugh! This is stressful.

Horse's hooves are his best weapon. I hope he's a street fighter. I have nothing, just feet and fists.

And here it comes.

The cliff edge at the apex of diminishing returns is rolling in.

In the final furlong, Ger son and Steff watch the chase. The Berliners are out there somewhere, no longer a problem.

Winnie and Paddington are at the edge of my vision. Neck and neck. Racing for first blood. Heat, sweat, slobber, teeth, and jaws. Sweat streams, eyes are mean. They are apex predators.

This is it.

Clarity is simplicity.

Race or die.

Horse brain and human brain in synch, firing straight and true, like an arrow. Any action, no matter how micro, will topple us to the turf.

Winnie and Paddington split to outflank us. Their speed is final, their judgement is the tension as muscles trigger, ready to leap.

Skin is tingling, heart racing, smiling like an idiot I know action is imminent.

Micro fractions of movement will spin us out of control.

Fate will play her hand.

Nature will decide the outcome.

Three, two, one. . .

Bam!

We break the sound barrier; the collapse of noise is clear; the sound of the silence is deafening. Freedom is fleeting. As we float, or fall, or fly, bracing for impact. . .

Which hits hard.

In the absence of attack.

Winnie the Pooh and Paddington Bear are gone.

Out of sight, out of hearing . . . gone. I dare not look. Horse closes the remaining metres and crosses the finish line. Pulling up alongside Ger son, he drops his head, as tension leaves his body. His flanks are heaving, breathing is slowing, and Horse nuzzles his companion for comfort. I want to climb down but wood burned thighs stuck to jeans and an explosion of lactic acid mean I will never get off nor back on to the horse.

Looking back, I survey the terrain.

Snapped back by invisible reins Winnie and Paddington stopped dead in their tracks. They are circling at the edge of an invisible fence. Pacing, growling and glaring along the inside of an indiscernible boundary. Ger son knows. Mischief sparkles in his eyes, and a smile creases his face. Many meters out beyond the boundary he sits astride his own horse in relative comfort. The race beyond the border was critical to success. Out beyond where the dogs have no jurisdiction. The wind that carried our scent across the grasslands also carries the trails of their territory. Winnie and Paddington knew we were coming long before we saw them. Leading by example, and with no time for explanation, he rode out to safety, Steff following. The Berliners, lucky in their choices, crossed over the boundary at a different place. Leaving me, the heaviest burden, to bring up the rear.

My legs are keening. Raw flesh inside my jeans, stinging me like a swarm of angry bees, getting worse as the adrenaline subsides. Under the watchful gaze of our Mongolian host, I smile then grin like a champion climbing up to the podium. Pain will come later. For now, the respect of the warrior nomad is the real medal of honour.

I like his mischief and feel a bond of kinship.

There is no room here for fakes. Mongolians are the real deal. Authentic adventurers, they are also courageous warriors and survivors.

Fussing Horse, who munches some grass, I stroke his muzzle and thank him for his courage. Standing up in the stirrups, we head slowly back home where Ger son regales his family with stories of our experience. Our hosts are gracious folk and that night we are wrapped in the warm embrace of their home. The old man and his spouse overnight with Ger son and his family a few hundred meters away. They are totally trusting, leaving us alone with their precious belongings. Heavy, loom woven rugs, handmade wooden furniture, and a clock lend a cozy comfort to the close confines of the ger. It is hot inside. We talk. Steff, face flushed, speaks with his country folk who are less stoic. They did not relish the thrill of the chase and as they decompress, Steff shoulders their burden. They are here on a romantic escapade; this is more than they bargained for. More than any of us expected to be fair. Steff gives them a good listening to. I respect his patience. Never complain, never explain is more my style so I judge them. Harshly perhaps but lived experience means my soft centre is hidden by a hard shell. As the Berliners chatter, and the heat rises, I head outside.

Prone under the vast ocean of sky, the stars are winking down. Horse is back with family munching grass and nuzzling his loved ones. They talk gently, whinnying and puffing in Mongolian horse speak. The noise is soothing. The glimmering constellations above challenge me to remember their names and shapes. Here in Nature's embrace peace and freedom arrive as pain and weakness leave the body. Sinking further into the stars, existence fades away and fatigue turns slowly into slumber.

Morning comes too soon. Waking with the dawn, horses and sheep meander through the grasses close by. Ger family's own dogs patrol their terrain. Sometimes running, sometimes playing other times just lying in surveillance of the land, sniffing the air. There is no breakfast. I have no stomach for bitter curds and sip a large bowl of airag for forced hydration. Today is a day of feasting and there is anticipation in the air, for the family will slaughter a sheep, a significant honour and we will dine together one last time. Animals are assets and critical to survival out here. The honour is real. Thinking back to yesterday I recall that Winnie and Paddington protected no livestock, just a homestead. Whoever lived there had a tough existence. The grasslands are mean. Steff translates the Ger family intentions as we watch the old man wander through the flock. With a noose on a long stick, we are witnesses to the reality of "farm to table."

Knowing what is around the corner, it is hard to tell who shows the most fear, the Berliners or the sheep. I have no real desire to witness death, nor can I turn away as this feels like an insult to Mongolian life. Steff observes with academic interest. The Berliners mutter. The boy pukes, the girl hides her face in his jacket as the noose finds a target and a woolly bundle is pulled from the flock, flipped over and stunned. Silent anticipation fills the air, as if all the animals around know the end of life is near, even the dogs have trotted in from the edge of territory. Ger son keeps them at a distance, with tongues lolling and tails wagging, they are excitable.

A blade appears in the older man's hand, slides under the fleece, and slits open the sheep's stomach. Reaching inside he tugs at the heart valve and blood pumps out, into the stomach cavity. The sheep fades away. No noise, no fuss, no mess. There is no blood either, the whole area is clean. Business concluded in a matter of minutes and the carcass is ready for the pot within another half lap of the clock. And, in that moment, the train riddle is solved.

Shocked at the speed of execution I make a vow to never upset a Mongolian with a knife. Bonding with the mischief is one thing, their brutal efficiency in killing another matter entirely. The dogs are bounding with excitement for now there is the very real prospect of a feast that includes them. The sheep's head is tossed in their direction. Excess blood, red gravy, is poured into a bucket for them to drink. Feast day has something for everyone.

Glancing away the remaining sheep are back at work, meandering through the grass chewing contentedly as they survive another day. Life is short for these animals. It is likely most of them will be slaughtered before winter. Sold or turned into food for the harsh months below freezing. What happens to the horses? They pay no heed and I presume are treasured beasts, safe from the prospect of execution. Turning back, all evidence of execution is gone, and the old woman and her daughter-in-law are already cooking. A fire was laid swiftly, and the aroma of mutton awakens my senses for the second time in a few days. A stew cooked with carrots and onions grown in a land that can yield only root vegetables. As for the base stock. I decide not to ask. Water appears unavailable and the only alternatives are blood, airag, and the juices from the meat.

We eat al fresco; the stew is amazing, and I am keen to eat beyond what is polite. Steff interprets all conversations. Enjoying the quieter non-verbal cues, eating slowly yet methodically, fantastic flavours trickle down into my stomach. Mild starvation is like fasting it heightens your senses, prolonged fasting of any kind increases taste sensations. In England we consume food without ceremony, here the feast is binding, familial, and a wholly different experience. Even the Berliners seem to have overcome their squeamishness, recognizing the preciousness of food, Steff for once can no longer eat candy and looks wholistically better after a few days without sugar. The love of food and family here reminds me of Italy without the luxury.

Before now, I had never met a Mongolian. It would have been a challenge finding Mongolia on a map. At the end of a long week, we have met smugglers, traders, doctors, nomadic farmers, and athletic warriors. Living and dying with a cultural freedom seemingly denied to others, these humble folks enjoy a proud heritage amid the complexity of relationships with their neighbours. Russians, subjugated by an ideology that brooked no freedoms are poor by comparison. Soon we will discover the state of play in China. A white van appears on the lip of the hill, our driver ready to return us to the railway exchange. Two days outback and these strange people have become family. A family who shared their treasures, home, knowledge, and ability to survive.

I will miss the noble and generous Ger folk.

Back on the train this locomotive is a new monster, a Chinese Dragon. Cleaner than the smugglers' train, it is also colourful and reptilian as it winds it way southeast towards Beijing. More than just standard rolling stock this dragon is a cultural symbol and also a display of local soft power from The Peoples Republic. Dragons demand a fastidious staff. The Chinese workers display a clinical officiousness absent in their Russian counterparts. Impressive as this is it sadly means the colourful sense of mischief enjoyed amongst the Mongolians is also gone. Within twenty-four hours the Russian threat of low-level menace and the Mongolian spirit are fading into history. Disembarking the train at the central Beijing Zhan a crush of people carries us towards exit gates about half a mile away. The oppressiveness of humidity and clouds of dust increase the discomfort. Crushed by the multitude of bodies, slow gradual movements are all we can manage. The distinctive thumbprint of China is a massive heaving population. The footprints of "The People" are an ebb and flow of humanity enduring over centuries the whimsy of Emperors, the cult of Communism, and now the influence of free market economics.

Maybe.

Liberated by the wisdom of Chairman Mao, "The People" have been purged of the landlord classes, re-educated, and repositioned for further struggle.

The avuncular Mao is everywhere.

In portrait form, he is visible on all public buildings looking down upon the masses.

The "Big Uncle" is omnipresent.

And Big Brother is watching you.

The inaugural head of the Chinese Central Communist Party, Russia's longest sustaining cultural export, rigorously pursued absolute power. In absolute imitation of the peoples' hero, Lenin, Big Uncle Mao perpetuated the widespread killing of his own people. Outstripping the efforts of Uncle Joe Stalin, through persecution, prison labour, and mass executions, Big Uncle Mao made a Great Leap Forward. Supplemented by failed economic strategies resulting in famine, he achieved an uncriticized peak of destruction with the death of forty to sixty millions of his own citizen comrades. As though he was made of Teflon all accountability slipped from his shoulders as the cult of personality reigned supreme over the requirements of responsibility.

Escaping the crush of the railway station, Steff and I head to a hostel approved for foreigners, a short taxi ride away. It is here we rediscover our traveling companions, last seen on the smugglers' train, the Swedes once more seize upon the opportunity to be depressing. Speaking of organ harvest in Chinese prisons, executions to order, and prison sentences cut short by the need for kidney, liver, or heart transplants, they deftly suck oxygen out of the room. Between shots of Absolut – which they forget to share – the mood is so heavy that even Bubble and Squeak struggle to be upbeat. Man's inhumanity to other men is hardly a surprise. Death is human. The method of death is cultural. No fan of the death penalty, I have some empathy. Humans are flawed, judiciaries are corrupted, and the arbiters of authority are erratic. To my mind, the execution of a single innocent soul removes all rationale for legislated homicide.

However, the Swedes are too much and with my constant companion Steff in tow, we head into the city.

BEIJING

Originally a trading post of military significance established more than two thousand years ago, Beijing is home and hub for nearly 20 million people. The central railway station, with pagoda towers of yellow ochre stone, sits in the crooked elbow of Ring Road Number Two, the second of five circulatory routes designed to reduce congestion and keep traffic moving like ripples on a pond out and away from the centre.

Beijing is hot.

The sun shines. The air is dusty.

The press of people is exhausting. A sharp contrast to the Eurasian Steppes.

Taxis line up against the kerb stones; they are older generation Volkswagens with caged interiors like American police cars. Yet to achieve the stardom of other international cities, Beijing locals are curious about foreigners. We are watched, observed, and confined to certain quarters and openly discussed. Our hostel is clean and functional, white without character and tiled like a public bathroom. Businessmen with business budgets enjoy well-appointed Sheratons and Hiltons where they are easily surveyed and tracked by the CCCP information gatherers. The contradictions of China are manifest and here in the great capital city a sprinkling of foreign brands illustrate the trickle of western wealth coming into the country. Among the alleyways behind our hostel, we hail a rickshaw which is pedaled west towards Tian'an men Square, up the broad eight laned Chang'an Street, large enough to drive several tanks abreast. Our man steers away from here onto darker cooler side roads.

Lean and muscular, his naked torso glistens with sweat as legs push hard against the pedals, steering through hutong alleys and stone slum dwellings. Old slum homes methodically razed are replaced with modern blocks as gentrification displaces generations of residents who are dispatched to other parts of town. The face of Sino-Communism must be proud, clean, and concrete as Western CAPEX washes into town. The dollar laced whitewash of the city adds a green sheen to the new breed of chattering classes evolving here under the red sun.

Hutong homes, the slum dwellings of The People, open onto the street, offering glimpses of shaded, small, skylit interiors. Running water is not evident and the tenements are jerry rigged to electrical poles. A snake's wedding of cables forms a latticework just above roof height. Reverberating with a rolling "thrum, thrum, thrum", flocks of pigeons fly low over the power lines. The birds regroup and return "en flock", flying low across the lines, creating a continuous loop in a hypnotic cycle of enthralling fly-bys. At ground level local citizens stand in the streets watching our passage. Fully clothed women, half clothed men, and naked babies are the population here. Generations intermingle around food stalls hung with unidentifiable fish and meats, squat on the curb side with bags of sunflower seeds, and smoke cigarettes around card games and cups of green tea.

On a journey of discovery rickshaw man winds and weaves a confusing passage through the hood. Life for the locals looks harsh and the winter months must be tough. In the boroughs of London or the banlieues of Paris, tourists wisely avoid similar areas. Here, we have taken a leap of faith and are easy targets in the open top transport. A few blocks and fifteen minutes later, close to the edge of Tian'an men, the large concrete plaza is surrounded by oblong concrete buildings, architectural monstrosities beloved of the regime. Rickshaw man stops, jumps down and lights a cigarette. Gesturing with his hands, we are at journey's end. Time to pay.

He demands four hundred renminbi – "The Peoples' Currency" – which is ridiculous. Forty euros for twenty minutes work is daylight robbery. Beijing, like London and other major cities, has its own tourist traps. We haggle on price and Rickshaw man gets animated.

Out of the corner of my eye the shadows get thicker. A crowd is gathering to watch the theatre.

We have offered him one hundred, a fair price for fifteen minutes of work, and easily a full day's pay for manual labour over here.

Rickshaw man throws down. He is agitated.

The shadows are thicker still. The mob presses in.

Yet to discover the dangers of a Chinese flash mob, I still sense we will be on the wrong side of history in this context. The crowd grows, the exit from the alley is disappearing in the shadows, and learning from Steff, I adopt rabbit camouflage. Still and alert I watch him continue negotiating unaware of trouble. Entry to this club was easy, getting out comes at a price. Steff is not wealthy, neither am I for that matter, and he is doubling down on the price. The atmosphere is thick with tension, and I whisper to him. Raising to two hundred, the release is noticeable. Rickshaw man is not finished yet and continues his tirade. The heat has dissipated though, and the alleyway exit may have opened. Two fifty brings us over halfway and puffing his next cigarette, rickshaw man eyes us both. His volume has dropped significantly, the shadows of the crowd have thinned, and it seems we have landed on a fair price. Rickshaw man grabs the cash. A few seconds later we walk into the sunshine bathing Tian'an men Square.

Gazing around the square I wonder if Rickshaw man works alone or how many of the crowd were paid agitators. The vastness of our location cuts off that thinking. On the south side, Qian Men – the front gate – is a Qing dynasty arch offering shade from the sun. Flanked on east and west by the National Museum of China and the Great Hall of the People, The Big Uncle Mao is preserved like Lenin for the world to revere; centre stage in this hundred-acre concrete flatland The Chairman, resides in his own mausoleum. Cornered by stone statues of muscular liberated workers reaching for the stars, hammers aloft in heroic praise to the cult figure, the reverence is real.

North of the mausoleum, several football fields away, stands the Monument to The People's Heroes. A large stone erection, higher than a house, with gold leaf poetry inscribed vertically down its column.

The monument is a classic symbol of the potency of struggle. Serving also as a navigation marker for anyone lost at sea in the crowd, the monument stands tall above "The People" who are all here. They form a tidal sea of flying kites, walking bodies, reading students, and sometimes paired ballroom dancers. The People are together but very obviously not assembling for any amount of time.

Gathering is illicit.

On the edge of the square a small troupe of young men appear. Like so many grains of sand they slip through the clenching fist that is the surrounding mob. Brightly clothed and moving like ninjas they drop down a large "ghetto blaster." At the push of a button they break out into choreographed dance. Unlike the flash mobs in the malls of America, nobody joins in. Like those flash mobs, people stare at the scene. I notice some folks edging away from the group. In short order the young men are an isolated island of movement in a fast-retracting sea. Their coloured clothes and lithe routine are individualistic and a sharp contrast to the blue and grey Mao suited citizens all around. As they distance themselves from the dancers, approved activities stop. Kites fall, dance steps cease, reading heads look up.

Creeping tension silences this part of the crowd. Danger is inbound. Melting back, I pull Steff into the mass as a white van hurtles across the concrete plain. Leatherjacketed gorillas leap out of the paneled side doors and muscular men hurl themselves upon the troupe tipping over the dancers. Two on one, they grab limbs, hair, wrists, and hands, dragging the wriggling bodies into the back of the van. The dancers are thrown into darkened recesses until, alone in the wilderness, the sound box stands timid beneath its tunes. The music continues unabated. Solitary testimony to the existence of those young men. The van driver climbs out of his cab, picks up the machine and shuts off the noise. Tossing it into the front of the van, he climbs back in and circles the white van around towards the road. Within a couple of minutes of their arrival, the dancers are gone along with all evidence of their existence.

The human sea closes in, readers heads return to books, kites appear in the sky, and the ballroom steppers slide around walking citizens. Normality has returned. Steff has donned rabbit camouflage. I tug him away, completely shocked at what just happened, unsure in truth about what just happened.

Walking a new trajectory, we say nothing,

think nothing,

and do nothing as we head to a smaller group of tourists.

Closing on them we hear spoken German. Busy with their cameras and offended by the curtailment of freedoms they are witnesses to the same show and are buzzing with indignation. Soft and plump, I guess they are Berliners. Before long, the buzz turns to whine. A new batch of Leatherjacketed gorillas emerge from the crowd and circle their hostages. For the second time in the shortest period we are perfectly still again. Rabbit camouflage deployed, we watch, ready to hop. No sudden movements, invisibility is static. Yet there are clearly watchers in the crowd. This shake down is real as cameras are snatched and memory cards are pulled, pocketed, and stored images are deleted. This is unreal. Protests are immediately silenced as firm, flat hands hold the Berliners at bay. Glancing around I see more leatherjackets moving amongst the Mao suits in the crowd.

How many?

It is hard to tell.

You have to look hard to spot them for the gorillas move silently in the jungle.

Like Moscow, the message is clear. Do not interfere with the business of State.

Steff and I are one clumsy move away from a trip in a white van and maybe our own disappearance. The protests here were many years ago. The reverberations are clearly still felt. Revolution is a bloody business, and the men of State maintain order amongst The People. Tian'an men Square, at the heart of power, is sacred, and expressions of colourful individualism are discouraged; freedom of expression is a distinctly foreign phenomenon. We walk north, away from danger, towards the Forbidden City. The Gate of Heavenly Peace stands in front of the Qing dynasty palace where Big Uncle Mao hangs once more in portrait form. A weird sight if you ask me. People are far from iconic; the human condition is all too frail. The colourful face of evil looks out for eternity over the wide Chang'an avenue and down at

The People enjoying approved activities in the embrace of the Regime.

The Forbidden City survived Communism, preserving a thousand years of history. Sloped tiled rooves, cornered by dragons, fronted by stone lions, and supported by wooden pillars varnished red, the palace stands the tests of time. The interior though feels empty. Free of artifacts, art, and atmosphere, large cobbled empty courtyards are cojoined by cobbled passageways to empty halls. The building is magnificent. The emptiness is indicative. Chinese Communism, like its Russian sibling, is devoid of soul. Spirituality, superstition, and the signposts to history have been removed. Ideology has been replaced by human iconography, Big Uncle Mao here, Stalin and Lenin over there, all in portrait and statue form. Reminders that Big Brother is always watching. In spite of all this I like the Forbidden City. Its survival resonates on a deeper level and I wonder at how folks may have lived here. Large enough to contain hundreds of people, Emperors, their wives and concubines, eunuchs, and administrators would have walked these halls for dynasties lasting hundreds of years.

The air here is sand coloured with a tint of coal, and outside of the Forbidden City we walk down alleys and side roads looking for food. Small restaurants have indecipherable menus with cages outside. Rabbits, snakes, turtles, and frogs are amongst the mournful creatures imprisoned behind the wire. Saddened by their plight we order a vegetarian meal with beer. A large litre bottle of cold Qingdao costs less than a dollar. Two large bottles wash away the dust and smooth out the wrinkles of our arrival in Beijing. Here to study Chinese, Steff and I will part company soon. I am heading on to Qingdao. The world is turning China into a global factory, and for my part I am hoping that learning Mandarin will secure employment and the ever-elusive chance for upward mobility. In England the myth is scuppered by the resistance to downward mobility and stuck on Maslow's bottom rung it appears that overseas opportunities are the key to future choices. Any increase in hope is directly proportional to the distance I am away from home.

Dislocation is real and necessary.

Out here at the edge of the Earth, beyond knowledge and experience, I wonder for the first time how to return. Without mentors, direction, or faith in institutions back home I am lost at sea. Bobbing along in a tide of torment my purpose of education through exploration takes me further and further away from home.

Lost in learning, the confusion is real.

Money counted in hundreds of billions is pouring into China. Dollars, Euros, and Pounds create moulds for Chinese capitalism. The coffers of Communism fill, infrastructure projects start, multiply, and signify the first steps in an arranged marriage of states. Marriages of convenience are complex contortions. The combining of families for the propagation of wealth and the forging of strong alliances is designed to make more wealth and power for those same people. History is littered with such stories; I wonder if there has ever been a time as unique as this one. In these arrangements much will be hidden from the extended clans to make sure the marriage goes ahead. Clashing cultures, irritable ideologies, and strange assignations will be the fodder, and it doesn't take a genius to see that the "lao bai xing", China's working classes, are no more likely to enjoy upward mobility in their society than I am in mine. Somewhere in our collective futures I believe the cost of this collusion will be counted in blood and bullets.

LATER

Clean and rested after a siesta in the hostel we wander dark streets near The Workers' Stadium. A dusty padlocked gate secures a tatty turf football field lapped by a ubiquitous pinkish red running track. The stadium is not unique beyond the high, whitewashed, concrete walls. The rumours of an Outback Steakhouse nearby have brought us here and appear to be greatly exaggerated. A fruitless search culminates in a couple of beers with local food. A solitary restaurant lit by a neon sign above a curtained door was easier to discover in the dark recesses of Beijing's lifeless streets than the elusive American brand restaurant selling Australian branded food "cul'cha".

Bubble and Squeak are asleep, drunk on cheap beer again. Never fully sure of their final purpose I presume they are flying home to Sydney from here. The Swedes are drunk on vodka again. Miserable and depressing, it is a relief to escape their harrowing stories. No doubt they will return to Stockholm soon and continue their tales of woe and torture. Steff, low on funds and leaving early tomorrow for his university enrollment, opts for a quiet evening alone. A quiet night freed of mobs, guards, and scoundrels is an attractive prospect. The Violinist from Holland is safe in her room, fatigued by travel.

Which leaves the Cellist.

Chatty, she is lithe, cat like in her movements and beside me. Privacy has been non-existent in these crowded countries, confined trains, and closed compartments. After dark in Beijing, the streets are empty of people and cars. We have stepped out together. An impromptu date. The curfewed silence suggests we are alone.

The Cellist is smart, green-eyed, and multilingual. Brown bobbed hair over pale skin, she speaks sometimes in Dutch and sometimes in English. She is full of positive energy and talks about music. I am invigorated by the melody of her language. Her movements and tone are suggestive. She speaks gently, with warmth and kindness, leaving meaning open to interpretation. Unlike conversations in London where meaning belongs to the loudest opinion, the Cellist is different, and opens a creative world that is alien to me. Neither of us own the podium of opinion but I am happy to listen, drunk on her voice.

Cold beer facilitates the cool conversation which electrifies the moment.

Reaching up, the Cellist kisses me. A kiss of sensitivity, intelligence, and sensuous warmth. More electricity runs through my skin, up my arms, across my shoulders, and down my neck.

Unexpected.

We click and talk more.

Curious about life the Cellist has an intoxicating passion for living. Her eyes sparkle with mischief and she kisses me again. Her story speaks of symphony and orchestra. A world of melody and magic. The Cellist is hypnotic and courageous for she too has crossed Russia and Mongolia on our Smugglers Train. Mutual respect binds us, as does the electricity of connectivity.

This is unnerving.

Everyone I have loved has been taken away.

Everything I have believed in has been broken down.

Friendships are fickle and relationships are painful. They come without operating instructions and I do not know how to proceed. Have I discovered a soulmate? I don't even know what that means

The Cellist is other worldly and an extension of the temptations of Switzerland, Italy, and France. Fate is at play in this dark landscape. Teetering on the brink of imminent happiness, her magnetic pull is strong. Ready to plunge headfirst into an experience without an exit, the Cellist fills my future with adventure and learning. Enthralled by her world with freedom from violence, the fullness of friendships, and the riches of contentment, passionate pursuits, and purpose.

I am in wonder at the thought of a world of warmth which for so long has been beyond my reach.

Symphony artists of exceptional talent, the Cellist and the Violinist are performing here on a cultural exchange. They will perform for VIP audiences at the Beijing Symphony Hall. Expenses paid by one government or another, cultural exchanges are a part of the soft diplomacy binding Sino-European relations. The Cellist is a part of that fabric and invites me to stay. We can be together and eventually return to Holland.

I have nothing to lose.

There can be only gain.

A strange thing happens when you are free from the constraints of society. Without the terms and conditions of established bureaucracies defining your life, the World becomes a place of magic. A magic formed by destinations. Destinations of choice. Choices that lead to pathways. Pathways leading to discoveries and exciting propositions that can only be found when you stray from the prescribed path of debt financing: go to college, get a job, get a mortgage, service your debts, and burn out to the beat of life passing you by.

When you stray off the path, you dabble with a new magic.

When you dabble with magic you ride the ripples of a melody that resonates on a different plane. No longer in your lane, you define the rewards of your own creations and the accountability of your own actions. This magic contains electricity. An electricity primed for the sensation of connectivity. A connectivity that pools deep in the eyes of the Cellist revealing a world of wonder, exploration, soul searching, and shared experience.

Fear of the repercussions of society obstructs the colour of magic for too many people.

For in this magic, where choices are abundant and destinies are dreams, it is only you who decides where and when it is time to land. Independence is empowering and liberating as you discover courage to make your own choices, to be your own person. Courage that strays beyond the edges of social constraint. The magic of seduction is powerful, and bathing in the gravity of that force I fall into the Cellists world.

Yet in the back of my mind is a cold voice. The voice of a fickle Fate. Or is it the angel, or maybe the devil? Surely no single person can be so full of magic, so loaded with laughter, and so replete with humanity. Where does the fall end and the landing begin?

A leap of faith is often necessary to bridge the gaps in rationality.

Recent leaps have restored my faith in humanity. A London lawyer, a courageous travel companion, mischievous Mongolians, an Italian family, and Spanish tourists have all proven that trust is home grown, and hope is in the hands of the many. Changes and strangers are opportunities for enlightenment not reasons for fear.

Affairs of the heart though? That's another matter.

Neural scars burn deep and when you have been branded by your own people, they burn deeper still.

I know there are no safety nets. With my heart and soul in the hands of the Cellist, what risks am I taking? She is the embodiment of culture and the bookend of a journey that started with a magical peace in the heart of Helsinki and is at risk of ending with a magical happiness here in the heart of China.

Yet Fate is fickle. Guns, dogs, weather, and watchers are fears which have been conquered. But love is a bridge too far. The devil on my shoulder is enraptured by the prospect of the sweet sin of honey. The angel too but for different reasons. The Cellist is intelligent, musical, sensational, and lithe. An artist to be enthralled by and a star to follow. Imagine the world of wonders never previously known. Still, the steadiness of industry and study brings the validation of society and the fulfillment of ego. Steady study equals steady pay and will repair the destruction of dysfunction that are mine by Fate, not by choice. Temptation leads to tardiness, says the angel, or is it the devil.

The messenger is unclear.

Ugh! This is stressful.

There is a generosity of spirit in the Cellist that makes me nervous. We are bound by a shared adventure which could continue into a whole new world that will get me off of Maslow's bottom rung. Just one giant step into the unknown and the sweet world of honey is mine to enjoy.

But what is love, other than a gateway to pain.

And what a price is that pain when linked to everyone you loved who has gone and to everything you believe in which has been taken away.

It occurs to me that Fate may be littering my path with opportunities for kindness. When trust is gone, your sense of worth is destroyed. It is in that destruction that the loss of self keeps you like a bird with a broken wing, unable to fly, stuck on ground level going around in circles.

The magic of the Cellist holds me in her orbit.

We walk into the night together as the next few hours define our future.

QINGDAO

The room shakes.

Qingdao, at the end of the Earth, is my stop. Steff, my constant companion, remained in Beijing.

The windows rattle in their frames as explosions scatter shrapnel. Rock fragments pepper the building. Sitting on the window ledge, I look down into the yard preparing for the next blast.

My north facing room is a square concrete cell, with a single bed, single sheet, and thin blanket. A veneer of grey plaster covers the walls. Across the way another white concrete hostel enjoys its fair share of the blast pattern. The cinder block room will be cold in winter and the plaster is barely dry and will provide no insulation. Shared showers down the hall have limited hot water. Long white painted corridors with tiled floors separate the rooms and complete the institutional feel. The building is foreigner approved. More prison than palace. It feels like a place of incarceration. Welcome to the foreign residence and study home for overseas students. Few folks are here yet. Early for the semester after my trans-Siberian adventure, the residence is mostly empty. Construction is underway. There is no heating. The latitude, around thirty-eight degrees North, runs through the Mediterranean countries so I guess winters are warm.

Outside the construction works continue blasting. Some wear safety hats. All smoke. A small red flag, handkerchief size, on a bamboo stick, indicates possible danger. No signs, no fencing, no warning lights. No indications that this is a place of labour, danger, and death by dynamite are visible. Sticks of TNT are placed, cartoon style, in granite bedrock. One man drops a heavy rope blanket over the top, another plucks a cigarette from his lips, leans down, and touches the lit tip to the combined fuse that runs through the charges. He walks back to his buddies twenty metres away, who stand facing the blast zone waiting. More cigarettes are smoked.

Boom!

The room shakes.

A blue flatbed truck sits by the road with more mats and a stash of explosives. White painted Chinese characters on the side shout a large message. I am guessing a company name, but my character recognition is not good yet.

Boom!

The windows rattle in their frames. Rock fragments pepper the building. Barring incident or accident, this will continue for some time. The workers move in, and the cartoon continues. It is addictive viewing and when the dust settles, there is no scorched cat or torched coyote, just smoking labourers going about their business.

Light the fuse.

BOOM!

Blast wave.

Shake.

Clear.

Reload.

Rinse and repeat.

The cohort laugh and joke, working without care, seemingly oblivious to the effect of the blast waves. The only ripple in frequency is the pause for cigarettes.

Light the cigarette.

Cigarette lights the fuse.

BOOM!

Blast wave.

Shake.

Clear.

Reload.

New cigarette as required.

Rinse and repeat.

Blood before breakfast is not my cup of tea so I exit my student cell and my dorm building on the south side. Overlooking the Yellow Sea, the local beaches is few minutes' walk downslope, and I turn left across the road and my run. Parallel to the coast heading North-northeast for a couple of miles, the path here is a paved concrete path. The train ride from Beijing allowed twenty-four hours in a clean comfortable bunk to reflect on my life choices. Alone. The Cellist is gone now. My heart hurts as a true treasure slipped away. Why? Here at the end of the Earth loneliness is real. Accentuated perhaps by a sense of loss. I want to go home but there is nothing there. Failing at conformity, from who am I seeking validation? A college degree, so we are told, will open more doors. A printed transcript is worth the sacrifice and debt. Why is this form of education of any more value than the lived experiences of my recent history? Answers are vague, for out here in life I have solved problems, managed risks, learned hard skills, made life changing decisions and evolved. The hollow reasoning of further education leaves my heart and my bank balance empty.

Reflecting on my constant companions, I recall Oscar, the joys of exercise, discipline, and love. Dogs are happy creatures, loyal and with the simplest of formulae are forever friends. I miss my dog. Why are humans so complex? Now I miss this woman whom I will never know. Ignoring my gut instinct I continued down the path of conformity. Somewhere in my future is a proper job and a mortgage. A debt financed future with no magic. It's enough to make me puke. I try to extinguish the thoughts of a magic barely understood. Ignorant that Fate may be offering kindness as healing, it is easy to rationalize the decision. Doubling down on exercise I can cure self-indulgent emotions, stay steely, and be rock hard. Like a real man. This is a trauma response, yet to be learned and understood.

Running lifts me. In the groove, recollections of happy companionship lift my spirits. Close to nature I am at my happiest and before long the golden sands of a beach appear. "Shi Laoren", The Stone Old Man, is an eroded rock out to sea. Visible from the beach, the Old Man represents age and endurance, an authentic reflection of Chinese civilization. Bitterness and hardship are part of the national identity. Generations who have survived under the heel of successive dynasties were liberated by Big Uncle Mao. Re-education did improve literacy. The trains are punctual too. Beyond that, cult ideology crushed individuality, and harsh conditions remain a collective burden of "The People."

As the Old Man stands sentry, keeping watch out to sea, I hand over two coins – roughly twenty cents – to access the private beach. Half a mile of golden sand runs in each direction. There is nobody else here. Twenty cents is a lot of money for locals who prefer the free access beaches where they can forage for shells and fish from the shore. Stripping down, I thank the Old Man for his diligence and dive into the Yellow Sea. The molten, brown-green glass coloured water is cold. The tide is strong. The autumn sea is coloured like beer bottles from the Qingdao brewery, a monument to German colonialism. Cold, strong currents pull my limbs, and the swells are three or four metres high. The surf crashes on the beach somewhere to my west and pulls me out east towards the next landfall. Which, beyond the Old Man is South Korea. No lifeguards here or coastguard either so, one hundred metres out from the shore, scribing figure of eight loops, I swim until fatigue forces me back to shore. In the troughs between the swells I relax, swim with the current, and surf along the crests of the waves. Rhythm beats fatigue. Gradually the yellow beach comes closer and gripping my toes into the sand, I wade, stumble, and tumble back on to dry land.

Here, prone on the deck, looking at the sky, an internal dialogue starts again. The interrogation starts with:

"What the fuck am I doing here?"

Escaping? Running away? Running to? Living? Surviving?

Unsure of the answer, a series of follow up questions such as:

"What the fuck just happened?

... is going on?

... am I eating?

... am I seeing?"

The onslaught of questions continue unabated until we come full circle back to:

"What the fuck am I doing here?"

I do not know. But if you are walking through hell, keep walking.

The Royal Navy was arguably my first great adventure. Crossing the Atlantic, Mediterranean, and Baltic, we reached as far as the heat waves of the Arabian Gulf and the watery graveyard of icebergs and growlers near the Antarctic Circle. Inspired by curiosity I sought out more challenges, which opened doors to new opportunities and a string of epic adventures. A surplus of questions remains unanswered, and the pursuit of answers leads to more questions. I have survived the severest of natural challenges. Witnessed the milk of human kindness through the generosities of strangers, unfamiliar loves, and foreign cultures. Fallen through the gaps in civilization. Faced down violence and threats and fought off the baseness of the human condition. Indelible sights and scenes with scars that run deep are the education not the solution. It is still unclear how to get off Maslow's bottom rung. Nevertheless, I am in fair form; curiosity is yet to kill this cat. Which brings me full circle to the original question:

"What the fuck am I doing here?"

Cut adrift from all things normal, it is up to me now to answer my own questions.

What I have learned is folks enduring hardship are often more honest than the chattering classes living behind the veneer of civilization. They are often the people in charge and many forget where they came from. Power is their insurance and authority is their escape from their insecurity. Given the choice they can be pain maker or pain reliever. Most choose the former, as it takes courage to be the latter. People who go without have a compassion and an empathy of understanding rarely found at higher levels of society. Of all these things, though, it is clear to me that humans are confusing, the human condition is complex. The natural world on the other hand maybe hard, but Nature is always authentic and contextually honest.

Back home the myth of upward mobility has triggered an unparallelled craving for material wealth and the condition of F.O.M.O. Greed is good apparently. As you leave the Western Hemisphere, there are no safety nets, and beyond the Steppe out to the Yellow Sea, there is real struggle. Energy and food security are as limited as clean water and health care. Poverty is the reality for most of humanity.

So, in answer to the question:

"What the fuck am I doing here?"

The answer must be authentic and honest:

"Who knows? I'm making it up as I go."

In my heart there is no going back. Physically I can return to Britannia and England's green and present land. Spiritually though, that is no longer home. There is no normalcy. Whatever that means. Keep calm and carry on is the only way forward. As Winston Churchill said, "if you are walking through hell, keep walking."

Vomited on to shore, the green-brown waters of the Yellow Sea crash down trying to drag me back under the waves. Flopping on the sand, out of reach of the clutching waters, I have created a routine that is like this every day and will remain so until it is too cold to swim anymore. Routines create constants and constants maintain sanity. Logically, therefore, physical fitness becomes the corner shoppe of stability and the harbinger of all good things. The fitter I am; the further I can explore, until here at the edge of the Earth, I stand on the precipice of sound judgement, the soul judge of what is wise and what is wipeout.

Dangerous it may be.

But life is short. It is not a dress rehearsal.

Risks are real, and here on the brink; this feels like real living.

And Fate has another go. Manifesting a different form of kindness, she brings two Frenchman into the void. Loic and Pierre.

Army officers. Loic, a Legionnaire from Marseille, Pierre an Engineer from Breton, they are also students of Chinese. Studying on behalf of their government, both are masters of cuisine. Lovers of seafood we connect here in China's seafood city, dining together. Under the roofs of Bavarian style villas - another homage to German colonialism - the two Frenchmen argue over the best preparations of Breton mussels and oysters: against a Marseillaise bouillabaisse versus a Qingdao squid hotpot. Observing the tableau, I listen at the edge of understanding. All dialogue is conducted in French or Chinese. No English is spoken. Ingredients are picked over, sampled and selected. Broths are compared, contrasted, and combined. Qingdao beer, a German brew from the nineteenth century is served chilled under Chinese ownership. Striving to keep up with the pace, the delights of shared cuisines and curiosities are spell binding. Shrimp, scallops, crabs, clams, mussels, snails, crayfish, and all kinds of coastal crawlers go in the pot. English is forgotten. As my head spins in the confluence of cultures, expression gradually becomes easier and what was once foreign becomes familial and a new safe space.

The City of Qingdao has a seaport, an airport, and a railway station whose architecture is Bavarian baroque. Back in the late eighteen hundreds the city was a German colony for sixteen years. Unique architectural features have survived the revolution in the form of villas, churches, and the railway station. The old city fans out from the main Zhan through narrow leafy streets. Like Beijing, taxis here are old Volkswagens with caged drivers in shirt sleeves and dark trousers smoking perpetual cigarettes. The local church is a surprising survivor of revolution. It appears Catholic, though may be Lutheran. It is astonishing to me that the building remains intact in spite of the whitewash of history. Spirituality and faith have been replaced by the cult of Big Uncle Mao and so the walls and alcoves are bare of pictures and statues. Whilst the church remains free of The Chairman's portrait, it is also devoid of any sense of spirituality. It is an empty and lonely building on top of a small hill.

The industrial heritage of the Germans remains strong, and heading east, the old city morphs into a new commercial cityscape. Shopping malls, wide avenues, and tall apartment blocks extend outwards towards industrialized areas, factories, and warehouses. Taxis are cheap and replace public transport. It is easy to explore the metropolis. Even down to the dockyards, which are a heaving and frenetic rainforest of activity. Here the hubbub and clamour, beneath a canopy of cranes, provide cover for the billions of dollars of concealed container goods destined for consumers across the globe. The Qingdao brewery is here, close to Hai'er, a soon to be famous white goods manufacturer. Both are fated to become wealthy exporters, providing jobs and steady incomes to a city population of five million people and further enriching the Chinese government.

Golden sandy beaches hug the coastline. Bathing populations and street walkers are denser closer to city centre. The crowds thin out near foreign enclaves and here, at the intersection of international business, the languages change again. Japanese and Korean dominate as stores and restaurants pop up with the unique signs and with the scripts of those nations. Their influence is significant as both countries have more than thirty billion dollars of investment in the region. Shandong, the surrounding province was formerly a concession territory on a ninety-year lease to Germany. It was handed over to Japan in 1918, which led to the May Fourth Movement of 1919 - an anti-imperialist student protest on Tian'an men Square which accompanied a nationwide upsurge in Chinese nationalism. Overlapping Manchuria, adjacent to Mongolia, Shandong is a contested land of fertile plains larger than England and Wales combined, with more than double the population. Three nations eyeing the soil for agricultural and economic benefits create real tensions at a subcutaneous level.

Yet, in the maelstrom of clashing cultures, crashing seas, and dynamite at breakfast, there is a resounding peace. With two unlikely Frenchmen at the heart of the peace there are also two other people bringing their own wisdom to the show. Americans. Like Boston John, they are different and contradict U.S. stereotypes. Mike and Mina are neither Irish nor Italian, nor are they Native American or Cowboy. They are intellectual, intriguing and blessed with curiosity. I move slowly into their orbit, observing them from a distance in introverted fashion, I tread carefully before engaging.

Mina is the doyen of the foreign student community. Calm and graceful, like a swan on a lake, she appears to be the centre around which a United Nations of female students circulate. German, Danish, Norwegian, Japanese, Czech, and American students all seem happy in her company. She seems to me an illustration of gentle leadership with never a cross word nor any outward sense of frustration. A rising tide lifts all ships and those around her all seem to progress rapidly. Unlike myself, they appear to be excellent students, with great grades and positive influence on the surrounding society. Academic learning has never been my strength. Mina appears to be at the head of a soft diplomacy where international and Chinese communities combine. I admire her from a distance. She appears to have set a high bar for learning. I follow suit and commit myself to one hundred percent attendance at class, followed by several hours of extra study. I rise early every day and run. Attend early morning and mid-afternoon classes. Run some more and swim, then study characters, reading and writing hundreds of words every day. When the books close, I head out to local restaurants and bars to practice new language skills. Sometimes with Loic and Pierre, other times alone. Karaoke clubs are prevalent too, punctuation between the restaurants and shops on the streets of new Qingdao. I avoid these. Studying at this level is hard and fatiguing.

The challenge is real.

The assimilation of a new language means rewiring the brain and an openness to new philosophies and ideas.

Unlike tests of physical and emotional endurance, academic discipline is the hardest mental tests. To read, write, and speak Chinese daily, without respite, is the expectation for all students here. The regime is strict. Hour after hour of disciplined rote learning is the expectation. Tests are daily, weekly, and monthly. Scores are published without empathy and failure is frowned upon. There is some margin of error allowed but there is nowhere to hide from the tutors, nor is there a home to go to if life gets tough. Student life in

Qingdao is a ride or die experience and I have no idea if I can survive the intensity of study. If I can get my language competency halfway close that of Mina and the students around her, this will be time well spent.

Loic and Pierre are professional and committed. The other male students, on the other hand, are less than inspiring. Less industrious, they are often lazy and, in a few cases, just here to party. Spoiled boys with easy jobs and soft mums back home are uninspiring.

And then there is Mike.

Mike is Mina's partner. Whip smart academically, he is intimidatingly well read and appears somewhat mischievous. Neither a grizzled gunslinger nor homicide detective with a hunch, Mike is unlikely to be found in a squad car on the streets of San Francisco or quoting lines from movies on 'Nam. Lean, smart, and like Boston John, Mike is worldly. Other worldly. We have only two things in common. Cold beer and Korean BBQ. The former from Qingdao enjoyed with the latter in Tu Da Li, a local restaurant.

Winter is closing in, exposing flaws in my assessment of our latitude. It is seriously cold. My north facing concrete cell gets icy as temperatures drop to the "freeze the balls off a brass monkey" level. Swimming stops and heat is sought in BBQ booths. Just a ten-minute walk from our hostel, by the time we reach the restaurant the tips of our fingers and noses are blue from the bite of north or onshore winds.

When caught off guard the freezing temperatures bite hard into my bones and awaken the demon virus of cold. The evil imp works his magic through the heart of my soul liberally sprinkling a permafrost of pain through the dermal layers of skin. Mostly dormant and ignored, the evil imp provides unwelcome reminders of the unexpected consequences of a blizzard in the French Alps.

In the restaurant, warm beer soon replaces cold beer, and a bottle of Soju infrequently finds its way to the table. Distilled grain liquor, the Korean national drink cuts the fat on the meat and adds a contrasting warmth to the world outside. In these more intimate moments, as icy winds freeze the air, Mike stretches my capacity for learning, which is already at breaking point. Communicating in three languages is a stretch. Daily Chinese peppered with French, and now another form of English, is a full immersion into a new world where Korean and Japanese are also heard on the streets.

The drain is emotional, mental, physical, and spiritual.

Which is not all bad.

For it triggers a second wind of resilience and the exploration of another depth of Sisu.

Sisu is not singular, it is multi-faceted, encompassing heart, body, mind, and soul.

An upshot of Sisu is gratitude.

Food and language are the fortification of that gratitude, for they are the gateway to culture and an entrance to adventure. I discovered this in France, then Italy, and it is no different here. Food and language create the shared environments where friendships grow and experiences are born. I like Mike for his intellectual advantage which exists on a continuum of subjects from Asian food to English and American literature. The latter of which I have very little frame of reference. The former too for that matter. I can remember some Shakespeare and Dickens, a bit of Wilfred Owen. With Mike though, I get a crash course on Gore Vidal, Aaron Burr, Henry Kissinger, Teddy Roosevelt, Franklin Roosevelt, Steinbeck, Vietnam, the Great Depression, Reagan-ism, Cuba, Civil Rights, the Slave Trade, rejection of Empire, and Boston tea parties. This is an unexpected and fascinating education which further tests my mental elasticity.

So far removed from Dark London the contrast is night and day.

In a world without internet and smartphones Mike illustrates a degree of learned knowledge that the world of accessible information has yet to undermine.

Under Mike's mentorship I learn about British culture and colonial influences from an external point of view. His capacity for mischief, not dissimilar to that of the Mongolian warrior, brings levity to gravity and humour in the face of adversity. The poignancy of the subjects into which we dive is expansive, intriguing, and enlightening. Amongst the bottles of beer and skewers of BBQ I learn to thrive in a cultural exchange of new ideas and new knowledge.

Imposter syndrome though is never far from the surface. Particularly in a world of academics. Life is simple. Study, sleep, study, exercise, study, study, study. Language learning is often undervalued in English speaking societies and, as the going gets tough, many of the students simply depart, heading home to the comforts of their own jungles. The Nordic nationalities continue. Stoic, like folk in Finland, the Danes and Norwegians here already speak three or more languages. The Germans are similar, many of them speak at least two languages. Some remind me of Steff and most of them remove the tarnish on the reputation made by the young Berliners out on the Steppe. Mina and Mike stay the course and I bring up the rear. This makes learning a new contest. Not used to being last, taking the exit is tempting but as other English speakers have given up, I refuse to be a statistic.

There is a magic in the air. Overwhelmed with Chinese calligraphy, grammar constructs, hours of homework, and daily testing, the allure of this magic is powerfully seductive. How can it be so powerful? Am I a weak fool unable to resist temptation?

Magic is like honey and honey is everywhere.

Sometimes in traps, sometimes in pots, even in the darkest of times honey offers a kind of magic that leads to light and a pathway out of hell.

The magic honey currently resides in the form of a sensual Cellist – she is an escape from the rigors of academic discipline; she is a linguist, artist, and gatekeeper to another world and is just a short train ride away. The devil on my shoulder, feeds the desire to dip into the honey. The angel is steadfast in her commitment to purpose and study. At the intersection of our journeys the Cellist has cast a spell - the strongest of charms in the briefest of encounters has created a conflict. My steely self is confronted with a new romantic version of my essential being, which wrestles with the true colour of this new magic.

After all, honey is meant to be enjoyed.

And as the devil on my shoulder says, “What could possibly go wrong?”

I fight back against a capricious Fate.

Immune to kindness and cautious around comfort.

It occurs to me once more that Fate could be working for me

rather than against me. But the sunk cost of that decision still feels like a bridge too far.

Instead of abandoning me Fate recognizes the density of my own personal stubbornness and offers a different kind of salvation manifesting kinship with food lovers and culture keepers. Loic, Pierre, and Mike are clearly on the side of the angel. With a steady moral compass they keep me pointing to the true north of discipline. The two Frenchman further fuel my love of France and Mike continues a global education from an American perspective. From dollars to donuts, nothing is off the table with Mike and his is the best kind of friendship in this cultural oasis at the ends of the Earth. He gives freely and is good company.

With Mike there is no quid pro quo.

Winter nights draw in, and the cold freezes my assets. Scratching at my letters in a small town by the Yellow Sea, a new sense of being is forged. Here, on the edge of an empire, scars heal. In the heat of this crucible, history fades.

In the warm camaraderie of foreign friends, I let down my guard and allow some peace into my soul. The yield of Sisu is the value of gratitude.

Nanjing

YEAR OF THE HORSE.

Horses are full of energy, albeit a bit too much. Both studious and athletic, they are strong believers in chasing after dreams. Rather than wealth and fame, happiness is what motivates them. They expect others to operate at the same speed as them and don't understand why they may not.

Horse people are ever-changing emotionally with short tempers and become angry quickly. But once it's over, they forget quickly.

Their biggest challenge is that they're blind to their own faults.

THE YEAR of the Horse is inauspicious. Born in the year of the Pig, I am a lover of freedom and adventure. Horses are lively, energetic, and independent in nature. Unique characteristics, yet there are turmoil and disruption to come. The year of the Horse will be a year of conflict.

DARK LONDON

The Irishman is angry. Seriously angry. Mad, like a cut snake, he is coiled, ready for action. He lunges, striking out to cause pain. I step out of range, dropping down from the threshold of the door. He's not large, but the rage in him inflates his body like a cobra, and the froth in his spit is tinged with a venom that stings as every cuss and brutal slur land on my person.

I do not enjoy being a hard man. Necessity breeds retribution, and if required, I will be this man's nemesis. The Irishman is a fraud rhino, and, after some considerable effort, I have tracked him to his lair.

As a part of his camouflage, he has adopted some particularly snake-like characteristics. His tendency for deviancy has enabled several years of freedom and reinforces his rage at the prospect of capture.

The threats are real, spoken in a harsh brogue. So many threats and so much rage. It is impossible to determine the end of one threat from the beginning of another. Finding him has not been easy, as his whole business is a façade. His lair is supposedly his mother's house, but after scoped the residence several times I have yet to see any evidence of her existence. His footprints, however, are large in this domain. A silver-grey Land Rover sits in the driveway, and it dawns on me how many of these fraud rhinos love a big car. Just as Burberry clothes became the garment of choice for discerning Chelsea football hooligans, the Land Rover appears to be the choice of vehicle for discerning fraudsters. The license plate on this one has confirmed ownership, and the regularity of "visits" to this address are indicative that the Irishman is more than just a casual visitor.

Reconnaissance saves lives and I have made several visits into this part of East London.

Not just to identify the rhino but also to work out entry and exit points. London may be home, but the eastern boroughs are enemy territory. Nothing is familiar and there are no friendlies out here.

The crisp air of pre-dawn is chilly and grey tinged with a slight mist. Still, before rush hour, it is quiet, and our friend, Mr. O'Brien – for that is what I name him - has been here overnight. Patterns of behaviour have been established, and O'Brien will be heading to work soon, off his guard. Dressed as a courier, I ride a red Yamaha. Motorbikes in London suffer significant risk from careless driving. They also offer the twin benefits of disguise and speed which are perfect for this task. Motorbike acceleration and agility get you quickly out of danger and into spaces and places cars cannot go.

> "Get out of here or I'll kill you. Come round here, to my mother's house, putting the fear into her. I'll kill you I will."

This has a familiar ring. Angry fraud rhinos just prior to tagging. I have been here before. Not dissimilar to angry men in uniform, they have a similar sense of righteous indignation. Levels of anger directly proportional to the level of disdain they employ or wrongdoing they have unleashed. Fraud rhinos are generally white-collar members of the chattering classes, mostly males holding on to prestige, aspiring to materialism and upward mobility. Some are female. All are angry and hold on tight to their fear of downward mobility.

The patterns are persistent and with each passing contract I am not sure how much more I can do. The money is good, but after many years of work in Dark London the quantity of neural scarring is now inversely proportional to an acceptable quality of life. There is a world out there with kind people. I have witnessed it firsthand and wish to return before that place becomes a mythical holy grail confined to my imagination.

O'Brien is stocky and wild. He is coiled to spring, and I take another half step backwards to remain out of reach. Caring little about his blows, I am more concerned about being dragged into the house. The lair of a fraud rhino is a minefield of dangers, and I never cross a threshold. It is not clear who is behind the door, nor the complications involved in order to exit.

O'Brien's words have meaning. They are visceral. He owes a lot of money. One half bar to be precise - which he seems to have forgotten to pay back. One half bar - or half of one million pounds: five hundred thousand sterling in short form.

That's a lot of cheddar.

Angry and feisty, O'Brien's language is littered with Fs. F for: found out, furious, and flying off the handle.

I see an older lady behind him in the hall.

"Morning ma'am, are you ok?" I enquire.

She says nothing, acknowledges nobody, and reminds me of another mother, also of Irish descent. That lady had one son who died not far from here, viciously murdered by unknown assailants. His behaviours were prolific too, as were his scandals - which transgressed the boundaries of law, civil society, and the rules of the underworld. His early termination was a violent death. Like O'Brien though, he was still his mother's angel. Unlike O'Brien, he chose blue collar rather than white collar crime, resulting in a significantly different outcome.

In both cases, the families appeared respectable to the neighbours, and both boys appeared to be successful businessmen.

"Feck you" froths O'Brien. "Feck you, feck your family. Feck off. I'll find you too and I'll feckin' kill you. Feckin' come round here, frightenin' my feckin' mother. I'll feckin' do you!"

The rage is tiresome. Time to move on.

"Alright Mr. O'Brien, I'm just making a delivery. Can you sign here please?"

I know it is him. The Land Rover is my first point of confirmation. The recalcitrance of the older lady and the neighbours have made identification harder. I tag him through other means. Preferring other points of confirmation, I chose to flush the rhino out of its lair and get the job done. Time stands still for nobody, after all, and the project needs to be closed. A signed affidavit with a warning of perjury is quality control - but I lie for nobody. In complex cases like this, it is a matter of professional pride to do the job properly.

"Feckin O'Brien," he spits. "Who the feck is O'Brien? Get the feck out of here, I'll feckin' kill you."

The rage is unreasonable. As he bunches up his fists, body inflating further, violence is obviously imminent. Rage is a form of arrogance, providing good cover for many men. Deployed as a cover for ignorance or wrongdoing, it is also a way to exert power. Defending his so-called mother is a false flag operation. There is no threat to her, nor has she committed any wrongdoing to my knowledge. Assuming this lady is his mother. He is the crim, and like a grenade with the pin out, ready to explode. I will tag him another day. Calmness is key. No more words are necessary and I back away slowly. Nodding to them both, I return to the Yamaha at the end of the driveway. The door slams and I turn my back to the house.

This is my mistake.

Replacing documents back into the holder - magnetically attached to the fuel tank - I slide the helmet over my head. Visibility is obscured now and inserting the keys, checking control panels, lights, and gear shift, I push the starter button.

The engine roars.

All is good.

Then a second engine roars.

All is less good.

O'Brien has a rush of blood to the head, and this could end in pain. Out of the house and into the Land Rover, he is backing out of the drive. Fast. I can see him through the windows, hunched up behind the wheel. The house is quiet; and there is no sign of the old lady. O'Brien - angry inflated fraud rhino - is glaring at me, I can see him working the transmission trying to turn fast. He is clumsy in his anger.

The road is silent. The residences nearby are quiet. It is early morning here but the main street at the end of the road is busy with commuter traffic. That is where safety lies.

Kicking into first I pull out and accelerate hard, the rev counter needle hits red, and I kick again into second, revs drop. Speed climbs. I stand on the pegs, crouched over the back of the bike, like riding a mechanical horse on the run from a mechanical beast. I can feel the heat of the Land Rover as it roars and leaps forward. Light and fast, the bike pulls away, peeling around the front of the big engine.

Revs climb again.

The engine screams.

Pulling on the throttle, speed climbs too.

The clumsy Land Rover is moving again, straightening up to try another charge.

Balanced on the back of the bike, the next minutes are nuanced. Pulling the head of the bike around, being evasive will give the engine time to bite. Staying low, I squat just above the saddle and allow the speed to climb. Agility is the adversary of clumsy. It is essential to stay mobile.

The fraud rhino is mad. I can hear him somewhere behind, roaring again - closing on my hind quarters, readying to pounce. Engine revs high, whining, I sit long enough to change up, then rise on the pegs, leaning forward over the bike. Revs drop, speed climbs, and the bike pulls away from the silver-grey beast. Tense, I wait for it to pounce. The main street is edge of its territory and the rhino will not be able to pull into traffic.

Balanced, holding my breath, the heat of the beast is a half-length behind me. No more gear changes, let the bike have its head. O'Brien cannot race into the commuter traffic so he will have to make his kill shot in the next few seconds. Cold sweat on my back contrasts with the engine heat which warms my front. The Land Rover roars again and, glancing back briefly, the glare of the mad Irishman is fixed on my back. He is tenacious for sure. His behaviours would have surprised me once. In a previous life I maintained a naïve belief that right and wrong were exercised by two distinct groups of people.

My world view has change - a global education and a growing understanding of the human condition has introduced the new reality that right and wrong are contextual and personal.

Every time the roar of the beast changes a gentle tug on the throttle keeps me just out of reach. We are racing towards two different goals - the rhino in a mad crush to escape justice, and me in a mad dash to escape the rhino. Streams of traffic up ahead run perpendicular to our road. Targeting the end zone, a five-metre square box where he will have to stop, I focus on gaps in the traffic.

No margin of error, this is a ride or die experience.

Read the space and escape to freedom or...

... miss the space or...

... get caught by the rhino and...

In either situation be on the underside of someone's car.

Senses heightened, everything slows, and my field of view narrows. The road ahead is busy, the spaces move like the gaps in frogger. Lights on full beam I am visible to the traffic. Accelerating, I edge further out from the rhino's spike. Leaning over the bike, fully engaged, details on cars and the faces of drivers are surprisingly clear. Who is attentive and who is not filters my decisions.

The beast behind is roaring but I forget him now. Crossing the end zone, this is no time to die.

I feather the brake and watch the nearest drivers. Instinctively they will slow and turn away from danger to protect their cars. I pick my man, watch his eyes go wide, see him grab the steering wheel, and know I am home. Dropping a gear, I tug the throttle and accelerate into the flow of traffic, cold sweat on my back, engine heat on my front, this is easy.

The car slows. The space grows. Sliding around behind the rear quarter of the front car, I edge into the middle and glance back. The rhino has stopped in the end zone. O'Brien glares from behind the wheel of his Land Rover. The car behind is moving again, closing the gap, and the car in front is oblivious to what just happened.

Humans are instinctive, predictable, and therefore, easy to read. I have pulled this maneuver a hundred times. Angry men though are a different beast. Volatile and often unaccountable, they are best avoided. Many play by their own rules, and they are found in all parts of the jungle.

Cutting through the traffic I swing round and, standing on the pegs, can see the big Land Rover wallowing in the traffic. Maintaining distance in the blind spots of his mirrors I mingle with the commuters, allowing other motorbikes to pass, until I am happy the rhino is absorbed fully in the confusion of traffic. Blind now to his surroundings he leads me deep into town and before long, turning right, I watch him exit the car.

Bingo!

This is his other lair. Accelerating away the rhino shuffles upstairs and is soon gone, as am I.

Scoping the premises, it takes a few short days to determine pattern of behaviour. In a new outfit, climbing the stairs, I knock on the door far down the corridor from O'Brien. A female voice is inviting.

"Delivery for Mr. O'Brien."

She barely looks up.

"Next door love." She says warmly. He is here, two doors down and just arrived. Second point of confirmation beyond the Land Rover and this is enough to close the deal.

"Thank you, Miss.,"

"No problem love, he's just arrived, probably drinking his coffee right now."

Stepping outside, I pull the door closed and take a deep breath. This rhino is angry and does not want to be tagged. Eschewing violence except as a last resort, O'Brien has already shown that he is the last resort kind of guy.

Deep breaths calm my nerves and I walk into his office. Speed is of the essence before he realizes our previous brief encounter.

"Mr O'Brien," he looks up.

Bingo! Third point of confirmation.

"Here you are boss, special delivery."

"Thank you, leave it on the desk."

The dream response as this gives me time to exit as I drop his personal invitation to Crown Court just at the edge of his fingertips. Turning away, I wait for the pin drop. Counting down the seconds I reach the single flight stairs as the crash happens. The roar of the beast. The indecipherable outburst of righteous indignation and a series of Fs.

"Feck, feck, feck. Feckin' feckin' fecker. . .. "

The machine gun burst of cusses precedes the thunder of a crashing desk and the swell of rage as he bursts through the door.

Reconnaissance saves lives though, and this time I am fully prepared. The Yamaha is alive, engine purring and ready to go. Helmet on, down the stairs, I jump onto the saddle, kick the bike and we race out of the stalls. The fraud rhino is roaring, running through the parking lot. To no avail. Revving the Yamaha, dropping into gear we pull across the asphalt and, waving goodbye, race into the traffic.

The rage is real.

Out of the gates, sliding through the cars I pull away from danger. The curses and cusses of the fraud rhino are loud. O'Brien disappears in my rear-view mirror and the growl of the Yamaha eliminates his noise.

Feeling sick and ready to collect a bounty, I am done with anger, rage, and fraud. Too many threats. Too much corruption. Too much pain. This is dirty work - as O'Brien fades away, so does my desire to keep doing it.

Neural scarring and lived experiences are making me edgy. A well-developed "spidey-sense" says it is time to leave Dark London behind. There is a new world out there. A new world of kindness and colour, mischief and magic.

Dark London serves a thin gruel, and this Oliver Twist wants no more.

Time to change the fare.

NANJING

Am I going to die?

Sniffing the air like an old bear outside his cave, the risk is unlikely.

Two leather jackets stand in the doorway, their purpose is still unclear, as is their form – are they gorillas or hyenas? Unlike their Russian counterparts, they do not carry guns. Like their London counterparts, a sense of low-level menace permeates the room. What is it about leather? What is the appeal of cowhide to plain men in positions of authority? Do they all get the same memo? Rule one when projecting power (according to "Authoritarian Vogue"): leather jackets are essential attire.

Wondering at their choice of garments, I greet them warmly.

Lu Lu looks nervous. She is a great asset and a fount of knowledge - my constant companion here. She brings an encyclopedic understanding to her role as office manager role: local government, labour law, and the mechanisms of Chinese Communism. A survivor of traditionalism, she has been raised under Confucianism but secretly embraces Christianity. Her business is her secret. The relationship with religion is a grey area to be managed carefully in this new "open

China." I respect Lu Lu's faith and trust her outputs. She works hard and is illustrative of young folks here. They are hungry for knowledge, opportunity, and contact with the outside world. Her ability to manage demands is impressive. The combined stresses of a patriarchal society and the increasing demands of Western businesses are unique, alien and counter cultural. Where I learn Chinese, she is learning English. Workdays are long and bilingual.

This does not smell like a shake down though.

Lu Lu's fear of authoritarianism is understood. Nanjing is different to Beijing and Qingdao, for here there is art as well as industry. The people are friendly, but the city has suffered. Occupied by nationalists, raped by Japanese forces, then purged by Communist forces, the scars of authoritarianism are pervasive and ingrained. The city is a red heartland controlled by the Peoples' Liberation Army. PLA Officers are China's new aristocracy. Their footprints are everywhere. Lu Lu's behaviours around leather jackets are reminiscent of Steff. She dons rabbit camouflage at the first sign of uniformed belligerence. I have learned to respect this method. There is no room for escalation in a zero-sum game you cannot win. It is in the heat of this crucible I have learned mediation skills. I have learned quickly that surviving China is a chess game where perception is reality. Everything is circular nothing is linear. Go head on at a goal and you are likely to die a death by a thousand cuts. Chinese people are natural traders, which to my mind makes them unnatural Communists. Everything here can be traded, repackaged, reframed, and reverse engineered. Wisdom is respected, as is intelligence and culture. If you win at their game, doors will open to higher influences and wealth distributors. The alternative to this reality means pack up and go home. Behave like an imperialist - Brit, American, German, Japanese - and doors will close; at which point it is time to move on. For if you choose to stay, unless you are streetwise, your pockets and purses will be emptied in ways that you could never imagine. Equally, thanks to the "Century of Shame", foreign behaviours in China have "刻骨铭心 (Engraved the bone and inscribed the heart").

Foreign interventions and territorial losses led to a national humiliation creating lasting memories profound experiences which have been handed down generation to generation. It is wise to tread carefully in the Middle Kingdom.

Lu Lu engages the leather jackets, though they look like gorillas they don't smell like them. I am happy for now, they are not hyenas, but their real form is yet to be determined. She offers them tea, comfortable seats, and drops two packets of cigarettes on the table. I prefer brick tea which is strong and black. We serve jasmine tea for these meetings -or chrysanthemum; these are the preferred flavours locally. The cigarettes are Zhonghua. A premium brand in red packets with gold lettering - Big Uncle Mao's choice and recognized nation-wide. Good tea and quality cigarettes give face to our visitors.

Lu Lu sits calmly beside me. She does that when she is nervous. Proximity to an illusion of safety means that she can speak quietly to me in English without being overheard. Duty-bound in multiple roles, I carry the burden of protecting my team as well as the business. Not something one considers in the Western world, but here, in return for unquestioning fealty, the boss has manager, protector, father figure, and big brother. In return for unmatched labour, it is on you to deliver comfort, wisdom, guidance, and income. China is nuanced and complicated, the country is both open and autocratic. Government control is everywhere as opportunities for free trade flourish. Optimism thrives as ownership is denied. Simultaneously open and closed, China is a mass of contradictions.

It is overwhelming, yet Western investors continue to drop billions of dollars into the rebuilding of this country. The dictators of direction seem to have little understanding of the world in which they operate, yet they throw down money in eye watering quantities. On the ground, we work long hours. Fifty, sixty, seventy hours each week, but never forty. Paid for one job, we do the work of three. This land of opportunity, experiencing its own industrial revolution, is evolving at lightning speed. Technology, infrastructure, and language are changing fast. Growth is phenomenal, like nothing else in the world. China is open and every professor, pioneer, entrepreneur, industrialist, chancer, and romancer is here riding the economic rocket.

There is a dark side too. Here at the crossroads of modern history, conditions are tough, sometimes brutal. Life is cheap, particularly for the locals. The pressure is immense and any cracks in the makeup of heart, body, mind, or soul are swiftly exposed and broken open. Blessed with Sisu, I am robust enough to survive. For each corporate survivor though, there are two or three people heading home each month. China is the ultimate test of perceived Western values.

And an early test for me is in the form of these two leather jackets, Mr. Wang and Mr. Li. Perhaps these are their real designations, perhaps not. Wang and Li, the Smith and Jones of Chinese family names, they are ubiquitous; I must assume they are genuine.

"We know who you are," Wang says.

"Why are you here?" asks Li.

I consider my response. There is no such thing as a straight question here. Shifting almost imperceptibly towards Wang, I think before I speak. Wang is the senior officer, around fifty years old, speaks calm and clear Mandarin. No local dialect, no slang. This sets him apart from local officers. Slim, just under 6 feet tall, his hair is thick, and black. Dyed to hide grey hair so he resembles a younger man. He accepts tea and cigarettes graciously. Pale skin, which indicates some education and a reasonable upbringing. His hands are those of an officer not of a field worker. Li on the other hand is darker skinned, shorter, and stocky. He is the muscle, mostly silent, watching, listening, sipping, and smoking.

Wang repeats Li's question: "Why are you here?

I have played this chess game before, on the other side of the world with men of law and men of lore, whose rules of engagement include questions, shake downs, and aggressive actions. Upskilled by Dark London, I am prepared for, but have no wish to enter, Dark Nanjing.

The rules on that side of the house were learned the hard way.

Still learning the rules on this side of the house, the depths of local austerity are yet to be determined.

I lean into the conversation and hope there are rules here too.

ARRIVAL

Pudong International Airport is vast and cavernous. A principal transit point for twenty-first century industrialists into the Middle Kingdom the experience is mundane. Uniformed militia scrutinize passports, check visas and facial features. Slightly nervous, I wonder what's coming. Unlike Russian border guards, the uniforms here are free of big hats and firearms. Entry to a country via train, car, plane, or ship mean protocol and process. These cross-border procedures differ by continent and country and with varying engagement: under armed escort, under threat of armed attack (no escort), processed at gun point, processed not at gun point, and "Hello! Anybody home?" in the case of unmanned checkpoints.

Thus, I scan the guards scanning me, looking for the crime I have yet to commit. A destabilizing thought. As they reluctantly approve my innocence, I keep calm and carry on through to the large arrivals hall. Officially I have arrived in the Peoples' Republic of China. Not for the first time. Airports are tedious though and Pudong is up there with the most tedious of hubs. I miss the train.

Once upon a time, "we" came here by ship: Brits, Americans, Germans, French, Dutch, Portuguese - via Hong Kong, Guangzhou, Fuzhou, Tianjin, and Qingdao. Foreign ships heading upriver from treaty ports spreading mercantilism through gun boat diplomacy. Today, in a more enlightened world, Capitalists have embraced the good Communists in a new form of "entente cordiale" known as globalization. We are all in it together. Mutual wealth and health are assured as the architects of geopolitical strategy have decided the CCCP are good Communists. And thus, billions in foreign currency flow into this nation, which is fast becoming the production suite and warehouse of the world.

It does not make much sense to me. As productivity leaves, creativity walks with it. That is my humble view. China presents the opportunity to achieve some upward mobility. So here I am.

If you ask me though, if something looks like a fish, smells like a fish, and tastes like a fish, it is probably a fish. And China smells fishy.

But what do I know? My knowledge of macro-economics is street level, not simply university awarded.

When Britain first met China, that Empire was wealthy. The U.K. forced trade upon a closed nation. When America first met China, the situation was similar. Both arriving nations needed global markets for trade. Britain introduced opium to the masses in exchange for silver and, unexpectedly, the discovery of tea. China's resources underwrote the cost of Empire. America on the other hand, always selling something, pillaged its own land of furs, and nearby islands of sandalwood in return for Chinese silver. When Britain was banished by the emperor, the Americans brokered opium for more silver.

When it comes to profit making, history is checkered, and the interpretation is variegated.

Both nations have returned today, but the situation is reversed as they bring the "silver" back to China.

Big Uncle Mao closed the country closed for business in 1949, when the Communists removed the emperor, kicked out the Capitalists, and purged the landlord classes. All ownership is theft apparently. I am not sure about that but at the least, all ownership is temporary.

This time America wields the crowbar, jimmying open China, and to those paying attention back home, all things Eastern are "de rigeur."

With a freshly minted degree in hand, I am ready to grease the wheels of industry, even though the future is unclear.

Retrieving baggage from the carousel, I step into a new world.

AT WORK

We have offices and an extra suite in the Suning Universal Hotel, a glass and metal alien construct beamed down at the intersection of the main Shanghai and Guangzhou roads. Squatting like a giant toad among flat-faced concrete facades and sloping red-tiled roofs of the surrounding buildings, the semi-circular lobby space is soulless with a lackluster coffee shop serving shit coffee.

I have two assistants. Long jet-black hair over pale moon faces, they are Lu Lu and Mei Mei – at just over five and a half feet tall they dress conservatively in uniform fashion of pastel, woolen sweaters, pleated wool skirts and patent leather shoes. Organizing everything, they are a valuable team, overseeing all business administration, government relations, finances, business licenses, payroll, even food and team dinners. They work incessantly to serve the team. Lu Lu is serious, Mei Mei somewhat flighty. Both mean well, fail-forward, bounce back, and bring a strength of character that is sometimes missing in the men, who often jockey for position and play politics for the smallest gain.

Lu Lu and Mei Mei take it upon themselves to look after me. Belongings, accommodations, cultural integration, information and intel, their service is exemplary. Discomfiting too, as servitude is not my deal. Ever present, quiet, and shy, Lu Lu and Mei Mei work uncomplainingly, and together we navigate the ebb and flow of modern Chinese culture. Sailing in uncharted waters, where a tidal stream of centrist economics meets the crashing freighter of globalization, there is no room for unwarranted servitude. The trials are hard, and I steer their priorities towards self-care and professional development. Setting boundaries that allow them to maintain face, they become role models for the company. From there we make groundbreaking changes to offset patriarchal influences. Smoking, spitting, and louche manners are eliminated. Equalized salaries and benefits are introduced and new concepts like maternity leave and accrued vacation materialize. As the team grows in stature and competency, outputs are improved, innovation becomes a central philosophy, and attrition reduces to the point that staff retention in terms of service is more than double the national average.

Topping sixty hours each week, survival for me means routine. Before dawn, I fumble for my laptop. Oasis, Madness, and the Jam belt out the tunes. Tea fuels the engine and a walk along the river gets me to work. Black tea from Yunnan is a strong choice; in secret, I add a splash of milk, and sometimes honey, imitating the English style of tea with milk and sugar. A taste of home for early starts which begin at seven. The work of the day is complete by the time the "third shift" kicks in. When London wakes up, they want attention, so the next few hours are spent in briefings, re-briefings, and micromanagement meetings. When clients in other countries wake up we are kept on hold for longer. China is expected to be available twenty-four-seven, so the rest of the world can maintain comforts and work eight-hour days. For their stoic endurance, I respect my team and my community, who are tireless and fearless. Leaving the office after dark, walking home, I can still get a haircut, a few groceries, or something to eat. Even at ten pm a barber will open or a kitchen will cook. As the intensity grows, formality is reduced. Office wear is really whatever anyone can afford to buy. Fred Perry polos, biking jeans, and a pair of old walking boots are my comfortable uniform. As the strain increases, delegation dawns and empowerment evolves, so team players can work independently in hybrid roles. As trust grows locally, morale stays high and so does productivity.

Yet, the consumer beast is always hungry, so we eat in the office. "Wai mai", ordering out services, ramp up fast and food finds its way to production and, before long, workers never leave. Dumplings filled with pork and celery, or chicken and coriander, doused with local vinegar from Zhenjiang, feed the team, breakfast, lunch, and sometimes dinner. Rest is driven by fatigue. Social lives are limited. Before long I am sending people home to be with their families and loved ones. There is no such thing as work life balance. There is just life and the quality of that life is important to those who live it. Often cruelly treated by their own system, I make it a point of being kind to my team and protecting my staff. As other emigres double down on their positions, I seek ways to make their lives better, remove obstacles to progress, and help them grow. I am not alone. Other enlightened souls recognize the benefits of team health. Kindness is a force multiplier, and as businesses grow, the industrious and the ambitious head to the brands that care.

Leaving the office in the nighttime, relishing the tranquillity of solitude, I walk several miles in any direction before returning to the soulless Suning. It is after dark, in cooler air, that exploration yields further discovery. Restaurants here and tea rooms there, on streets with no lights, rely on lanterns outside their doors and flickering fluorescent building signs to provide illumination and navigation way points. Quiet of traffic, safe, and almost empty of pedestrians, a natural curfew exists in the darkness. Walking for hours, quartering the city, I form my own map and grid reference in the web of streets beyond Guangzhou Lu, out and around Gulou District.

It is in the darkness I reflect. Life may be tough, but not too long ago, I was in a world of pain. Corrupt policemen, good gangsters, bad brigands, and factotums of fraud contrived with flawed institutions to shatter the illusions of civilization. Foreign friendships here have restored faith and healed wounds, but neural scars are slower to mend than their physical brethren. Out on the edge of the world, I have a shit salary, and a few benefits which contrive to maintain the veneer of cozy comfort once more. The value of the pound means I have ten times the buying power against the yuan. That increases by another factor when combined with the retail costs of clothes and consumables. With this new wisdom I can maintain a high standard of living.

Yet, the power of the English to shit on their own people though is legendary and within three months my company CEO wants to devalue my earnings by paying my salary in local currency, I decline his generous offer. Not enjoying any rebuttal, he targets benefits next, the nice apartment is the first to go. Then the rental subsidy. Then the nice office. Anything that resembles the luxuries that other expats receive is removed. Anything that pushes me closer to a Chinese level of living is applied. This happens fast.

There are no safety nets.

With nothing to return to England for, my exit is somewhere here in this strange new world. As I yield the office and apartment, my salary and currency remain intact. Boundaries have been established and I look to break the contracts on the office and apartment.

Lu Lu looks uncomfortable when I tell her the news.

The face of the company is important and integral to relationships. A prestige location opens the door to higher level government relationships. It is important to the staff too, for they wish to stand apart from their peers. Of large value locally, this is small beer to London who wishes to press ahead with cost cutting. Back in the land of two faces, nobody gives a flying frosty about life on the ground in China.

Lu Lu is resolute with her concerns. She continues, in the face of all adversity, to be diligent and honest. Wise beyond her years. If we lose face, or cause face to be lost, then we lose "guanxi" – relationships. Your relationships in China reflect status, which define the ease or complexity of successes. We talk, I listen, and London wins. Lu Lu, despite her concerns, is loyal and together we work at breaking our lease agreements.

Breaking contracts and moving locations may be relatively straightforward elsewhere. Out here though, who you signed with, and who is involved, could be different people. Deals are done in the dark, and, as we break the contracts, we have no idea who's fingers we are breaking and whose faces we are shading in the process.

In the new, open China, with lightning-fast growth, gaps appear in the fabric of society leaving holes through which integrity may fall.

Navigating the opaque nature of local contracting, we find a new office. A strata-titled building, which means units on each floor have separate landlords. Which makes price negotiations individual and arguably easier. It also presents challenges on utilities and property management, as individual landlords bicker over responsibility and price points. Still, London wants cheap and that is what London gets. This is a big step down from the foreign-approved office space and we lose some staff in transition. HQ behaviours undermine on the ground efforts and the message here is interpreted as lack of care or lack of wealth and prestige. Small beans make big pills and this is a bitter pill to swallow. Lu Lu stays but Mei Mei goes with the brain drain. Instead of a relatively comfortably émigré enclave we are now in the real world. No foreigners allowed.

Who cares?

Nobody.

The West wants cheap.

Cheap rents, cheap bills, and preferably, cheap labour. The cheaper the better, as that means more profit for those who need it least. It also means happy words for those paying the bills. Whatever the exchange of choice, London, Frankfurt, and New York, shareholders love happy words. Bad reports are not permitted.

With the deal done and the contract "chopped" by the landlord and me, it is replicated in triplicate, we can return to business as usual. Lu Lu and I set about rebuilding the team, the trust, and the product turnover. Mr. Li, the landlord, is a short, dark man, who wears dark woolen suits, pale pastel shirts and smokes eternal cigarettes - Zhonghua of course, which he magics up from a faux-leather clutch bag. Marks of status for him, like the bundles of bills which can be seen every time he draws open the zipper. Cash is King. Landlord Li wants to be the King of Cash, and his fingers are agile as bundled notes disappear into the darker recesses of his outfit. Six months' rent disappear within three puffs on a cigarette, and I am left to wonder if this a factual payment or fallacious belief. Chopped contracts are legally binding; un-chopped are not. In this world of fast growth and loosening morals, getting a chopped contract is like drawing blood from a stone as there is no guarantees the persons you are dealing with are the same as the names on the papers.

In this world, dialogue is protracted and nothing happens fast, just in case a better mark is coming around the corner. Tea, cigarettes, and time are all drawn out, until, exhausted of any other options, the landlord receiver of your coin realizes that you are the best deal for now. My signature is Mandarin, my name for documentation is Chinese, but my outer packaging is still Western, I cannot though hide my skin. Li is suspicious of foreigners – the architects of the Century of Shame. Even with cash paid and an office space full of computers and people who indirectly pay all his bills, he cannot get beyond the fact that this is an unapproved zone. Foreigners are rare in this world.

Peering at me through the curling smoke of his eternal cigarette, he calculates and scrutinizes. There is money to be made. The contract is signed and chopped, despite Lu Lu's best efforts to warn of the unintended consequences of cheap behaviour. I know that Landlord Li may not even be the landlord. Nor even a Li. We have a contract with someone who may or may not be the man in front of us, who may or may not be the owner of this unit.

Welcome to the real China!

The deal is fishy.

But London gets what London wants.

EATING THE PEANUT

Somewhere in this transition I have received some photos.

Photos of a man.

A man, eating the peanut.

For you, dear reader, that will conjure up an image: maybe a cool bar, with a cool beer and a dish of snacks; maybe a ball game or a trip to the theatre. For eating a peanut is probable in those situations and death unlikely - unless of course the man has a nut allergy. For which there are precautions.

Not in this case though.

For the peanut in this phrase is the bullet from a gun. Direct to the back of the head, kneeling, face towards an earthen wall. There is no cure for this allergy.

It is not clear from where these photos have come. Nor the message I am being sent. It is for sure a warning.

"Watch out my friend."

But for what?

It is hard to know.

China is an opaque conundrum where the rules change daily. Have we moved into someone else's turf? When we broke our contracts whose fingers did, we break - and in which pie? Who lost face? Who is whose guanxi? The ripple effect of a single action travels far across the pond. Disgruntled employee maybe?

I have heard whispers of executions in China.

The executions of undesirables in football stadiums, where peanut eaters are trucked in from out of town. The local citizenry are there too, forced witnesses to the washing of dirty laundry, where the detergent is a 7.62mm shot to the back of the head. Peanut eaters are washed out in the public view of second and third tier cities. Rumours come from the hinterland, and a few expatriate friends have heard about them too.

On closer inspection, the peanut eater in these photos is alone. Political prisoner maybe? Or unwitting organ donor? I think the gun is an AK, a Chinese version of a Russian staple. The gun carrier is uniformed. The uniform may be militia or army. Could be Wu Jing too. It is hard to determine which organ of government is pulling the trigger.

Who's taking the photo? To be determined.

So many questions. I destroy the pictures and keep mum.

The world is grey and there are no safety nets. In the absence of support from London, and a punishing work routine, there is little to gain from over processing the message. I vow in the minute to strengthen my guanxi network and, in the absence of Brits, find new friends in the émigré community.

Autumn is cooler, and Nanjing is a beautiful mélange of colours. Sap sodden Plane trees shed their leaves, harvests are collected, and markets stocked with unfamiliar seasonal products. Fruits and vegetables that taste as good as they look.

The cool air is speckled with microdots of coal dust.

A by-product of China's industrialization, coal fuels the power plants and the needs of the big dogs providing the jobs. Situated on the North Bank of the Yangtze River, factories and plants overlook a continuous convoy of barge trains loaded with brick, sand, concrete, and coal. A ceaseless supply chain fuelling growth, like an overworked, water powered, sushi conveyor. When the wind blows north clear skies are enjoyed, sometimes for several days. When the wind blows south, or flags to nought, a creeping cloak of coal dust taints the air.

A FLUSTERED LU LU enters the room.

She looks pale, maybe frightened. This is alien to her standard demeanour.

Behind her, two leather jackets fill the space. Sniffing the air, I sense no odour. Police? Maybe. Authority? Definitely. Corrupted? To be determined. This looks like a shakedown but does not feel, nor smell like one. There is nowhere to go so we roll with the punches. Lu Lu makes tea, offers cigarettes, and makes room for the men.

Mr. Wang and Mr. Li. They show me identity. I assume it is real.

"We know who you are." Wang says.

"Why are you here?" asks Li.

Calmly I wait to respond. Wait until my stomach has finished a few back flips - and a front flip for good measure.

My exterior is calm; my belly is nervous. Officers Wang and Li of the Gong An belong to the public security bureau. The Gong An is an FBI type organization responsible for social order. Under the leather jackets they wear dark clothes over tan shirts. Li is the muscle, although I am not sure what he makes of my size. Big for a local, he is nothing like the giant men of Shandong. Up there I can hide my six-foot stature. Here in the "Jing" that is harder to achieve. Sitting down I try not to dominate the space, for I am keen to understand their purpose. Li likes tea almost as much as he likes the ciggies, so we feed him as much as he desires. Wang is different. Perhaps fifty years old, educated and articulate, he steers the conversation. He enjoys tea and cigarettes too, but like all things in China it is worth noting nuanced behaviour – small changes can mean big differences. Wang consumes with polite refrain. Hands and skin are pale illustrating the life of an official, not the toil of the fields. Li is "lao bai xing" for sure, his skin is browner and tougher. Escaping the farm, he has somehow found favour and joined the ranks of service. Wang is a selection from somewhere. The right education? The right family? Maybe both. For sure though, he will be ideologically sound and therefore here as a watcher with a warning. Behaivour is what sets them apart from their fellow leather jacketed gorillas in both London and Moscow. This is a smooth operation. No fists, no sticks, no guns.

A few minutes of small talk, sips of tea, and puffs on cigarettes and the tension leaves the room. Lu Lu interprets, which is our modus operandi and a practiced deceit. There are very few Chinese speaking "lao wai" in the region. "Lao wai" are foreigners. Those learning Mandarin are growing in number. Those who sustain the learning are fewer. Those who have reached my level of fluency are rare. Fluency though, like many things in China, is a debatable concept. The language, like everything else, is evolving at lightning speed. For the non-linguistically inclined it is a struggle to keep up. Outside of Mandarin, dialects are plentiful. Nanjing has its own patois; so does

Suzhou, just a few hours down the road, and Shanghai adds to the confusion with words that look similar yet sound totally different and undermine any shared meaning.

You are playing with fire when you mess with the local lingo.

Immersed deep into society, fluency is a ghost, and I glance with disdain at the "one-minute wonders" who finish a semester or two, then sell their expert knowledge to the Western world as "Old China Hands". They are clowns at best, deceivers at worst.

Back to Wang and Li, we move them along. As Lu Lu interprets, I have time to listen to their speech, know their tone, and get a feel for their nuance. The method is sound but lasts only as long as I choose to keep quiet. Once the cat is out of the bag, it does not go back in, and another pool of people know about the "local lao wai" who lives among them.

"Why are you here?" asks Wang. It is time to break the ice. I reply directly.

"To manage this small company."

"You have computers and internet?" A rhetorical question, for that is all visible. I choose to answer anyway. Landlord Li was instrumental in the set-up of the latter and may be a reason for our visit.

"Sure. We produce computer imagery, moving pictures, animations and such for customers in Europe and the Middle East. Real Estate developments mainly."

Lu Lu, dons rabbit camouflage and sits quietly. She is a great listener and will pick up any nuance or connotations that I miss. When necessary, we confer in English, and she guides the right answer. She has saved me many times, and I am protective towards her and the loyal members of our team.

Inside I worry about "eating the peanut." More specifically the pictures I was sent. Was it a form of intimidation? Did they come from Wang and Li? That seems unlikely. The next question surprises me

"What do you know about Falun Gong?"

So here we are. Small talk is done. Face has been given, and the room has been fully scoped. Down to business.

The Falun Gong: a cult group of qi gong spiritualists that have been outlawed in China since 1999. They have no official membership, administration, hierarchy, or governance that follows a strict doctrine; in fact, anyone, including members of my staff or even Wang, or Li could be a member, and we would not know.

"I know nothing." I lie. "Never heard of them. In fact, I do not go to church nor know Christianity."

It is important to tread carefully. Eating the peanut notwithstanding, there is Lu Lu's hidden faith to consider. Glancing over she is calm. The rabbit camouflage is good. That said, she must be feeling nervous.

"Nothing? But you have computers" notes Wang, "and internet access too" which he presents as evidence of my guilt.

"Now look here my old friend" says I and perhaps lean into the room. "Young Chinese people, with good jobs, good salaries who I look after daily both here and beyond the workplace. They are my purpose as I am theirs. For sure, I cannot deny the evidence in front of you. But we have no secrets. Our servers and our ledgers are unrestricted. Please feel free to open the books or check the screens and determine for yourself who we are."

Openness and freedom are rare concepts in the new "free and open China." The talk is good. As yet, not everyone is walking the walk. The infusion of these words permeates their thinking. Li is silent, staring into the production suite. Wang is silent, looking me over. His eternal cigarette in his hand.

Leaning in, I pour him tea. A symbolic gesture, for this is Lu Lu's role. "Da lao ban," the big boss pouring the tea is a message to be interpreted. Wang has a sparkle in his eye. The gesture is noted.

"Foreigners are not allowed here you know. This building is for Chinese only." Wang again, Li remains silent. Like a hound on a scent, he is scanning the production team.

"Sure. I know that," says I, "but we are friends." I drop in the word "peng you" to test the water. A loaded word for in the right context the meaning could be totally opposite. Wang and Li are streetwise. Our landlord wants more fish on his hook, he smells a money opportunity, and I am sure he is the grass who called the Feds. London wants savings though, and that is what they have. Personally, there are no safety nets - barely holding on to Maslow's second run - I need a network. Not just foreign friends but local law. It would be good to have a couple of local Feds on my side, men who know the rules.

Topping off the tea, I hear Wang continue:

"...instinct suggests you're a good man, Lao Kong." Using my Chinese name, the word "lao" suggests we could have a relationship. "Lao" means old, as in old buddy, old friend, or old man, a gentle patronym. "It is important to us that you respect Chinese culture, Chinese traditions, and Chinese law. It would appear from how you treat our people that you are good "lao wai."

Pressing my hands together Confucian style, I nod slightly and thank him for his graciousness. China is a chess game. Which game you are playing is never totally apparent. Nor are the pieces with which you play, nor the board on which you are playing. Sometimes you think you are playing, but in fact you are being played.

"Thank you, Lao Kong," says Wang. "We do not need to see your ledgers today, nor your servers. Do not prove my instincts wrong old friend."

He stands, ending the encounter but not the farewell. Handshakes mean nothing in China, so I stand and nod. Pressing my hands together again, I thank Wang for his attention to duty, their diligent visit, and most importantly for preserving social order.

Picking up the cigarettes I gift the packets to Wang and Li. Lu Lu pulls two new packets from somewhere and, double respected, our officers turn to leave, just as Wang fires his parting shot:

"Your brother is a good man too. A policeman I believe. Like me?"

Clever and shrewd.

A little drop of personal knowledge sends the biggest message. "If you know your enemy and know yourself, you need not fear the result of a hundred battles." Sun Tzu, the Art of War.

I take the hint. Wang and Li are gone. Playing by their rules I ask Lu Lu to discover birth dates, cigarette, and tea preferences. "Send them cards and a carton of cigarettes every birthday, Spring Festival, and Golden week" are my instructions.

The cost of these gifts is a tiny expense yielding ten times the protection. Lu Lu laughs but knows we need guanxi and follows up.

We are in China now; we play the house rules here but two problems remain unsolved. Whose fingers were in which pies when we left the foreign approved enclave. Additionally, neither the progeny nor the purpose of the pictures is clear.

MARKET DAY

Market day is Saturday.

Early in the morning, a short walk to Hankou Road brings me to the top of the street. The market is colourful, noisy, simultaneously odorous and fragrant. Full of foreign friends and local traders, the market reinforces the mass of contradictions that make this great country. A soft touch bumps my elbow. Wang appears from nowhere, eternal cigarette at his lips.

"Shangwu hao, lao pengyou," he says. "Good morning old friend."

Old enough to be my father, Wang has other similarities. Men of law, both are no stranger to violence or retribution. Both have been part of an indoctrination process. Both have been purged by their own. Both have survived re-education.

Wang offers a cigarette, I take it. I offer to buy him coffee. He does not like it. We stand like old friends looking down the market.

"The world is changing" says Wang. He's a survivor. And a grandpa. At his age he outlived Big Uncle Mao's political purges and the re-education camps in the countryside. With average life expectancy he has ten years remaining. Perhaps a few more. For all the tea and cigarettes some lean old boys consume, they still push through their seventies and into their eighties. Found in the parks working the parallel bars, doing tai chi, and dancing with their beaus they look like men half their age. Off duty, Wang is one of those for sure. Lean, green-tea drinking, ciggy smoking, Wang will see his grandchild grow.

That said, if he survived the purges, he could have blood on his hands.

Of the right age, Wang may be a red guard.

The red guards were student led paramilitaries - militant youths whose overzealous suppression of intellectuals and traditions led to violent rendition, humiliation, torture, and death. Teachers, officials, and party leaders were targets and several hundred thousand people died during the persecutions. Eventually deemed too radical, even for Big Uncle Mao, the movement was put down by the Peoples' Liberation Army. Backlash from the radical students was savage, wild, and nationwide. The Red Guards were outlawed, the army got tougher, and mass executions ultimately squashed the movement. Power was restored from the barrel of a gun, and more than sixteen million youths were sent to the country for re-education.

I look closely at Wang. Kindness is there today. His past is not obvious, nor is any zealous radicalism. His history is hidden well. No judgement there for I hide my own history too. Perhaps violent ideology is Li's line of country. Scanning around though he is not present.

Wang is alone.

"A purge is happening" he speaks quietly. An unexpected opening.

"Corruption. Be careful old friend, we are cleaning house." Graft is significant. Bribes and facilitation payments have reached staggering levels. Millionaire bureaucrats have joined PLA Officers in the ranks of the aristocracy. This is too much for the Party to ignore and an early indicator that perhaps, "something is rotten in the state of Denmark."

"They took a judge today." He tells me.

A snatch squad on a Saturday! That's just mean. Snatched over breakfast - no tea, no cigarettes, no cornflakes. Just heavy judiciary. I recall the ruthless efficiency of a white van gang on Tian'an men square. The judge here is powerful, so the snatch squad is from another province. Big men of Shandong are the enforcers. Wu Jing, I guess, but do not ask. "He will be eating the peanut soon," continues Wang. "We are sending a message. The family pay too. They will be invoiced for the bullet. A symbolic cost but a strong message."

The delivery is quiet. This is not a warning; it is shared intel to cement a camaraderie.

"You'll be alright Lao An" he uses the familiar version of my name. "From our side of the house that is. You are trusted, stay the course. Be good to our people and we will take care of you."

I believe him. There is no reason not to.

If I was going to be cleaned, I wouldn't see it coming.

Looking down the marketplace, a sea of peoples collide, western cultures of all persuasions intermingle with Chinese students, and peasant farmers.

The fragrance of flowers and fruits combines with the smell of blood and offal from the wet market, producing a malodorous soup of scents. In this soup I notice young Chinese people at play. Laughing with Western friends, they wear brighter colours. Dyed hair, punk fashions, slogan tee shirts, Japanese cigarettes, and Anglo-American music is everywhere. The youngest generation embraces change. With that change comes freedom of expression, interracial mingling, and freedom of love. Unintended consequences of growth, these are perhaps too much for the old Party man and conservative watcher by my side. The market is street theatre, and I love its implications. For it is here in an autocratic world that I have freedoms never enjoyed. These freedoms are compound by excess buying power in an affordable city. As dollar, euro, and sterling currencies strengthen I buy wholesale volumes of the Peoples' currency and live well. Here in Nanjing, upward mobility is not a risk; it is a reality, and with a friend like Wang I perch on Maslow's second rung, savouring some security.

"How's your brother?" asks the older man "the Policeman."

I know he's a policeman. Wang knows he's a policeman. He just wants me to know that he knows.

"He is fine, thank you" I respond without knowledge.

It dawns on me that, slave to a wage, I have not seen a Brit for months. Nor am I aware of any condition at home. Trapped in Nanjing, overseas communications are complex and difficult to maintain. Phone calls, internet, and snail mail are functional, flawed, and surveilled.

Privacy is never guaranteed.

In fact, nothing is guaranteed.

It has been too easy to disappear. That's a daunting thought.

My disappearance tomorrow would engender no curiosity or create any alarm, and, in real terms, it is entirely possible. Cash is king in China and the ability to buy a solution to your immediate problem is essential. If you have the cash almost anything can be bought, if you negotiate wisely. Then there is guanxi, a simple concept over complicated by academic thinking. Guanxi is about networking, maintaining good relationships. Without good guanxi you quickly discover China is a money pit. A drain down which you can quickly lose all you have earned. From micro to macro and back again, that is reality. Ivory tower bankers burning billions of other peoples' money have no guanxi, just data. But the People are masters of manipulation and can make data dance. The People will discover whatever your belief may be; conscious or unconscious, they will learn your tastes, feed you like a fat baby, and relieve you of your money.

Forget complaining.

The People are survivors of servitude and repression. If you are stupid enough to be conned, then more will fool you. Survivors are wise - street wise - and wisdom is a respected quality. The chess game is a crush of wills in a clash of ideologies. A frenetic accumulation of wealth and status, common to all kin. It is a crush that flushes out all manifestations of the human condition - the good, the bad, and the ugly. All are caught up in the same tidal stream of personal endeavour. Relationships here are forged, beaten, remade, or ground to dust. Your choice is simple: endure and evolve or pack up and go home.

On a quiet market morning, a good guanxi relationship is established.

Wang joins the team.

Recalling a Norwegian woman, brave in the face of Russian bullies, she understood how to manipulate strength. Knowing the rules is more than blind obeisance. How you use them for purpose is the skill. Wisdom is knowing when to play the game and when to leverage the frailties of the directorate. My guanxi network may be small but it is strong.

After an exchange of cigarettes, Wang moves on as quietly as he arrived.

Stepping into the market maelstrom, I stop halfway down the street at the German bakery. It is still early enough to sit. In a town of five million people this is the only place to enjoy good coffee. Rich, strong, black coffee with flavour. Not the brown piss in a cup served by chain outlets and poor hosts. Real bread too. And in the absence of a French patisserie, the baker makes croissants. The wee café and bakery is a little piece of heaven to be enjoyed once a week, and from this vantage point I watch the street, drink my coffee, and smoke a cigarette.

I have Sisu with street wisdom. I will survive.

SHAKEDOWN

Lu Lu looks nervous as she enters the room.

She has no time to speak before the two leather jackets storm in. Are they hyenas or gorillas? No need to sniff the air. This is a shakedown. The real deal. Intent is obvious as the two men barge into the office and stand glaring at me.

I stay calm. No response is necessary.

For I have no idea why they are here.

Nervous faces can be seen in the production suite outside. These are not smooth operators like Wang and Li. My new friends are here to cause a splash and create some terror. Having worked over the staff outside, they gained entry to the inner sanctum and, in guttural, localized dialects, they spit abrupt sentences and curt phrases. I smile inwardly for this is "the Sweeney Todd" – Chinese style.

Staff leave the premises creating problems I will have to solve later. Lu Lu stays, stoic and loyal. She is clearly frightened. The bullish men are glaring, demanding, and really irritating.

"Sit them down Lu Lu, make some tea please."

A simple task removes her from the line of fire and, standing up, I play dumb. Human body language is easy to interpret if you pay attention to the human condition. Too many of us cannot see beyond the packaging of race or the stain of stereotypes. In the silence, I scan Bob and Benny, or Double B, for that is what I name these intruders. Brown skinned heavies they seem young and, therefore, lower down the rank structure than say, Li and Wang. Whatever is coming next can wait. Saying nothing nor responding to their manners means silence calms the room.

"The supreme art of war is to subdue the enemy without fighting." – Sun Tzu, the Art of War.

Lu Lu returns, kicking off the standard routine: seats, cigarettes, and tea. Bob and Benny sit down. That's a first win. Lu Lu though is clearly concerned. She leans in.

"Labour bureau."

"So what?"

"They are the largest department in the country. Very powerful, demanding, they can close us down."

"What have we done?" I ask

"Nothing. But they are here for a reason."

"Well let's find out" says I.

The Labour Bureau, there for the protection of the People, are bureaucrats and, in some cases, militant unionists. Zealots with anti-foreign tendencies they may be, but Bob and Benny are all about the money. The cause though, and the rules? Those are to be determined.

Reeling off a list of charges, complaints, and angry issues, Lu Lu interprets diligently. Sitting quietly, listening, I determine how to play this game. Double B bristle with indignity, like a couple of savage dogs. The imperious attitude of foreign nations, international businesses, and negligent companies is a scar on the honour of the Chinese nation. Their rage is real for they truly believe we are bad actors.

Or want to believe.

Truly.

For that fire brings fuel for the shakedown.

"Have we done these things Lu Lu?" I ask. In a fishy world, anything can happen. I know there is much I do not know, but abuse of the People and contravention of labour laws seems a bit of a stretch. We have been deliberate and strategic in our efforts to be model employers.

Bob, or is it Benny, thumps the table. The cigarettes remain untouched. A rejection of etiquette. These fellas mean business.

"Of course not!" says Lu Lu, slightly annoyed. I believe her, for we have been diligent in transparency, taxation, and resisting temptation.

In a dirty world, where short cuts are rife and some form of fraud is a standard behaviour for many, the strongest weapon is cleanliness. Be clean, be open, and be consistent. In my encounters with Old Wang, I have learned that the best defense against a coming purge is a good spring clean. Behind the scenes Lu Lu and I have spent hours combing over ledgers, accounts, transactions, and operations, seeking and eliminating any opportunity for exploitation.

Purges come in many forms. International business is a massive cash cow to be purged on a regular basis. Westerners are extravagant and degenerate; they have money to burn and secrets to discover.

We are clean.

"Appear weak when you are strong, and strong when you are weak." Also, Sun Tzu.

China is not a place for small business. Small is weak and means easily crushed. Without the punching power of the big dogs we are open to exploitation. A hangover from Soviet Russia, Chinese Communism employs "the man with the biggest fists wins" philosophy. Bob and Benny are big fists. Survivors of Empires, the People are unnatural Communists, but in this new world order all sorts of characters come out of the woodwork. Adaptability is essential. Be agile and able to pivot, for in the crushing changes one must run to stand still.

Our porcupine defense is an impregnable integrity. Double B are the Feds. The Feds fed by grass and I wonder who the snake in that grass might be. Are they new fingers in new pies? Old fingers in new pies? Broken fingers in old pies? Or is this just a random lottery shakedown in the world of Bob and Benny? I have no idea. Fuck 'em. Nor do I care. Nor will I lie for anybody. Nor will I kowtow to bullies.

Bob and Benny have no idea that I can play nemesis to their hubris.

Whoever or whatever the cause of today's shakedown, the outcome is the same. It is all about the money. It is always all about the money.

Once the list of charges has been read, the demand for compensation is made. Not surprisingly a considerable sum is expected in return for all the indignations we have heaped upon the People and our young staff members. The sum itself is well within the range of international business. Roughly one hundred thousand in local coin, that's not a lot of cheddar. It is though, a couple of years salary for both Bob and

Benny, assuming they divide the spoils equally. I wonder if this is the real reason for their entrepreneurial spirit. As the Western world pours billions into China, the perception of wealth is coupled with a perception of carelessness. The round-eyed, fair-haired "lao wai" are profligate and reckless.

"Ok" says I. "That seems fair."

Lu Lu looks at me. Shocked. Close by for safety, there is a desk between us and Double B, adding an extra barrier of security. "What?" she says, astounded.

"Trust me Lu Lu; there is more going on here. Let's play the game; see where it takes us." She is loyal, we have been through much together and are trusting of each other. We share all news and have worked hard to stabilize this company, look after the staff, and stay sane. Equally, Lu Lu is liaison to Wang and Li, so we share similar intelligence.

That said, not all intelligence reaches her ears.

"All war is based on deception." More Sun Tzu.

"We can do that" I say to Double B, via Lu Lu, for I shall handle this in English. Wishing them to perceive me in the light of whatever prejudices they burn with, I bumble through this in clumsy fashion. "How does the process work?" Lu Lu, though concerned, is diligent in her interpretation.

Bob and Benny break their stares. Benny reaches for a cigarette, Bob follows.

Bingo! The heart of the matter. Actions are nuanced in the Middle Kingdom. As the rules of etiquette are engaged, I know the charge sheet is fake. It is all about the money. In the gaps between sentences, as Lu Lu interprets, I watch their every move.

"Well," says Benny. "Cash, in a bag; there's a bank downstairs." Bob nods, excited, until he checks himself and pulls another cigarette. He likes the tea and sips regularly. Maybe he is nervous.

"Sure, sure" says I, "肯定啦! - kending la!"– of course - but that is a lot to carry. We should break it down, manageable loads perhaps." Benny and Bob are hooked on my helpfulness. Lu Lu thinks I am mad. "We have some red envelopes here somewhere, a few big ones for VIPs, that should do the trick." Bullies love intimidation. Double B have hit the jackpot, and like old friends they lap up the tea and cigarettes reserved for VIPs. These young men are in the driver seat now, convinced that dumb "lao wai" number one is on the hook. "More tea, Lu Lu, keep it coming. We'll have this ship shape in no time."

She pours.

I watch.

Bob and Benny draw down on good tea and better tobacco.

Biding time, staying calm, it is clear they are in no hurry now. Double B are ready to milk the cash cow.

"So, I do have one question, about the paperwork?" I ask carefully. They stop. Lu Lu looks.

"You know, paperwork? The confession to crimes, the apology, and self-criticism, signed and chopped documentation. All standard stuff, no?"

The strength and frailties of bureaucracy are in the rigidity of their regulations.

"If you know the enemy and know yourself, you need not fear the result of a hundred battles" – you guessed it. Sun Tzu – the Art of War.

"No matter, no matter" says Bob "'Mei guanxi.' Not an issue, we will sort that and bring it back in a few days."

Of course you will. I beam happily at his suggestion.

"Marvelous, marvelous! And of course, we can trust that these accusations are true, yes? You have verified information and ascertained your evidence." Lu Lu raises an eyebrow, remains inscrutable, and interprets carefully. Loyalty merits protection, and the nuance is in the language. I am making an accusation, testing the water; maintaining an English approach she has the buffer of blame. Plausible deniability as one of the People enduring under the heel of this foreigner. Blame is not in her nature, but this risk is necessary. To close this down I have to read all of the signals.

"没关系，没关系 - Mei guanxi, mei guanxi," says Bob swiftly. He is the weakest link. "不用担心 - Bu yong danxin" - No worries, no worries, do not be concerned. All is good. It will be fine."

He is too cavalier. Nuance is important. Bureaucracy does not allow for personality.

"Well, that's good" says I, "We really must do the right thing. Let's get about it and get this done. Oh, and just one more thing. What about the receipt? The "Fapiao"?

The dreaded word falls through the air. Fapiao, a coded piece of paper recording official transactions, in business and government, in triplicate. Fapiao, little paper tickets from coded books that are distributed through the bureaucracy like a report. No matter how slow it moves, once the Fapiao is issued it will show up somewhere. One day it will appear on a desk. Behind that desk may sit an auditor, or a Party accountant, or even worse, someone cut from the game. Whilst our sum to be paid is not yet in the realms of peanut eating, if Bob and Benny are running their own racket, the "fapiao" will trace a path to an unknown face which could have repercussions.

A risk worth taking perhaps.

Let's see.

No noticeable change in temperature.

Let's continue.

"And of course I need your 'ming pian'" - name cards - "as you appear to have forgotten those on the way in." Bob is bobbing up and down, counting money from an easy mark. Fear pays, he knows. Cavalier, he flips his card onto the table. Benny is still. Lights are coming on over there.

"Of course, I trust you men and fully understand the situation. Most important you know to respect Chinese law and show respect to the People. It is truly terrible how some of us behave. Yes, you are of course right; we would not allow this in our countries. Now, let's lay the money out here, shall we? If you could just lay down your ming pian, and start counting, Lu Lu can draw up a fapiao. How about that Lu Lu?" She is frowning. But Bob is all about it, cards on the table, fingers in the dough. Benny pulls his card but is yet to lay it down.

"Now, let's get this straight, shall we? One hundred thousand? Yes? Yes? Excellent. And, I think we have all the admin sorted. Good, good. So, we can just lay the money out here, by the red envelopes and cards on the table, we should be good to go imminently.

Oh, and just to reassure me of course, this will not happen again. The matter will be all cleared up. No return visits? This is all legal, yes? Good, good. One and done! As they say, no return visits. Marvelous."

Bob is a mess, puffing away at expensive cigarettes, his face is shiny with glee. He cannot believe his luck at my obvious stupidity. Benny finally puts his card down on the table. Lu Lu is robotic. My madness beyond her. The stage is set.

For if it looks like a fish, smells like a fish, and tastes like a fish, it is probably a fish.

Benny feels it but the lure of cash is just too much for him to stop moving towards the prize.

"Super. All righty then. Marvelous. Now before we pack up" the table is laid like an evidence room. Double B, drinking tea, smoking exclusively, stood behind the biggest stash of cash, smiling, with cards on the table.

"One or two quick photos, I think.

I am terrible with names you know. and of course, I need to record the transaction and you gentlemen must be in a terrible hurry."

I snap a couple of photos on my phone.

The room freezes over. Bob is confused but Benny sees what is occurring. The rage of the fraud rhino builds in his brain. I have seen this before. Fraud rhinos are ugly beasts when they are angry, prone to volatility, and possible violence. The Asian rhinos are a wee bit smaller than their Western counterparts but equally deadly given the right provocation. But there is something in the air out here and, thanks to Wang, I know to look out for trouble. It is on me to protect my team, myself, and our assets. The burden is real. London cares only for the two faces of demand and critique so survival is now personal.

If I head off Double B, we know more of the game and how to play.

Phone in pocket I continue the dialogue.

"Now, I understand there's a new judge in town." Mouth agape, Benny stops talking before he begins.

"Some corruption issues I believe, money I heard, peanuts too, a right old mess, isn't it? The old judge they say has gone to Shandong. It gets cold there in winter. Who knows what's happening. Re-education maybe?

I am sure you have heard.

Oh, and don't worry about the photos, we wouldn't want any confusion arising now, would we? Best for all of us if I keep these photos for now. I can send you copies if you like. Lu Lu, please make sure we forward copies of these photos to Bob and Benny. At their office.

Please do keep the Fapiao, they are most important you know. Unbelievable how so many get forgotten or go missing when money changes hands."

Lu Lu thinks I am nuts. She interprets faithfully. Bob is reaching but Benny stays his hand. Anger fighting the confusion on his face.

"Do you know the new judge? I heard he is an ardent Party man. A legalist. Yes, no? Strongman, eh? The best kind. I think it is wonderful, you know, that we are on the same side. Respect the People and the Law. Together we can grow a better China."

I press my hands together Confucian style and give a short nod to Double B.

The trap is closed, and Benny withdraws his hand. Bob, somewhat dimmer is looking around. What just happened? Benny breaks the silence with a muted response.

"Yes, it is good. We should leave this for now though. I did not realize you knew the judge." An error of interpretation that I allow to pass. Benny restores some professional calm and stubs out his cigarette. Bob is confused but follows suit. Eyeing the money, he tails Benny to the door.

"Show them out Lu Lu, please." She stares at me, mad and amazed. For we are safe. Somewhat stunned she thanks Double B, gifts them a carton of smokes, closes and locks the door behind them. All the staff have gone. A carton of cigarettes for the preservation of a hundred grand feels like a good deal. Even better when you think we would have been on the hook to Bob and Benny forever. On the hook for thousands. Who knows how many others are stuck in their web. Fate is fickle. Nevertheless, I say a small prayer of thanks, for she has taught me some lessons.

Sitting down, I light a cigarette, pour some tea, and breathe a sigh of relief. Alone here, with just a few friends, China is a matter of survival. As billions of dollars, euros, and pounds sterling rush in from overseas, everyone wants a seat on the gravy train. With few friends, no Brits, and one foot on Maslow's second rung, it is today, more than any other, that I relish "the need for security, stability, and protection from danger or harm."

China. Open to the West is not Western. Nuance is important.

The game may be similar here; there is money to be made. But the rules are different, and the game is played another way.

Nanjing, a former capital city is in the grip of revolution. A revolution in culture, history, politics, and business. A revolution at the crossroads where East meets West and a new Silk Road is being laid.

Stuck in a geo-political furnace under an autocratic government, freedoms are temporary, and the law is arbitrary. Yet, I feel alive. More alive than ever. Stuck in a world that is not mine, far from home, life is a risk. The protection of others, their wellbeing, and their assets means upward mobility is a possibility. In exchange for a ticket to the chattering classes, there is no return ticket to the comforts of convenience.

The destination to which I am headed is yet to be determined. The future is yet to be written but it is in front of me now.

Frightening as that may seem, life is not a dress rehearsal. Life is an adventure.

A series of epic adventures.

If you enjoyed *Sisu – A Series of Epic Adventures*, please enjoy this extract from *Sisu – When the West built China*, where the web of intrigue and mayhem that is China's industrial revolution grows and reaches a dramatic climatic conclusion.

ZHENGZHOU

Am I going to die?

Maybe. In fact, it is a distinct possibility. The message was clear:

"You need to leave. Soon.

If you do not leave soon, then you will never leave."

In Chinese terms, this is not subtle. Over dinner with drinks, in a closed room, I have heard the words. Delivered by a man of business, he is our partner. Joint venture partner to the fools in England, he has all the power here. Those arrogant men, stupid from greed, have dropped me in this world of pain. They have left me with nothing. Their arrogance and desire blind them to a very clear reality: China is not Britain. Their contracts are a tissue of falsehoods, of no more value than a chocolate teapot. Yet, like many international business "brains" they are pouring money into the Middle Kingdom. Right into its dark heart. Not a new occurrence. The West is bleeding money.

Who cares?

I do. For they have royally screwed me.

I miss Nanjing.

The colours, the people, the connections.

Yet after the stresses, and years of making money for someone else, fatigue coloured my judgement. A judgement honed to spot a fish, to notice a nuance, and know the scam. This time though I missed it and the hook is in me now. Not just one hook, many hooks, and deep into my skin.

No passport.

No visa.

No status.

No business.

What is it about men in business? Men with a pervasive arrogance who defy logic in the pursuit of profit and are ready to burn their own people for a bit of extra coin. I wish upon them retribution. Zhengzhou is a dark place. A dangerous place. There is a confidence growing nationally. Confidence in the weakness of the other hemisphere. China is wealthier. The production house of the world is strong. Everything is made here now. The consumer babies are well fed, nice and fat. Turkeys ready for Christmas.

The signs are there, easy to see if you know where to look. Western men eating the peanut. It has happened: American, English, a couple of Europeans. This would not have happened a few years ago, for fear of retribution. The temperature is changing now as a new man seeks power. His name is Xi.

Xi Jinping.

Foreigners eating the peanut means imprisonment. I know from experience that the law is arbitrary and freedoms are temporary. As Chinese confidence accelerates, incidents will escalate, and the existence of the émigré could be endangered.

For those washing money via Frankfurt, London, and New York, the threat is unseen. Billions of dollars still flood into China and, even now, I still wonder at the impossibility of that.

Where does it all come from?

How much more money can there be in the world?

These questions will be answered soon. A global financial crisis is around the corner. For now, though, the threat is visible – and direct - and the existence of this particular émigré is truly endangered.

Our business partner organized the shakedown. A very personal meeting, most impactful.

More impactful when you realize that our dinner companion is a member of the judiciary. A senior court judge on the provincial circuit. And partner-in-crime to our joint venture partner. They are making good coin. Passive income if you like. As the money floods in, topping up their bank accounts, a cash cow is being milked. My presence on their grass means a disruption to the flow of currency. They have been doing very nicely for a few years now and wish to continue.

Passive income is the billionaire's choice and works well for the fraud rhino too. When opportunity presents itself, they seize it with both hands.

Standing in the lee of a tree, I shelter from the heat and humidity.

Cold with fear, I am also drinking too much.

Totally alone, I am in danger of disappearance.

Zhengzhou is a real shit hole. Nobody wants to be here.

Even Old Wang cannot get me out.

Zhengzhou is the capital of Henan province, on the banks of the over-irrigated Yellow River. It is a rail junction through which every piece of cargo passes. Toxic, like the water of the river, it is a "wretched hive of scum and villainy" the likes of which you have never seen. The damage to the natural environment here is a lesson to the world of unchecked greed and corrupting power. Not only has money been diverted, but there is no incentive for betterment. The land is scorched and crops don't grow. The trees are gone and the desertification of the environment means the air is full of grit and sand. There are no birds, no animals. Nature here has been raped, and it will take many years for the Earth to heal – and only if the power dynamic changes. There is nothing left in this bankrupt city. Yet, through a quirk of Big Uncle Mao's policies and rail engineering, hundreds of millions of product units flood through this hub which serves the entire continent, and out into the world.

Wealth and power are locked in the centre of this web.

A web, at the heart of which are some big spiders.

Alone amongst the spiders, my fear is real.

It is time to leave.

But how?

A sandstorm has blown through the city. The orange-tinged air leaves sand grains on my skin and in my eyes. From the safety of the shadows, I watch a policeman across the road, his body hangs between two colleagues. He can barely move as they walk towards the waiting car.

White, with blue and red flashing lights on the roof rack, the car is inscribed with the words "jingcha." Police is the word emblazoned down the side of the vehicle. Disheveled uniform, he is slumped and ragged, blue shirt stained, collar undone, and tie hanging loose, he is drunk. So drunk he cannot stand. Vomit stains his front. He vomits again, loudly onto the street, and collapses onto the floor. As his buddies scoop him up, I remain discreet beside the tree, in the shadows of a building.

The police here rule with impunity.

Power is truly autocratic.

Our business partner is a part of that power, and his cohort includes a senior court judge. Fraud rhinos are dangerous beasts, particularly when threatened. Here in the home of Shaolin Kung Fu, the fraud rhinos walk with the spiders. Big, hairy, poisonous spiders.

This time Fate has dropped me in to a dystopian jungle, from which I am not sure I can find the exit.

About the Publisher

TACTICAL 16

Tactical 16 Publishing is an unconventional publisher that understands the therapeutic value inherent in writing. We help veterans, first responders, and their families and friends to tell their stories using their words.

We are on a mission to capture the history of America's heroes: stories about sacrifices during chaos, humor amid tragedy, and victories learned from experiences not readily recreated — real stories from real people.

Tactical 16 has published books in leadership, business, fiction, and children's genres. We produce all types of works, from self-help to memoirs that preserve unique stories not yet told.

You don't have to be a polished author to join our ranks. If you can write with passion and be unapologetic, we want to talk. Go to Tactical16.com to contact us and to learn more.

All of Tactical 16's books are available on our online bookstore, T16Books.com. Visit it today to see more books from our selection of authors and to find a new adventure to read!

www.ingramcontent.com/pod-product-compliance
Lightning Source LLC
Chambersburg PA
CBHW051242050726
47594CB00001B/276